The New Social Face of Buddhism
A Call to Action

The New Social Face of Buddhism:

A CALL TO ACTION

Ken Jones

Wisdom Publications • Boston

Wisdom Publications
199 Elm Street
Somerville MA 02144 USA
www.wisdompubs.org

Library of Congress Cataloging-in-Publication Data

Jones, Ken (Ken H.)
    The new social face of Buddhism : a call to action / Ken Jones.
        p.cm.
Included bibliographical references and index.
    ISBN 0-86171-365-6
    1. Buddhism —Social aspects. 2. Religious life—Buddhism. I. Title.
    BQ4570.S6J65 2003
    294.37—dc21

                                                    2003001394

07 06 05 04 03
5   4   3   2   1

Cover by Roger Dormann
Interior by Gopa & Ted2

Cover painting, *Fire Beyond,* by Kazuaki Tanahashi. Copyright held by the artist; used by permission. Illustration on page 64 by Andrew Campbell

Wisdom Publications' books are printed on acid-free paper and meet the guidelines for permanence and durability of the Committee on Production Guidelines for Book Longevity of the Council on Library Resources.

Printed in Canada

Dedicated to All Followers of the Way

Go forth on your journey, for the benefit of the many,
for the joy of the many, out of compassion for the world,
for the welfare, for the benefit and joy of mankind

Shakyamuni Buddha (Vinaya I, 21)

CONTENTS

FOREWORD

By Kenneth Kraft

IN A THIS TIME of violence perpetrated in the name of religion, we are painfully reminded of the dark side of humanity's religious impulse. We may wonder if organized religion has the ability to reform itself, to recover lost threads of spiritual insight and strength. Yet religion at its best is creative, visionary, and liberating. As we grope our way through the maze of modernity, just to see things more clearly would be a blessing and a source of hope.

Like other world religions, Buddhism is being tested by a new era. How are wisdom and compassion expressed today? What is right livelihood? Are there situations in which war, however abhorrent, is justified? What does the precept to cherish all life mean amid the loss of species and the collapse of ecosystems? Rooted in once-great Asian civilizations, Buddhism may at first seem unequal to the complexities of present-day social, political, and environmental crises. Nonetheless, it is evident that this ancient tradition contains abundant spiritual and practical resources. How can these resources be actualized most effectively to meet current needs?

Ken Jones's 1989 book *The Social Face of Buddhism,* was one of the very first attempts to synthesize Asian spirituality and Western social thought. *The New Social Face of Buddhism* is based on its predecessor but has been almost entirely rewritten. Returning to the same central issues with greater clarity and maturity, Jones draws upon—and exemplifies—the remarkable growth of engaged Buddhism in recent decades. The Buddhist term "skillful means" refers to the ability to communicate timeless teachings to a particular audience, whatever the circumstances. With this new book, it is clear that Ken Jones's means have become more skillful.

Jones starts by asking, How much social theory does one find in traditional Buddhism? The short answer is: not Not much. So he undertakes an ambitious task—developing Buddhist insights about the nature of the self into a theory of society. Not content with a Buddhist-inspired patchwork of ideals, he seeks a fully authentic Buddhist social theory. In Jones's view, engaged Buddhists should aspire to social forms that are expressive of enlightenment and conducive to enlightenment—in other words, radically liberating.

Gathering material from diverse sources, Jones bolsters the new Buddhism that is emerging in Asia and the West. In some spiritual traditions, the awakening of nondual awareness is described metaphorically as the opening of a "third eye," and many contemporary Buddhists aspire, with undiminished ardor, to open this eye. Jones believes that a spiritually mature person in today's world cannot stop there—he or she must also awaken to social awareness and social responsibility, in effect opening a *fourth* eye. If the potential for individual enlightenment is beyond dispute, what are the possibilities for some kind of collective awakening?

In the latter half of the twentieth century, an unprecedented number of Westerners were attracted to Buddhism. For many, it seemed to offer a safe haven from a crazy world. The prevailing attitude was "Stop the World—I Want to Get Off," the title of a Broadway show in the 1960s. Scholars, Buddhist practitioners, and artists initially assumed that true Buddhist practice entailed somehow "leaving" the world in some manner. The traditional way to leave the world was to become a monk or a nun, but few Westerners chose to take this step. Lay practice became the most viable option.

As Western lay practitioners deepened their understanding, unexpected things began to happen. Personal relationships, daily activities, and the natural environment acquired new luster. The world became reenchanted. Buddhist teacher and activist Joanna Macy titled her 1991 book *World As Lover, World As Self.* From this standpoint, leaving the world is impossible, because we *are* the world. Stated another way, we can leave the world at any time, by entering so deeply into the present moment that the imagined distinction between "self" and "world" evaporates.

By showing how scholarship and spiritual practice can illumine each other, *The New Social Face of Buddhism* helps to dispel the misconception that one of the goals of Buddhist practice is to abandon thought. In meditation, it is of course essential to allow the dusts of thought to settle. Yet thought itself is not the problem; identification with thought is the problem. Those who have experienced the mind unfettered by thought find that thinking has its place just as other human activities have their place. Jones demonstrates that intellectual rigor and analytical complexity are not alien to the contemplative life.

Indeed, Jones's work makes a strong claim that contemporary Buddhist teachers and leaders must be conversant with the heritage of both Asia and the West. Just as he recognizes the shortcomings of traditional Buddhism, he exposes deficiencies in Western intellectual history. If the West's understanding of the self is flawed, as Buddhism would assert, then social theories based on those mistaken assumptions are destined to miss the mark. East or West, human folly abounds. But, broadly speaking, Buddhism has failed to address the impact of *collective* greed, anger, and delusion, while Western society has failed to address the roots of *individual* greed, anger, and delusion. For engaged Buddhists, there is a link between the violence of others and our own anger, between oppressive economic systems and our own greed.

A well-known Zen koan asks, "What is your original face before your parents were born?" Like all koans, it challenges us to see clearly into our deepest nature. Ken Jones poses a new question: "What is the social face of Buddhism?" This too is a kind of koan, one that points to the potential for liberation in societies as well as individuals. We must work together to bring it forth.

Kenneth Kraft

Kenneth Kraft is a professor of Buddhist studies at Lehigh University and the auhor of *The Wheel of Engaged Buddhism.*

ACKNOWLEDGMENTS

I am grateful to David Loy for his companionship on a lonely endeavour. Thanks are also due to my editors Josh Bartok at Wisdom and Susan Bridle, for their helpfulness and courtesy.

PREFACE

THIS IS A COMPLETELY REVISED edition of *The Social Face of Buddhism,* published in 1989. It is about the contribution of Buddhism to understanding and transforming society, and is written for both Buddhists and non-Buddhists. Though written to be accessible to people of any background, it is particularly addressed to the many Buddhists who feel torn between the requirements of a personal, privatized Buddhism and their deep concern for the suffering in the world which gives rise to the need for a positive response to it. In this book, I assert that the distinction between personal Buddhist practice and social activism for the benefit of the world is illusory; in fact, there is only one practice to be done. The book is also written for people who are trying to understand the problems of our society, who are concerned and wish to change it, and who may know nothing about Buddhism particularly, but would like to explore perspectives and responses beyond the horizons of the familiar landscape of secular rationalism. Perhaps most importantly, *The New Social Face of Buddhism* is written for those who suffer frustration and despair at the prospects for our planet and our seeming inability to do much about them, yet still long to act.

The original edition of this book, written over fifteen years ago, was an argument for a socially engaged Buddhism that at that time was little developed and not widely accepted. Since then, engaged Buddhism has come more fully of age, as attested by a steady flow of books on the topic. Socially engaged Buddhism is now more in need of constructive criticism than special pleading. The original edition, moreover, was written in a world colored by the Cold War, "new age" promise, and the birth of the "green" movement. The present book engages with a world characterized by postmodernism, free market globalization, and transnational terrorism.

This new edition retains the general purpose, ground plan, and main topics and themes of the original—that the work of inner liberation must necessarily be one with that of social liberation. However, much outdated and marginal material has been replaced, and the contents have been rearranged to give a more concise exposition. Thus, this is a substantially new book while meeting the same needs as did the previous edition in its time.

Any discussion of "the new social face of Buddhism" requires a thoughtful, critical, and comprehensive engagement with modernity—the predominant global culture of our time. This entails, first, a sophisticated social analysis that originates in and parallels the Buddhist diagnosis of the human condition itself. Secondly, I argue that the Buddhist goal of what the *Vimalakirti Sutra* calls "inconceivable liberation" and modernity's humanistic project of social emancipation are complementary. The former is liberation from the root fear and anxiety that characteristically afflict human beings. The latter is freedom from poverty, social injustice, and ecological degradation. Thirdly, I believe the prime task of an engaged Buddhism is to promote a whole "culture of awakening" that will support the flourishing of our full human potential. This inner work of profound awakening will be capable of sustaining an outer work of no less radical social change, toward an ecologically sustainable and truly democratic commonwealth. I do not, however, share Albert Einstein's view of Buddhism as "the cosmic religion of the future." What I have in mind is a convergence with and within modernity of a broad spectrum of spiritualities (and humanisms) in an overarching culture of existential awakening. In this process I believe Buddhism has a unique value as a catalyst.

Throughout this book *spiritual awakening* refers to a path of inner transformation, in contrast to institutional, metaphysical, or ideological religion. I have focused on Buddhism as a nondogmatic, nontheistic spiritual tradition that appeals to personal experience. As such, it is of interest to humanists and agnostics and also to open-minded people of other faiths who can feel at home in its perennial spirituality. More specifically, the writing is informed by my own thirty years as a Western Zen Buddhist practitioner.

Part one of *The New Social Face of Buddhism* eases the reader into the journey ahead and establishes some key Buddhist ideas. Part two sketches a Buddhist social theory and provides some analytical tools for the remainder of the book. It also offers a Buddhist understanding of the contemporary culture of modernity. In part three I explore various perspectives on the work of inner transformation. First, I examine contemporary spirituality and psychotherapy from a Buddhist point of view, and then review and discuss a variety of spiritual training practices. Part three continues with a consideration of Buddhism in different social contexts, emphasizing the importance of cultural awareness and the context-dependent nature of morality. Part four is concerned with active social engagement. It includes several chapters of critical discussion about socially engaged Buddhism itself. In the final chapter, on building a radical culture of awakening, I draw together the many themes developed earlier in the book.

I have been critical of attempts to "update" and "reinterpret" Buddhism and am concerned, instead, to examine social phenomena in the light of root Buddhist teachings. Engaged Buddhism is not presented here as some new kind of Buddhism, but simply as the logical extension of the traditional teachings of morality and compassion to twenty-first-century conditions.

Buddhist social engagement necessarily requires a Buddhist understanding of history and society. Therefore much of this book offers a Buddhist perspective on a range of urgent topics, rather than an explication of Buddhist doctrine. Engaged Buddhism is now attracting the interest of scholars hitherto preoccupied with Asian Buddhist texts, at times drawing the criticism that this contemporary expression of Buddhism is not grounded in traditional Buddhist literature. There are two responses I would like to make to this objection. First, this book is addressed primarily not to scholars but to spiritual practitioners, social activists, and anyone else who is intrigued by the subject. It is a tough exploration, and some of my readers may at times find the going hard enough without the added baggage of unfamiliar scriptural documentation. (I'd also like to note that I generally have chosen to use English rather than Pali or Sanskrit terms, and have tended to use common phonetic English spelling of those terms when used, in order to make the book more accessible to lay readers.) Secondly, my priority has been to base my argument on the existential Buddhist analysis of what it is to be human and the goal of awakening, inviting the evidence of the reader's own life experience and drawing upon my own practice. Though citations of the Buddhist canon do not abound in *The New Social Face of Buddhism,* nonetheless, as Buddhist philosopher and social commentator David Loy asserted, "Buddhism is so thoroughly integrated into other dimensions that it tends to disappear" and hence plays "an undercover role." In the bricks and mortar of this presentation there are deep Buddhist elements, notwithstanding the sparsity of doctrinal scaffolding.

I invite the reader to explore further and at firsthand the important contribution Buddhism can make to understanding and transforming this complex and troubled world in which we live, and I hope to more solidly build a vision of Buddhist social engagement than has been possible in this initial sketch.

Ken Jones
Spring 2003

PART 1

FOUNDATIONS

Chapter 1

MAKING A LIFE

"WHAT IS THE SELF?" or, more personally, "Who am I?" These are the questions around which the whole argument of this book revolves. Though well-worn, these questions are also always new, weighty, and gritty. Let us start by taking the question of the self very personally, and then extend the investigation of the self to its function as the prime mover of history and society.

We begin with the words that Siddhartha Gautama, the Buddha, began in the fifth century B.C.E., addressing the problem of being human, of having to live out a life: "Suffering, and the Way out of suffering, I teach." *Suffering* is the usual translation of the Pali word *dukkha*. And yet this translation is unavoidably misleading, as will become clear as we see the compendious and suggestive meaning of *dukkha* unfold.

The first noble truth proclaimed by the Buddha is the fact of suffering, of which there are several kinds. There is the suffering that arises from gross physical and mental affliction: the "objective" pain of disease, famine, bereavement, and so on. There is the suffering that arises from change, the vicissitudes of life, the impermanence of all phenomena. As the Zen saying goes, we are all fleas on life's hot griddle—the fleas that jump must fall, and the fleas that fall must jump. And most fundamental, there is the existential suffering and gnawing sense of lack arising from the fruitless struggle to create an enduring self from the flow of transience.

The Diagnosis

We tend to feel that it is the affliction or deprivation itself that causes us to suffer. However, the Buddha's second noble truth was that suffering arises not from these afflictions themselves but from our characteristic response to them: trying to escape from them, and trying to get less of what we don't want and more of what we do. You may want to confirm the second noble truth by undertaking a simple experiment. Identify in your life some small but well-established indulgence, perhaps something as simple as the regular enjoyment of a cup of coffee. Now deprive yourself of it for a period of time until you can feel, almost physically, the raw emotions of frustration, irritation, and longing. If this experiment is done with total attention, it will become clear that it is the feeling of frustration, the feeling of being deprived, that causes the suffering and not the actual experience of simply going without the cup of coffee. Contrariwise, it is our frustrated attempts to evade what is unpleasant—say, for example, the experience of being ill—that cause us suffering, though we mistakenly believe our suffering to be due to the unpleasantness itself.

The third noble truth is that suffering disappears when its root cause is eliminated. If somehow we cease our (inevitably futile) attempts to escape from what we don't want and to cling to what we crave, then either our suffering will cease entirely or, in the case of gross physical and mental distress, we are at least likely to suffer in a way that is more manageable. For example, in the same hospital wards there can be very different responses to much of the same painful illness: the same amount of pain causes less suffering depending on one's relation to it. We shall see, however, that this truth by no means implies that by ameliorating our suffering in relation to these gross forms of distress we should accept the fact of them with indifference and therefore do nothing to remedy them.

We may discover, perhaps in meditation, perhaps in a personal crisis, that all our specific fears feed from a single taproot of fear—which itself arises from the underlying sense of vulnerability, of transience, and of powerlessness in the face of all that resists our efforts to control, possess, or reject. Fear often conceals an underlying sense of meaninglessness, of existential emptiness. The nature of the self-delusion characteristic of the ordinary human condition is precisely described by German poet Rainer Maria Rilke in his poem "Tenth Duino Elegy": "Strange, alas, are the streets of the City of Suffering where, in the sham silence of sound drowned by sound, there swaggers the cast poured forth from the mould of emptiness."

Living Out the Human Paradox

This terrifying sense of lack stems from the human paradox of having an animal body while at the same time being vividly conscious of the fact, and from being able, at least some of the time, to dissociate mind from body and reason from emotions.

Most people are impelled—from the very depths of their being—to evade the experience of reality, and their evasion takes the form of whole constellations of behaviors and imaginings. The particular manifestations of these behaviors and imaginings are in turn guided by the particular historic culture in which they occur. In our culture, those who struggle but are unable to share the problematic support that these delusive constructs give are labeled "neurotic."

This existential paradox, which has been central to much twentieth-century psychology (the schools of Carl Jung, Erich Fromm, Rollo May, Abraham Maslow, and Norman O. Brown are examples). But it has been left to the poets to express it most graphically—as in Rilke's "Ninth Duino Elegy": "Oh, why *have* to be human, and, shunning Destiny, long for destiny?" This human paradox was particularly tangible to many Renaissance poets, who were acutely aware that man's newfound sense of mastery brought with it a yet deeper sense of alienation and helplessness.

In his Sonnet 129, Shakespeare illustrates the suffering of wanting and of transience:

The expense of spirit in a waste of shame
Is lust in action; and till action, lust
Is perjured, murderous, bloody, full of blame,
Savage, extreme, rude, cruel, not to trust;
Enjoyed no sooner but despised straight;
Past reason hunted; and no sooner had,
Past reason hated, as a swallowed bait,
On purpose laid to make the taker mad:
Mad in pursuit and in possession so;
Had, having, and in quest to have, extreme;
A bliss in proof, and proved, a very woe;
Before, a joy proposed; behind, a dream.
All this the world well knows; yet none knows well
To shun the heaven that leads men to this hell

Three hundred years later Philip Larkin keenly expressed the suffering of impermanence in his poem "The Life with a Hole in It":

Life is an immobile, locked,
Three-handed struggle between
Your wants, the world's for you, and (worse)
The unbeatable slow machine
That brings what you'll get.

Both *in* nature and yet transcending it, we humans have to live our own lives; it is not lived for us, as with the animals. We are doomed never to find real peace until we have faced and truly responded to the human paradox—that is, until we have wholeheartedly accepted our humanity.

Every kind of human ingenuity is exerted, all unconsciously, to mask and deny what we are. The normal, characteristic human condition is that of delusion, of inauthenticity. Delusion is sustained by the drive to acquire, to possess, to cling to all that will apparently strengthen our sense of self, and to reject all that threatens to undermine it. We instinctively struggle against our experience—be it a wave of depression, a bronchial condition, the loss of a job, or unhappiness in a personal relationship—in order to maintain something of an inviolate and separate self, whether outraged or saintly. "I" tend to respond as if somehow separate from my condition, making the threat into an alien "thing"— the *bronchitis*, the *unemployment*, the *disagreeable marriage*. This has the effect of making the condition even more alien and even more threatening. We are instinctively opposed to what could bring relief and enable us to cope better, through a total acceptance of the depressed me, the wheezing me, the idle and frustrated me, the self-pitying and guilty me. We feel that we would become too vulnerable, that we would "lose control."

The struggle to sustain delusion is carried on with ill will, aggressiveness, bitterness, and anger, and in the virtuously repressed and transmuted forms of these emotions that make them socially acceptable and relieve us of guilt. The incessant coping with threat and feeding of desire to maintain the sense of well-being and control is our developmental (and historical) project, our lifelong lawsuit against reality. While diversions, drugs, entertainments, daydreams, and the playgrounds of what was and what might yet be are endless preoccupations, most people most of the time are engaged in a struggle to "come to terms with life" that amounts to fortifying their identity both in terms of "belongingness" and "making their mark in life."

The lifelong formation of belongingness identity is described as follows by Adam Curle in *Mystics and Militants: A Study of Awareness Identity and Social Action:*

> We become what we belong to and what belongs to us: our civilization, our nation, region, family, church, political party, wife and children, school, university, neighborhood, community, house, land, books, profession, clubs and societies, social standing, investments, tastes in music and literature, views on the meaning of life and the immortality of the soul, preferences for brands of cigarettes or gin, friends, reputation, dress, eccentricities, honors, hobbies, way with the opposite (or the same) sex,

pictures and a thousand other things. From these we fabricate a sense of self, an identity. It is by this that we define ourselves to ourselves.

We find self-identity both through belongingness and through "standing out" or "making our mark"—whether as the president of the golf club or a wearer of stylish attire. The most favored and more or less socially licensed ways of "standing out" have not changed much since St. Augustine of Hippo in the fourth century C.E. identified them as the acquisition of more power, prestige, wealth, and sex than the next person. Similarly, fifteen hundred years later, Helen Gurley Brown, editor of *Cosmopolitan* magazine, claimed that "what every woman yearns to learn" is how to have for herself "love, success, sex, money."

What is at issue here is not necessarily a lifestyle itself, a particular pattern of behavior, but what meaning it gives to our lives and how it daily sustains that meaning. Myokyo-ni, a renowned contemporary Buddhist teacher, makes the following distinction: "Because we have never clearly experimented, never clearly differentiated, between *like* as a *preference,* and *must have* as a *compulsion,* we mistrust our natural preference or else impulsively abandon ourselves to it. Both ways we lose.... 'To laugh, but not to be carried away by laughter; to cry but not to be carried away by grief.'"

Buddhism teaches that each of us has a true nature, a buddha (awakened) nature, revealed when we become aware that mortal fear is not a necessity of the human condition. More or less masked in each of us, this true nature is always there, always our potential, and always capable of manifesting itself. (But it is best not dwelt on, for there is nothing that the hungry self, or *small mind,* as we say in Zen, would wish to do more than to dress up in that Big Mind.) In each of our lives, what we do out of self-need may indeed be alloyed with a relatively self-less fellow-spirit, which partakes of our true nature, in service and in friendship. Buddhism is not a religion of good warring against evil, which all too easily becomes the "top dog" of ego beating the hell out of the "bottom dog" of id for not being good enough. Through meditation, we can become more aware of the self-need that we have been obliviously driven by, and conscious of its destructiveness. Then, through the befriending and gentling of this self-need— "the despised and rejected shadow," as Jung called it—we can begin to move forward to integration as a full human being.

The Remedy

And so we come to the Buddha's fourth noble truth—the remedying of the suffering that is the human condition. Just thinking about the self confines the investigation to a closed loop, like the arm trying to pick up the body. "It is as though you have an eye that sees all forms, but does not see itself—this is how your mind is," remarked the eleventh-century Zen master, Fayan. "Its light penetrates everywhere and engulfs everything, so why does it not know itself?" However, if we sit quietly for a few minutes, trying to observe it, something of the self, of mind, is speedily revealed. Even if we try to focus attention on some external object, or the rise and fall of the breath, attention is soon swept away by a host of random thoughts and feelings, and an underlying restless energy. Some emotionally charged thoughts may fixate and become obsessive—whether some nagging anxiety or some pleasurable prospect or should I do this instead of that? Dahui Zong-gao, another of the old Zen masters, describes an all-too-familiar scenario:

> [People], ignorant of their true self, pursue things, willingly suffering immeasurable pains in their greed for a little bit of pleasure. In the mornings, before they've opened their eyes and got out of bed, when they're still only half awake, their minds are already flying about in confusion, flowing along with random thoughts. Although good and bad deeds have not yet appeared, heaven and hell are already formed in their hearts before they even get out of bed. By the time they go into action the seeds of heaven and hell are already implanted in their minds.

Even a fairly brief experience of practicing meditation gives a glimpse of the extent to which our lives are shaped by a profound, restless anxiety. Most of us, for most of the time, are able to engage a lifestyle that covers it up tolerably well. But from time to time a chunk of our support system drops away, whether it be through bereavement, divorce, losing a job, or any other significant loss. We can then appreciate the degree to which our sense of self was affirmed by the supportive and confirming experience that has now disappeared.

We are born into a trap, and like most trapped creatures we keep trying to escape in compulsive ways that only tighten the grip. And yet as soon as we see that the trap is of our own making, we can step sideways, as it were, and without any fuss we are free. Contemporary Tibetan teacher Gendun Rinpoche writes:

> Only our searching for happiness
> prevents us from seeing it.
> It is like a rainbow which you run after
> without ever catching it.
> Although it does not exist,
> it has always been there
> and accompanies you every instant.

Our "inconceivable liberation" is the total acceptance of, and opening up to, the transience and fragility of our human condition. It is the emptying of the wants and desires of the clinging, agitated, and opinionated "I," so that the world is experienced undistorted and unfreighted by self-need. All that is other is then seen in its *own* light. The self is restored to the self, to the body, and to what the thirteenth-century Zen master Dogen called "the ten thousand things." Then, as the renowned writer and translator R. H. Blythe described, "Things become beautiful, but not desirable; ugly, but not repulsive; false, but not rejected; a task may be boring and trivial, but we do it without anxiety or alienation."

In the awakening to the realization that there is no fear, there is a great sense of release and gratitude, although, at the instant, this transcendence seems a leap into oblivion. When we cease to struggle, the water buoys us up, and then we are ready to really learn to swim, instead of thrashing about to keep afloat in the belief that we are getting somewhere. This "coming home" to reality and our restoration to our true nature is the dawning of what Buddhists mean by *wisdom*. And the transpersonal social face or aspect of this revelation is compassion, which arises as deep fellow-feeling for the driven folly and suffering of humanity and all living things.

Chapter 2

MAHAYANA:

THE GREAT WAY OF LIBERATION

MAHAYANA BUDDHIST PHILOSOPHY is the intellection of advanced meditative insight, accessing a profound level of consciousness. Most familiar in the West in the form of the Zen and Tibetan traditions, it provides a vital foundation for a socially engaged Buddhism, in terms of both intellectual understanding and insightful action.

The Mahayana school, sometimes called the Northern school of Buddhism, originated in India somewhat later than the Southern school, which is represented today by Theravada Buddhism and the Pali scriptures. (For four centuries after the Buddha's death in 480 B.C.E. Buddhism existed only as an oral tradition.) While the Theravada and Mahayana schools retain a unity in core Buddhist tenets, they evolved distinctive forms and philosophies. At their different levels of abstraction Theravada and Mahayana Buddhism offer, in my view, complementary rather than opposed perspectives on Buddhist social theory and activism.

Liberative Emptiness

Nagarjuna, one of the most important Indian Buddhist philosophers, developed a doctrine of the void, of emptiness. This teaching is central to the first of the Mahayana schools, the Madhyamika, which originated in the second century C.E. It asserts that phenomena exist only through their mutually defining relativity. Black is black because white defines it; so with good and evil, empty and full. Phenomena are "empty" of independent, intrinsic being; it is difference that defines them. In the words of the *Lankavatara Sutra:* "False imagination teaches that such things as light and shade, long and short, black and white are different and are to be discriminated, but they are not independent of each other; they are only different aspects of the same thing. They are terms of relation, not of reality. Conditions of existence are not of a mutually exclusive character; in essence they are not two, but one." For example, the doors and windows of a house are only such because there are walls to define them, and the house itself is only defined by its constituent parts. Similarly, the utility of a pot or other vessel lies in the empty space it contains.

By attributing separateness and solidity to phenomena and emphasizing their differences we seek to confirm self by strongly affirming all that is other. The strong contrasts and opposites reflect the push and pull of attraction and aversion in the hungry and fearful ego. The nature of reality as commonly experienced is thus a (distorted) reflection of existential need. The doctrine of the void is paradoxical and cannot be grasped by logic. It can only be experienced through meditative awareness in which the "I" recedes and dependence is reduced on solidly structuring and differentiating our experience.

There are two erroneous interpretations of emptiness, both of which are relevant to a socially engaged Buddhism. Mystics tend to turn their back on a world that they perceive as unreal, a mere transient illusion. Of all religions Buddhism has long been associated with this quietism, this flight from the world, and the institutionally embedded conservatism that commonly accompanies it. Related to this is the reification of emptiness into something more real than the world of manifest reality, of form, so that the humanity and well-being of individuals come to be seen as being of little account. At worst such a perspective can become an accessory to social injustice, as in the case of Japanese "Imperial Way" Zen, which we will examine in chapter 10. This one-sided metaphysical understanding of emptiness has been denounced by the contemporary Japanese school of Critical Buddhism, as well as by a number of Western proponents of engaged Buddhism. However, some of these critics have not only rejected that metaphysical caricature of the doctrine of the void, but they have rejected emptiness itself as dangerously opportunistic mystification. Thus is the baby thrown out with the bathwater, and a true understanding of emptiness, the foundation and safeguard for any Buddhist social activism, rejected.

Though strenuously denied by its monk-scholars, there is indeed a tendency toward nihilism in the Madhyamika. The emergence of the next great Mahayana school, in the third and fourth centuries, may have been a reaction to this. It is variously termed the Yogachara (referring to the yogic insight on which it is founded), the Vijnanavada (consciousness doctrine), or the Chittamatra (mind-only school). By the eighth century a synthesis with the Madhyamika seems to have occurred, reflecting a complementarity of the two perspectives.

The mutually defining attributes of phenomena are explicitly recognized by the Yogachara school as "form"—as distinct from (and yet identical with) the "emptiness" of the interrelationship phenomenon. Thus, war and peace are empty of meaning except insofar as each defines the other. Later the Chan (Zen) school of the Mahayana strenuously maintained the need to maintain a sense of balance between emptiness and form, and was particularly concerned lest meditators identify with emptiness and lose touch with the phenomenal world. Thus Chan master Sengcan warned: "If you get rid of phenomena, then everything is lost. If you follow after the Void you turn your back on the very substance of things."

Emptiness is also a rather misleading translation because of its negative connotation. The original Sanskrit term *shunyata* also carries the meaning of swollen, or pregnant—and it is indeed pregnant with the potentiality of liberative, energizing creativity. It points the way out of the oppressive prison that the self-protecting ego supposes to be reality. It is experiential realization that makes the shift. The "new" world that is experienced—which has been present all the time—is more manageable and has a liberative lightness about it. Living and acting in it have been likened to play, not in any frivolous sense but in the sense that phenomena are no longer experienced in strenuous and labored resistance. The Japanese call this lightness *karumi,* and it is much valued in their art and literature.

Paradoxically, the world emptied of self-construction actually has a vivid *suchness*, a *thusness*, a pungent reality, which contrasts with the pale, devitalized world that reflects underlying fear and anxiety. Fifteenth-century Zen master Ikkyu Sojun describes:

If your eyes see
And your ears hear
Not a doubt will you cherish—
And how naturally the rain drops
From the eaves!

Every creature, every thing in the world, is there in its own right, its own *rightness*. It is not to be seen with the eye of implicit comparison that detracts from its unique dignity (or falsely enhances it!). It is not seen as better or worse than it might be, or than something comparable. This is characteristically expressed by the great thirteenth-century Japanese Zen master Dogen Zenji: "No creature ever comes short of its completeness; wherever it stands it does not fail to cover the ground." This is the humanism of emptiness.

For the Yogacharans it is only consciousness, "mind," that we experience. Scholars appear to be divided as to how far Yogachara philosophy is an "idealism," but in the later period of the Yogachara school, and certainly in Ch'an, the reality we experience is mutually created by self *and* phenomena, subject and object. Objective reality exists, but only as the experience of self. Neither has separate and independent existence. This typical Mahayana paradox is nicely spelled out by Chan master Sengcan in the famous poem *Hsin Hsin Ming*:

> The object is an object for the subject;
> the subject is a subject for the object;
> know that the relativity of these two rests upon one Emptiness.
> In the one Emptiness both—mind and things—are One;
> all the myriad phenomena are contained in both.

When self (subject) gives up its struggle to sustain its sense of separation from all that is other (object) it opens to an at-oneness, to unity consciousness. In Dogen Zenji's words, from the *Genjokoan:* "When the self advances, the ten thousand things retreat; when the self retreats, the ten thousand things advance." He further elaborates:

> To study the Way is to study the self;
> to study the self is to forget the self;
> to forget the self is to be enlightened by all things;
> to be enlightened by all things is to remove the barrier between
>   self and others

However, since self and other exist in mutuality, if self is enlightened by opening to other, then other must be enlightened also. The buddha nature—the existential authenticity—of all things must necessarily be revealed simultaneously. This was most thoroughly expounded by Dogen, though it is found much earlier in the *Avatamsaka Sutra:* "Owing to its self-expanding and self-creating power, a great loving heart transforms this earthly world into one of splendor and mutual fusion, and this is where the Buddha is always abiding." In most religious traditions, where there is an opening to unity consciousness, such testimonies flow quite naturally. There is here an immense potential to transform our awareness of reality, and for this radically different consciousness to sustain the vision and confidence to effect previously impossible social changes. Finding the Higher Third.

The *higher third* beyond *this* versus *that*, is a nondualistic perspective in a conflict situation, where we are not needily drawn to identify with either of the contending groups. It observes how such contending parties mutually define one another in a single reality, and is alive and empathetic to the existential need that ultimately drives them both. It is thus free to examine dispassionately the origins of the conflict in the overall situation.

The higher third is not a halfway compromise but a radically different awareness of this *versus* that, us *versus* them—a shift from a black-and-white perspective to a polychromatic outlook. In social and interpersonal problems we readily get locked into what our hard-edged subjectivity perceives as the hard-edged objectivity of "facts." Yet in such situations we discover there is my fact, your fact, their fact, and these all change their shape, size, and color with the passage of time, with changes of circumstance, and with shifts in perspective. It is in the liberative "emptiness" of facts that the power of the higher third lies.

Where appropriate, the higher third involves the active, ethical response of taking sides. For example, there are countries in the world in which the *this* of a dictatorial regime and the *that* of a violent popular resistance are mutually defining. Years of confrontation have polarized the middle ground out of existence. Each side denies the full humanity of the other. But the conflict and the suffering have been initiated and maintained by the dictatorship, which has thereby brought upon itself the violent retaliation. So, if wisdom is informed by compassion, the higher third must ultimately take the part of the oppressed, of the relative good, though *without identifying with it,* that is to say: it is not drawn into a one-sided partnership.

From the higher third we view the overall situation without the subtle bias of wishing it, and seeing it, other than it is. But we may also be passionate partisans of one contending party that we believe has right on its side—though without needing the belongingness identity that it offers, or being blinded by rancor or ideology. From the perspective of the higher third, we can also clearly see what moves our adversaries; we can empathize with them; and maybe, having dropped our personal addiction to the struggle, we can still go on resolutely opposing them, in the nonviolent tradition of Gandhi.

This is a shift in awareness that can strip away the stubborn and implacable ego investment in a conflict. It can take the violence out of it. It can even enable us to pursue the conflict more realistically and effectively. And, above all, it can facilitate a resolution. Conflict resolution as a way of life, a social norm, is essential for resolving the intractable problems of the contemporary world, but it is the higher third that offers an approach that goes down to the roots.

The higher third implies a paradoxical situation, if by paradox we mean a contradictory statement or wordplay that is an explicit denial of logic, as with the identity yet difference of form and emptiness, or being both an impartial observer and a passionate adversary. Jung, in "Psychology and Religion, West and East," had no doubt about the spiritual significance of paradox:

Oddly enough, the paradox is one of the most valuable spiritual possessions, while uniformity of meaning is a sign of weakness. Hence a religion
becomes inwardly impoverished when it loses or reduces its paradoxes;
but their multiplication enriches because only the paradox comes anywhere near to comprehending the fullness of life. Non-ambiguity and
non-contradiction are one-sided, and thus unsuited to express the incom-
prehensible.

Many paradoxes will be found in this book. But a paradox is only such to the
logical mind. Frustrating paradoxical formulations are best reflected upon in an
oblique, light, and poetic manner—or else swallowed in a single gulp.

The nondual embodiment of emptiness and action is the essential and distinctive characteristic of a Buddhist social activism. This kind of "engaged spirituality," declared Erich Fromm in *The Revolution of Hope*, is "the strength and
joy of people who have deep conviction without being fanatical, who are loving
without being sentimental…imaginative without being unrealistic…disciplined
without submission."

Indra's Net

Indra's net is an engaging metaphor for emptiness that first appears in the
Avatamsaka Sutra (third century C.E.) and was later developed by the Chinese
Huayen school (sixth to eighth centuries C.E.). The Huayen school has been
claimed as the intellectual culmination of the Mahayana, with Zen Buddhism
as its actualization.

In the heavenly abode of the great god Indra is a wondrous net that has a
light-reflecting jewel at each of the infinite intersections of its threads. Each
jewel exists only as a reflection of all the others, and hence has no self-nature.
Yet its existence as a separate entity sustains all the other jewels. Each and all
exist in mutuality, and since none casts its light by itself, it cannot cast any
shadow that would deny the light of others. Each has no existence separate
from the whole, the one—which exists only through the many, yet the many
create a whole that has its own significance and value. The energy that sustains
the net is not generated outside the net or in any one part of the net but is,
again, mutually generated through the interbeing of the entire net. Not only is
the net infinite, but in each jewel is reflected another infinite net, and so on ad
infinitum. The net is thus a metaphor for a paradoxical interbeing—a mutuality in which entities do and do not have an independent existence, are empty
and yet exist.

The metaphor of Indra's net can prompt our understanding at different levels. Three are noted by Buddhist scholar Francis Cook in his book *Hua-yen Buddhism*:

> The intellectual lure attracts the aspirant to the practice which will presumably culminate in an existential or experiential validation of what was before only a theory. At the same time it guides the aspirant in actual relationships, serving as a kind of template by means of which the individual may gauge the extent to which his actions conform to the reality of identity and interdependence.

And scholar and translator Thomas Cleary, in *Entry into the Inconceivable: An Introduction to Hua-yen Buddhism,* emphasizes its "instrumental value" as

> a set of practical exercises in perspective—new ways of looking at things from different points of view, of discovering harmony and complementarity underlying apparent disparity and contradiction. The value of this exercise is in the development of a round, holistic perspective which, while discovering unity, does not ignore diversity but overcomes mental barriers that create fragmentation and bias.

At the personal level we actualize Indra's net to the extent that we treat other people and things with the same scrupulous and intimate attention we normally reserve for our own bodies. Indra's net is the making of the taken-for-granted—the chopping of carrots, the turning off of taps, the chairing of meetings, the writing of tedious letters. This sacredness born of Indra's net is the quality of attention we give to the most casual and the least satisfying of encounters and tasks. To the extent that we can do these things without getting in our own way, we actualize Indra's net. The world is re-enchanted.

From the standpoint of an engaged Buddhism the net is valuable as a working ideal for society and its organizations, in which we are brothers and sisters in mutuality. The network of autonomous groups is now widely regarded as a more appropriate response to many task situations than the traditional model of hierarchical bureaucracy. Economist E. F. Schumacher proclaimed that "small is beautiful," yet the problem remains of effectively managing and coordinating extensive networks in the larger interest without the coercion of a "free" market or a centralized state. The answer for such a commonwealth must surely lie in a high level of public-spiritedness—for which Indra's net provides the ultimate metaphor.

The wisdom of Indra's net is an emptiness that frees us from self-absorption, and the prime Buddhist virtue of compassion is the everyday face of that wisdom. Compassion is responsive appreciation drawn forth by the need of others and not skewed and flawed by our need to be compassionate.

The Bodhisattva Ideal

The active sense of compassion in the Mahayana is also expressed in other features of that tradition. Enlightenment, for example, lies within the reach of everyone, not only monastics and recluses. The heroes—and heroines—of the Mahayana are the bodhisattvas. These are mythical personifications of wisdom, compassion, and selfless action who inspire the spiritual aspirant to faith, energy, and patient endurance. They take upon themselves the cares of suffering humanity. "May all sorrows ripen in me," exclaims Shantideva, the eighth-century Indian ascetic and poet, in his *Guide to the Bodhisattva's Way of Life*. His words seem less extravagant when set against the course of human history in the twelve hundred years since he wrote them. Consider:

> I take upon myself the burden of sorrow; I resolve to do so; I endure it all. I do not turn back or run away, I do not tremble.... I am not afraid...nor do I despair. Assuredly I must bear the burden of all beings...for I have resolved to save them all. I must set them all free. I must save the whole world from the forest of birth, old age, disease, and rebirth, from misfortune and sin, from the round of birth and death, from the toils of error.... For all beings are caught in the net of craving, encompassed by ignorance, held by the desire of existence; they are doomed to destruction, shut in a cage of pain.... [T]hey are ignorant, untrustworthy, full of doubts, always at loggerhead one with another, always prone to see evil; they cannot find a refuge in the ocean of existence; they are all on the edge of the gulf of destruction. I work to establish the kingdom of perfect wisdom for all beings.

Powerful female bodhisattvas are prominent in several of the Mahayana scriptures, such as *The Lion's Roar of Queen Srimala*. These extraordinary beings, with the help of such miraculous demonstrations as instant gender change, maintain that women—even ordinary laywomen—are as capable as men of attaining and teaching the highest levels of spiritual realization. In the *Avatamsaka Sutra* there are revealed to the young pilgrim Sudhana "innumerable bodhisattvas walking, sitting, engaged in all kinds of work, doing charitable deeds out of a great compassionate heart, writing various treatises whereby to benefit the world...[and] praising worldly business and all forms of craftsmanship which would increase the happiness of all beings." There is nothing here of the quietistic indifference commonly imputed to Buddhism!

Buddhist scholar Stephen Jenkins, in "Do Bodhisattvas Relieve Poverty?" notes "the enormous relative preponderance of passages in Mahayana texts that express concern for the broader physical and mental benefit of sentient beings," identifying the relief of poverty as "the role of the ideal practitioner, the bodhisattva." He cites evidence for the "clear distinction between material and spiritual benefit, with attention to their interrelationship," and continues:

As in Pali sources, the satisfaction of material needs is seen as a prerequisite for moral development, and its absence is seen as the cause of moral decay. The role of the bodhisattva is to relieve these material needs not only through moral leadership but also through direct action, in order to prepare the conditions necessary for preaching the Dharma. These points are made most strongly in regard to *The Large Sutra of Perfect Wisdom*, with secondary reference to several other major sutras.... It is a reasonable generalization that in the Mahayana scriptures there is a broadly attested concern for poverty as an obstruction to spiritual progress and a clear mandate for its direct relief as a prerequisite for addressing the more subtle roots of samsara.

Jenkins quotes as typical the following timeless passage from the Suvaranaprabhasa Sutra:

May those who are in danger of being threatened or killed by kings, thieves or scoundrels...those who are beaten, bound and tortured by bonds...distracted by numerous thousands of labors, who have been afflicted by various fears and cruel anxiety...may they all be delivered; may the beaten be delivered from the beaters, may the condemned be united with life.... May those beings oppressed by hunger and thirst obtain a variety of food and drink.

The buddhas and bodhisattvas occupy a vast pantheon, and their wonder-working exploits are described in colorful and extravagant language in the Mahayana sutras. They are the subject of devotional folk cults, but their visualization also provides a means for more sophisticated practitioners to access higher meditative states. They embody myths that support practitioners in actually experiencing the intellectual constructs of Mahayana philosophy. The Mahayana tradition's emphasis on compassion, egalitarian orientation, and the bodhisattva ideal all point to a preoccupation with everyday affairs as both an expression of spiritual maturity and as a practice for ripening it.

The ideas introduced thus far are no more than conceptualizations of a radically different way of experiencing reality. They do, however, provide an intellectual tool kit that has value both personally and as a means of understanding and deconstructing modern society at a very fundamental level—with positive implications for what might evolve beyond it. Delusion, the sense of existential lack, emptiness, the higher third, and the metaphor of Indra's net are among the useful ideas that will be taken up again and again throughout the arguments of this book. The case study that follows illustrates in an everyday setting the application of some of these key ideas.

Don't Take It Personally:
A Case Study of Emptiness in Action

None of those who teach or learn in the "school" of samsara doubt its grinding, in-your-face reality. Take for example, a "real" school—a crumbling, inner city high school. Many of its teachers and pupils experience bitter resentment, and each day can be hell for them (though for the ambitious new head teacher it may be a stepping stone to a better job). Each has built up his or her own mental image of the school to make sense of their experience and to explain to themselves their role in it. And for each, the school has emotional meanings also. Through all these shared (or divergent) meanings, those who work in or attend the school experience it as a solid and mutually confirming reality.

Since the school is objectively such a strong experience for everyone, it is understandable that each is little aware of how his or her deep existential need for a secure self colors that experience, and so for the most part they experience their behaviors exclusively as responses to the external conditions with which they have to cope. This kind of evasion is the cause of *dukkha* (suffering), entailing a delusive way of experiencing reality. These behaviors in turn further shape the realities of school life, such as a heavy reliance on harsh discipline arising out of a siege mentality. Thus the school itself becomes an institutional embodiment and inflamer of the "three fires" of greed, aggressiveness, and existential ignorance: each struggles to get what he or she can out of the experience; is filled with rancor and rage; and is deluded as to the personal origins of these negative mental states that make the discouraging realities so much worse. At the same time, one can't deny that the school is underfunded, the teachers are overworked and poorly paid, and the building is dilapidated.

There are, however, a few teachers more able to open themselves to the bleak and painful realities of this samsaric school, and to experience without evasion their own fear and anger. This more wholehearted acceptance of how things actually are gives them strength to do positively what they can. They are open in compassion to the predicament of colleagues and pupils. Paradoxically, although they are more open than anyone else to the unvarnished, vivid reality of working in this school, these realities are for them empty of self-need: they are insubstantial, shifting, contingent shared meanings. They let go into this reality passionately, *but not personally:* they recognize and let go of the habit of solidifying reality *out there* so that there is something hard and tangible against which to define themselves. They have a lightness of spirit. It is manageable—there are possibilities!

As one of those elegant Zen sayings has it:

Though we lean together upon the same balustrade
the colors of the mountains are not the same.

Chapter 3

THE KARMIC DYNAMO

A CENTRAL TENET of Buddhism, as we've discussed, is the dynamic interdependence of phenomena, which are in a process of continuous, mutual redefinition. This interdependence is a paradoxical dialectic, and one way to understand it is in terms of cause and effect. The Buddhist literature distinguishes five different orders of cause and effect, one of which is *karma,* a much-misunderstood concept, both within Buddhism and in the Western culture that has adopted (or co-opted) the term. Most people view karma as an experience of misfortune that is the consequence of misdeeds done in the past—as an adjustment on a cosmic balance sheet, so to speak.

For individuals as well as cultures, misfortune may seem disturbingly arbitrary. This is especially so when fate seems to strike a random blow of adversity, perhaps resulting from simply being in the wrong place at the wrong time. "Why me?" we ask. And so, out of a craving to make sense of an unjust world, the Buddhist doctrine of karma, a subtle teaching involving a specific dimension of the law of cause and effect, was perverted into a belief in retributive justice.

According to this mistaken understanding of karma, there are inevitable, negative karmic consequences, as a kind of universal retribution, for misbehavior or evil intent—earlier in this life or in a previous life. Contrariwise virtuous behavior somehow accumulates "merit" toward a more favorable future rebirth. Since the events of previous lives are unknown to us, reward and punishment occur through the functioning of some mysterious fate. This is a fatalism that diminishes one's free will and responsibility for one's own future, which is so important in Buddhism.

This retributive tradition encourages a calculative, fear-driven ethic in which "good" actions are undertaken to accumulate "merit" in one's karmic bank account. Buddhist scholar Melford Spiro documented this phenomenon in his study of Burmese Buddhism: "Many Burmese keep merit account books…these are exclusively concerned with *dana* [offerings to the monastic community]…almost any villager can say how much (and for what) he has expended on giving." The following statement is a typical expression of this mentality, attributed by Winston King in his book *In the Hope of Nirvana: An Essay on Theravada Buddhist Ethics* to a prominent Buddhist layman in Burma: "A person who steadfastly and continuously observes the Five [ethical] Precepts can gain the following beneficial results: [1] he can gain great wealth and possessions; [2] he can gain great fame and reputation…;[3] he can die with calmness and equanimity; [4] after his death he will be reborn into the world of Devas [Gods]."

Retributive notions of karma flourish in traditional and fatalistic cultures—and sustain them. If your children are sick it is bad karma, and unrelated to unhealthy environmental conditions or inadequate medical services. If you are low-caste, or consigned to the "under-class," or the wrong race, then that is a result of your karma and not a cultural predicament pertaining to specific unjust social and economic conditions. The fate of whole peoples and nations has thus been explained simply in terms of a retributive karma, whether they be Jews or Cambodians.

Yet the teaching of the law of karma is a valuable element in Buddhism, and it offers some interesting social and historical perspectives. It is important, however, to disassociate the true Buddhist teaching of karma from the above common perversion of the doctrine, which is both contradicted by the letter of canonical Buddhism and wholly alien to its spirit. Thus Walpola Rahula, a Sri Lankan monk and Buddhist scholar, has noted that this mistaken view has theistic overtones and warned that in the context of karma, "the term *justice* is ambiguous and dangerous, and in its name more harm than good is done to humanity. The theory of karma is the theory of cause and effect, of action and reaction; it is a natural law, which has nothing to do with the idea of justice or reward and punishment."

The Buddhist understanding of phenomena is essentially integral and naturalistic, reflecting a perspective of interdependence. There is no element of manipulative fatefulness suggestive of a supernatural "other" acting from outside. As the familiar saying has it: "Sow a thought and you reap a habit; sow a habit and you reap a personality; sow a personality and you reap a destiny."

The notion of causality is intrinsic to Buddhism. And, as I mentioned at the beginning of this chapter, Buddhist doctrine defines several distinct orders of causality, which include: the physical, inorganic order; the physical, organic (biological) order; the nonvolitional mental order; the volitional mental order; and the transcendental order. The Buddha declared that although every willed action may produce an experienced effect, not all experienced effects are products of willed action. (Willed action issues only from the volitional mental order, and only willed actions create karma.) Consider, for example, a fatal but unexplained plane crash. It might have been due to metal fatigue in a critical mechanical part; this would be an event issuing from the physical, inorganic order of causality. Or the pilot may have had a heart attack, which is a physical, organic causality. Perhaps an overworked ground controller may have accidentally overlooked giving a directive, which would lie within the nonvolitional mental order. Or the crash may have been the work of a hijacker, which would indeed belong to the volitional mental order of causality. The karmic condition of the passengers would be irrelevant in this instance. Furthermore, it is contrary to the whole spirit of Buddhism to go hankering after some "meaning" for the "coincidence" that it was those particular passengers of the thousands safely flown by the airline who booked onto that "fateful" flight.

Some understanding of karma—stripped of crude notions of retribution—is essential in order to make sense of our lives. Karma is willed mental activity (which may or may not be behaviorally expressed) that leaves a trace, or "karmic residue," in the personality. Such a residue is usually accompanied by dispositional tendencies to act according to patterns established by reactions in the past; these patterns are referred to as "karmic complexes." One kind of dispositional tendency is defilements. These are negative and emotionally charged thoughts and attitudes that are triggered when conditions arise that are similar to those in which they originally evolved—which then become the ground for the accumulation of further karma. In this way, habitual patterns of behavior become deeply ingrained, shaping a distinctive personality. As Freud observed, we may experience repetitive compulsions, such as being drawn again and again into a kind of personal relationship that brings us grief. Or, a child may experience self-pity and discover that its manifestation attracts welcome adult attention. Then every time a situation arises that arouses feelings of self-pity, the habit of manipulative behavior kicks in. These behaviors may become highly refined over the years, and become so much a part of the person's way of living their life that they are taken for granted. They become a specialized, delusive way of relating to self and to others. It is typical of such karmic situations that blame is projected elsewhere by "Poor Me," the perennial victim, or is turned in against the self. "I'm not good enough" and "If I get too close, I'll be exploited" are familiar life scripts. Negative, life-shaping karmic energies are commonly driven by the fires that sustain a strong sense of a separate, alienated self. This can have harmful consequences for ourselves and others. Similarly, by positive behavioral conditioning, positive karma can be created. Moreover, through clarifying our awareness by meditation or therapy, negative dispositional tendencies can be gradually dissolved. For we do enjoy conditional freedom and have the ultimate responsibility for making something of our lives.

Organizations, and society at large, are shaped by complex conditioning forces of which the karma of their members is only a part. But it is the delusive *volitional intent* of each generation that is the flywheel that drives the follies of history. Thus, in the modern era, a seemingly helpless, relentless acquisitiveness fuels the accumulation of wealth and the expansion of technology. And even though some of us may personally be free of the consumer itch, we still bear some causal (though not karmic) responsibility for sustaining the consumer society to the extent of having to participate in it.

Social structures and cultures are both shaped by karmic volition, and promote it, as in the case, say, of oppressive laws and institutions, which may appear to take on a life of their own. The intent of past generations remains embedded in cultural norms and social institutions—though eroded, more or less slowly, by subsequent generations. The persistence of such social karma can be impressive, as with the endurance and reemergence of national identities submerged by centuries of alien government. There is a stubborn inertia here that ensures continuity and frustrates would-be change agents. This perseverant nature of cultural habit is most eloquently voiced by the eighteenth-century political philosopher Edmund Burke at the time of the French Revolution. In response to rationalists like Tom Paine, anxious to construct their utopias from first principles, Burke warned in *Reform of Representation in the House of Commons* that society "is made by the peculiar circumstances, occasions, tempers, dispositions, and moral, civil and social habitudes of the people, which disclose themselves only in a long space of time." He believed "innovation" becomes desirable when "the general opinions and feelings will draw that way." The different revolutions in England in the seventeenth century, in France in the eighteenth century, and in Russia in the nineteenth all pushed social change beyond the limits of historical continuity, and thus failed and fell back to some more sustainable level of social evolution. Contrariwise, when underlying change in the society has robbed a regime of its credibility, then revolutionary achievement becomes irrevocable, as with the collapse of the apartheid regime in South Africa and of the communist regimes.

Socially engaged Buddhism developed as a "radical conservatism" out of the struggle of Third World Buddhists to develop a synthesis combining the best in their traditional cultures with the best of modernity. Radical conservatism recognizes the need for radical change, but also acknowledges the complexity and slow momentum of social development and is sensitive to the potential growth points of a new society, and thus seeks change that goes with the grain. It is an example of the Buddhist "middle way," which is a higher, third way, rather than mere compromise.

As it is with individual lives, so it is with institutions, societies, and cultures: They may be swept into ruin by karmic and other tangled conditionality even though they have the objective means to avert their fate and more than enough warning of it. The actors are driven by addictive behavior and a kind of tunnel vision that is ultimately self-destructive. And when the majority is locked into mutually affirming karma it may be particularly difficult for even a well-informed minority to achieve a change of direction.

The most striking example is the ecological crisis, particularly global warming, that threatens global modernity. Although the danger is widely acknowledged by governments and industry, it has proved impossible to secure emission reductions of greenhouse gases at a level that would come anywhere near to averting irreversible and possibly catastrophic changes. No amount of rationality seems able to change the direction and momentum created by ingrained mindsets and the cultures and institutions in which they are embedded.

The fate of Easter Island provides a graphic case study. This South Pacific island, two thousand miles away from the nearest land mass, is so small that its perimeter can be walked in a day. Even when first settled by Polynesians in the fifth century C.E. its natural resources were limited. Raising only sweet potatoes and chickens left the islanders with plenty of time. They used it to create over the centuries a remarkably sophisticated social and religious culture. Its most impressive achievement was the construction of hundreds of huge, carved-stone heads—each ten to forty feet high and weighing up to fifty tons—on ceremonial platforms. By the time the population peaked at around 7,000 at the end of the sixteenth century, the original extensive woodland had been cut down in part to meet the islanders' economic needs. However, the greatest consumption of trees was evidently to make the trunk-ways along which the statues of competing clans could be rolled across the island from the quarry. The consequences of the approaching deforestation must have been quite clear to the inhabitants. However, such was the karmic intensity of the need to sustain ritual belief and of one clan to compete against another that they went on to the bitter end, leaving several unfinished statues in the quarry. The loss of the forest deprived the islanders even of the means of escape in ocean-going canoes. The soil deteriorated, and by the time the first Europeans arrived in 1722 the population had sunk to 3000, living in squalor and engaged in perpetual warfare and cannibalism in order to keep alive.

Traditional and canonical Buddhism extends the span of karma through successive rebirths. The succession, however, is that of a vital energy, not of a reincarnated personality or essence. It has been likened to the phenomenon on the billiard table when one ball suddenly stops dead when striking a second that immediately speeds away.

K. N. Jayatilleke, a contemporary Buddhist scholar, writes that

Buddhism, while granting that "the laws of heredity" *(bija-niyana)* condition, on the whole, the physical and physiological characteristics of the
person, holds that the temperament and such personality characteristics
including aptitudes and skills are, on the whole, conditioned by the psychological past of the individual.... According to the texts there is mutual
interaction and integration of the two in the formation of a new personality. It is said: "Just as much as two bundles of reeds were to stand erect
supporting each other, even so conditioned by the (hereditary) psycho-
physical factors is the consciousness and conditioned by consciousness
are the psycho-physical factors." (Samyutta Nikaya II.114)

Although modern social scientists differ about the relative significance of
nature and nurture, all would give at least some weight to the latter. The notion
of the two sheaves quoted above is therefore no longer adequate, and instead we
have a tripod of reborn consciousness, nature (hereditary physiology), and environmental nurture supporting the personality. This is, however, still a preliminary understanding, for the social environment is itself recreated by successive
generations. Each individual inherits at birth certain karmic and other causal
social conditions, a collectively created past at work in the present.

There is, I believe, in both the teaching of karma and rebirth a perspective
that can bring a deeper, psychic dimension to a socially and historically engaged
Buddhism. This awaits future exploration.

PART 2

SOCIAL UNDERSTANDING

Chapter 4

TISSUES OF THE SELF:

A BUDDHIST SOCIAL PSYCHOLOGY

THE BUDDHIST MODEL of the mind—in which the personality in its entirety is constituted of five *skandhas* (aggregates)—presents a continuous, sequential process wherein patterns of conditioning and reconditioning construct a distinctive, individual personality. The skandha model is typical of Buddhist psychology in that it derives from the advanced meditative experience of mental processes—slowing them down, separating them out, and labeling them.

The first skandha is physical sensation, and in Buddhism the mind itself is regarded as a sense organ.

If the first skandha is about sensing a happening, the second skandha, *vedana*, is about feeling it happen. The emotions are engaged—we feel the irritation of the pain of, say, a toothache. A kind of elementary response begins. Feeling, for better or worse, does confirm that "I" am here and alive. Already, at this point, there is some solidification around a sense of self.

With the third skandha, perception, there is recognition of the feeling as good, bad, or indifferent; desirable, aversive, or neutral. A volitional response takes place. It may be a grasping and consuming urge; aggressive feelings where ego feels threatened; or the indifference, apathy, and numbing of awareness that sometimes masks a sensitive area. We may have learned to dis-identify our response to the feelings at this point, disassociating self from them to some extent and hence not being unduly moved by them. Thus, with a toothache, we may sense tactile pain, become aware of some sense of annoyance, recognize it as an undesirable occurrence, and appropriately make an appointment with the dentist. That is all. However, if we take the pain as a threat to our inviolable "self," a whole torrent of negative reactions could well come into being.

This brings us to the fourth skandha, commonly translated as "conception" since here the wide range of ideas, feelings, attitudes, and so on, are identified and classified. Together they amount to a distinctive ego or personality—a whole history of residual cognitive and emotional associations. The most relevant of these residues is drawn into awareness as a mental impression, further modified by the feeling of the moment. The association may well have a strong volitional character, thus consolidating a particular karmic disposition. The experience of a toothache may be associated with a painful visit to the dentist on an earlier occasion, in which case we may now experience fear that is disproportionate to the actual discomfort, and which may turn out to be groundless. Such a minor misfortune may also trigger (and reinforce) some "life script" theme such as "It's just my luck—it's always me who gets tough breaks!"

The fifth skandha organizes the contents of the fourth into a comprehensible pattern, and is perhaps best translated as "dualistic consciousness," or "discriminative consciousness." It is dualistic because it can only be meaningful to self and make self meaningful if it is organized in terms of "this" and "that"; it is an experience of relativity in which phenomena are classified according to their similarity or difference. The most significant of these dualisms is self/other.

The foregoing is a laborious deconstruction and conceptualization of a subtle and entwined process. Self clings to the process, tries to manipulate and control it, and gets "sucked in" at the level of the third and fourth skandhas. The cultivation of meditative awareness tends to dissolve the fixation of the self on consolidating and defending the self, exposing these processes to awareness, free of self-identification. Self *can* operate without all the smoke, noise, and trouble of this ego process—but we have a deep-rooted fear that if we were to allow it to do so, everything would somehow fall apart.

Big Mind, Small Mind

The Yogachara school of Mahayana Buddhism offers a model of mind that locates the skandhas and karma in a wider context. It also provides a basis for further discussion about the nature of "the self." And, it informs some new and tentative reflections about the scope of a socially engaged Buddhism.

There are three aspects of this model that concern us in this discussion. At the center is *manas,* perhaps best translated as *attentive energy.* Next there is *analytical consciousness* (called *manovijnana* in Sanskrit), the cognitive faculty that enables attentive energy to differentiate the experience of phenomena. Then there is what is variously known as *store-consciousness, the collective unconscious,* or *the universal consciousness (alayavijnana).* The *Lankavatara Sutra* offers the following simile: "Universal Mind is like a great ocean, its surface ruffled by waves and surges, but its depths forever remaining unmoved. In itself it is void of personality and all that belongs to it, but by reason of the defilement upon its face it is like an actor and plays a variety of parts among which a mutual functioning takes place and the mind-system arises."

In the deluded mind-state attentive energy struggles to establish a strong sense of self through the differentiating function of analytical consciousness, which weighs, polarizes, and solidifies this and that. The collective unconscious is an ever-changing stream of energy "perfumed" (to use the idiom of the scriptures) by karmic residues, from whence attentive energy draws forth karmically appropriate volitions. Note that all three elements of this model are aspects of the self. When meditative calm and attentive energy weaken the urgent, alienating structuring of reality which it effects through the differentiating function of analytical consciousness, the emptiness of the collective unconscious is exposed to consciousness—and we are opened to the oceanic depths instead of struggling in the turbulent surface waters.

Scholars' understanding of this model of mind is varied and controversial, but the idea of a collective unconscious is crucial. It is particularly relevant to determining the nature of the self in Buddhism. The doctrine of *no self* is emphasized in order to put in question our strong attachment to a solid self-identity, which the Buddha saw as the origin of suffering. However the Buddhist scholar D. T. Suzuki argues in *The Field of Zen* that it is equally possible to take the contrary view: "Without self there will be no individual; without an individual there will be no responsibility. Without the idea of responsibility morality ceases to exist; so the idea of self is deeply involved in our idea of moral responsibility…. We must in some way have a self, but when self is analyzed…and the senses and the intellect are taken away, no self exists." Thus there are several warnings in the early scriptures (the Pali Canon) that either denying or affirming the self could lead to misunderstanding and confusion. The Buddha made it clear that despite his silence or deliberate equivocation on this matter it did not imply that he did not consider the question of great importance.

The self that accepts phenomena without the least reserve and becomes totally at one with phenomena no longer stands out as a separate self. And yet a person does undoubtedly remain, and often with a quite distinctive personality, free now to be wholly him- or herself. In Zen this unity consciousness is sometimes called *Big Mind,* in contrast to the alienated *small mind.* In "Self the Unattainable," D. T. Suzuki explains:

> The emptied self is simply the psychological self cleansed of its egocentric imagination. It is just as rich in content as before; indeed it is richer than before, because it now contains the whole world in itself instead of having

the world opposed to it. Not only that, it enjoys the state of being true to itself. It is free in the real sense of the word because it is master of itself, absolutely independent, self-reliant, authentic and autonomous.

Finally, in the light of this understanding of the self as separate and yet not separate from the collective unconscious, there are some observations I should like to offer.

There is a view, common among Buddhists, regarding the need for the self to "guard the senses"—lest, out of the root fear arising from an existential sense of lack, the fires of hatred, grasping, and ignorance should flare up. Yet it is a common experience that at times, when the fires of the passions (anger, grasping, and aversion) flare, there is no sense of the self conjuring them up or appropriating them: The experience is rather one of being overwhelmed, invaded, and carried away by powerful energies that flood in. In these moments, the self seems to "forget itself" in aggressive rage or lustful passion.

Other individuals, perhaps when abandoning themselves to service or self-sacrifice in some way, may find themselves flooded with an entirely different but equally overwhelming experience—of unity consciousness and love.

In both instances, the self has done something or had something done to it that triggers a powerful invasion from the collective unconscious of whatever karmic proclivities are being magnetized. The murderer and the saint are both accessed from the collective unconscious, whether in its "tainted" or its "pure" aspect. The power manifested in these situations is a wonder to the many folk who are able to keep their feelings decently under control.

For this reason it is misleading to assume that there is One Pure Consciousness, an immaculate Absolute, from which little ego is alienated. Little ego is all too often shocked to find itself a mere manifestation of the reckless energies of a karmically driven collective unconscious, from which it is and is not separate. Its delusion is that of the collective unconscious and vice versa. When delusion vanishes the collective unconscious is experienced as undeluded or "pure" consciousness.

There are noteworthy ethical implications here. We do have some responsibility for our karmic condition and its manifestations. But a morality of the will can only hold the ethical line more or less precariously, building up defensive conditioning. My argument supports the antinomian view of Far Eastern Buddhism: that intrinsic morality has to be spiritually realized. In traditional Zen training the moral precepts receive the most serious attention only after many years of practice. But the understanding of the collective unconscious offered here implies a deeper sense of compassion for self and others, a more profound insight into the Mahayana belief that "the passions are our buddha nature" (again, the twofold nature of the collective unconscious), and a recognition of the need to cultivate meditative clarity to reveal the underlying benign nature. This statement from the Tibetan Buddhist *dzogchen* meditation tradition, quoted by Keith Dowman in *The Flight of the Garuda,* illustrates further implications of this point: "How ridiculous to expect to find primal awareness and emptiness after you have suppressed passion! How tragic to spend your life searching for something in a place where it is inconceivable that you should find it!"

Sociology and modern historiography imply the unfolding of the collective unconscious through the sociohistorical supercharging of millions of individual wills generation after generation. The immense folly of history is no mere aggregation of personal delusion. The collective unconscious is a subtle and controversial concept, sometimes dismissed as mere speculation. It engages interestingly with the Buddhist social theory developed in this book, but is not essential to it. That individual delusion is inflamed by the sociohistorical process and swept along by it is sufficient explanation alone for the delusive follies of the human race.

The Social Construction of the Self

The skandha model, like the rest of what is essential to Buddhism, refers to the perennial condition of humanity, whatever the social context. It was originated by scholar meditators to assist an inner liberation wherein the social milieu was of little significance. This is not so today. If the model is to underpin our understanding of modern, socially dynamic cultures, we shall need to relate it to contemporary models of mind that are focused on the interaction between self and society.

For the modern mind what is strikingly absent in received Buddhism is any *social* explanation that enlarges insight into the predicament of the individual person. There are historical and cultural reasons for this, which apply more or less to all the great world religions, and which will be discussed in chapter 10. A major concern of this book is to make a modest start at fitting a social "handle" to received Buddhism—to establish at least the framework of a compatible and serviceable body of social theory. This means selecting and employing contemporary social theory that is complementary to Buddhist teachings and that in no way detracts from its historic insights.

Let's begin with phenomenology, the study of the way in which phenomena—the things of which we are conscious—appear to us. It seeks to explain how a world of meaningless sense experiences is translated into a meaningful world of objects—a translation that occurs from birth in our individual consciousness but that increasingly depends on interaction with others. Phenomenology views reality as personal invention made possible in collaboration with others: it is an intersubjective construction.

A phenomenological model of experience (associated with the German philosopher Edmund Husserl), became influential in the later nineteenth century, when the sharply dualistic subject/object paradigm, predominant since the Cartesian revolution in science and philosophy, began to break down. Phenomenology is clearly a hospitable Western landfall for Buddhism, whose starting point is also the observation of the flow of experience, without assuming a separate self experiencing what goes on "out there." The content of our awareness is all that we can know for sure.

Our concern is how phenomenology has been applied to an understanding of social processes. A central figure here is Alfred Schutz, a pupil of Husserl who emigrated to the United States after the rise of Nazism. In Schutz's phenomenological sociology the individual creates and inhabits a "life-world" that is the total sphere of the individual's existence, public and private. Schutz maintained that it is through a process of "typification" that we construct meaning for ourselves out of the basic stream of experience. We classify experiences according to their degree of similarity, and the resulting typification simply becomes "common sense," taken-for-granted knowledge. Beyond a certain stage of individual development, typification necessarily becomes a social process. To communicate with other people and actively relate to them we need to learn and accept their established typifications. From out of a jumble of personal sense experiences we *inherit* a world of shared meanings, socially acceptable feelings, and rewarded behaviors and strategies for coping in a life-world that is relatively stable and predictable. Schutz illustrates his point about shared meaning with the experience of a stranger shipwrecked into a culture totally different from his own; the new culture is unreal and deeply disorienting to him, down to understanding what even the smallest gesture might signify.

The vital energy of the person struggling to be and to do, as reflected in the five skandhas, is the ultimate source of making meaning. But the meanings themselves, and the kinds of meanings, beyond heredity (and what we perhaps might identify as past-life karma), are conditioned by the social culture into which he or she is born. Schutz, in *On Phenomenology and Social Relations,* describes this social inheritance as follows:

> The social world into which man is born and in which he has to find his bearings is experienced by him as a tight-knit web of social relationships, of systems of signs and symbols with their particular meaning structure, of institutionalized forms of social organization, of systems of status and prestige, etc. The meaning of all these elements of the social world in all

its diversity and stratification, as well as the pattern of its texture itself, is by those living within it just taken for granted. The sum-total…constitutes the folk-ways of the in-group, which are socially accepted as the good ways and the right ways for coming to terms with things and with fellow men. They are taken for granted because they have stood the test so far, and, being socially approved, are held as requiring neither an explanation nor a justification.

Later developments of phenomenology, which in turn led into postmodernism, have emphasized the fragmentary nature of intersubjective knowledge—that it is inherently unstable and created anew through each encounter. Authority, for example, which was formerly understood as something imposed upon others, is now seen as depending upon an accepting state of mind in those over whom it is exercised. Unless legitimized in this way it can only be exercised through power, which is much more difficult to sustain.

Phenomenological sociology is hugely significant for Buddhism. It means that how we experience the world is not a creation of the self in isolation but is a social and historical undertaking. *The forms and also the extent of delusive consciousness are not only personal to the individual in their origin but are also socially inherited.*

Some societies are manifestly more delusive in the Buddhist sense than are others. These societies condition delusion more irresistibly, through the socialization of particular norms, values, and ideologies and through the controls and compulsions of their laws and institutions. Unregulated violence, theft, and deceit are condemned, but are glorified in their institutionally legitimized expressions. Ideologically driven totalitarian societies demand of their citizens a very high level of uniform self-identity and promote enmity and violence toward allegedly inferior out-groups. Similarly—but much more insidiously—"slash-and-burn" free-market capitalism glorifies an entrepreneurial acquisitiveness that subordinates ethics to the ideology of the market. Each of these kinds of societies nurtures a restless, insatiable, sensation-hungry, and escapist kind of humanity, undermining and trivializing its capacity for active and compassionate at-oneness.

Psychoanalyst Erich Fromm, writing from a humanist perspective in "Psychoanalysis and Zen Buddhism," describes the human predicament as follows:

The average person, while he thinks he is awake, is actually half asleep. By "half asleep" I mean that his contact with reality is a very partial one; most of what he believes to be reality (inside and outside of himself) is a set of fictions which his mind constructs. He is aware of reality only to the degree to which his social functioning makes it necessary. He is aware of his fellow men inasmuch as he needs to co-operate with them; he is aware of material and social reality inasmuch as he needs to be aware of it in order to manipulate it. *He is aware of reality to the extent to which the goal of survival makes such awareness necessary....* The average person's consciousness is "false consciousness," consisting of fictions and illusion, while precisely what he is not aware of is reality. We can thus differentiate between what a person is conscious of, and what he *becomes* conscious of. He *is* conscious, mostly, of fictions; he can *become* conscious of the realities which lie underneath these fictions.

A significant discussion has developed about the relationship between Buddhist and Western psychology. So far there has been very little parallel discussion with respect to social theory, although David Loy has recently addressed this topic. This would need to refer not only to Buddhist psychology but also to compatible applications from Western psychologies and therapies. For example, concepts like *projection, rationalization,* and *role-playing* offer useful tools for a Buddhist social analysis founded on Buddhist psychology.

We can look at the projection of repressed existential fear and rage by an in-group upon an out-group, expressed and amplified in myths and ideology. Or, we can examine rationalization, in which there is a distancing and repression of feelings in creating a social myth that masks an otherwise unacceptable reality. Thus, the Nazis created a whole technical and bureaucratic vocabulary of mass extermination, wherein the various functionaries could get on with their work without exposure to the truth, which would have been disabling emotionally as well as politically. More mildly, the welfare bureaucracies of democratic states attempt safely to cerebrate in an impartial rationality all the misery and rage that it is their business to alleviate. Indeed, the operation of complex social systems is dependent upon the cold rationality of their public and private bureaucracies, which safely distance realities on digitized computer screens. Suffering has indeed become a much more sophisticated and many-layered phenomenon since the Buddha preached in his *Fire Sermon:* "All is burning...burning with the fire of greed, with the fire of hate, with the fire of delusion."

Of the shared meanings that structure reality, behavioral roles are of particular importance. A behavioral role is a set of actions, attitudes, thoughts, and feelings relevant to a person's situation or occupation. They are maintained more or less consistently and are more or less acknowledged by others who can be relied upon to respond in a particular way. Thus in the doctor' s office, we play out what we suppose is the role of a patient. When lightly carried, roles are a convenient, instant shorthand for everyday transactions. Played lightly and humorously they can even be a bridge between strangers. More commonly, however, roles provide another means of securing the self in socially endorsed, guilt-free behaviors. Roles ensure a secure, orderly world in which even subordinates may be glad to "know their place." The white coat, the badge, the clipboard, and the official smile ensure that we shall at least be recognized as *some* kind of somebody. However, role becomes ultimately delusive when it takes over the whole identity, so that one is dependent for one's entire personhood on one's roles: one *is* one's persona.

Role-playing, rationalization, and projection are among the forms of social conditioning that enable, permit, or pressurize individuals to feel, think, and behave in particular ways out of their need to sustain a sense of self. Buddhist teaching rightly gives priority attention to the individual person. But for how much longer can it continue to ignore the delusive social forces with which that individual has to engage from birth, conditioning our lifestyle and our life-world more than we know? If the existential roots of greed are to be exposed, why not the consumerism that fuels greed and feeds on existential anxiety? If we are to ameliorate personal truculence and rancor, then why not the "up front," "in your face" culture-with-attitude that stokes it up? Conversely, why does modern Western society so rarely support the kinds of political and economic conditions that encourage compassion and generosity? Is it really possible to believe that modern society is no more than a collection of individuals, so that if enough of us try to behave decently to one another, oppressive regimes will cease to oppress and transnational corporations will cease to exploit? Lifestyle change is a good start, but it can never be enough without a commitment to radical structural and institutional change. The Buddhist teaching, if it is to be sustained into the next millennium of our crisis-ridden planet, must be socially and ecologically engaged.

The Social Fallacy

Thus far, I have argued that Buddhism needs a social psychology. Yet I would also like to assert that social psychology needs Buddhism.

In 1859, in the Preface to his *Critique of Political Economy*, Karl Marx pronounced that "it is not the consciousness of men that determines their being but, on the contrary, their social being that determines their consciousness." It has been a persistent tendency in contemporary social thinking to reduce the person to a social product, malleable for social engineering as the New Man or New Woman, or a mere theatrical creation on the stage of life. The *social fallacy*, as I call it, is the belief that human well-being is to be achieved primarily or solely through social development. It is deeply ingrained in modern social theory, and seeks to explain social phenomena (and remedy its ills) exclusively in social terms—particularly economic and political terms.

The social fallacy is of much more than theoretical interest. It is a commonplace mentality that has grown up over the past five hundred years with our increasing mastery over the objective world and the decline in religious belief. It is the belief that most afflictions can sooner or later be fixed "out there." As spiritual self-transcendence and the consolations of exoteric religion have receded, together with magic and fatalism, the range and power of our external fixes have expanded. These fixes and consolations include everything from the optimism engendered by a vision of a better society and the peace of mind offered by life insurance policies to faith in the power of modern medicine and the instant distraction of a multitude of television channels. And progress promises that what cannot be done now will certainly be done later. In the world's richest country it is common to put the mind in for routine servicing by one's psychiatrist, much as the car is put in for servicing by one's auto mechanic, so that it will run more smoothly and won't disrupt productivity. Only old age, death, and the diseases that medicine still cannot cure remain outside the mentality of quick-fix scientism.

But the question persists: What is it that animates this social and linguistic animal to struggle so fiercely to create a meaningful life-world? The self has its own existential dynamism, and phenomenological sociology is doomed to failure unless it includes the self that makes social reality. Buddhism implies that unless there is some significant personal, individual change in the ways we feel and think about ourselves and others, we shall go on evolving societies that express and reinforce the futile struggle of each of us to escape from our root fear. Buddhism and other kinds of spiritual paths are not about social liberation but about human liberation, about the release of human potential trapped in the delusive suffering that arises from the root human condition. Secular social psychology is by contrast superficial, for it does not go down to the roots of human behavior, and is narrowly confined when set against the real concerns of our lives. We can be bereaved as well as unemployed. We can be terminally ill as well as threatened by war. We can experience deep inner loneliness as well as poor housing conditions. We can suffer from corrosive self-hate, self-pity, and bitterness as well as from an insufficient pension. We are human beings before we are citizens; the inevitability of our death (to the extent we can open to it) is often infinitely more significant to us than whether it will be nuclear or not.

It is not just that both these contrasting pairs of afflictions trouble us, but that the "remedy" for both lies ultimately in how we experience and live our lives. The tacit assumption that we have spirituality for the first of each pair and social development for the second blights the effectiveness of both and deludes us into supposing they are separate. The self is the ultimate reference point for the social structures and processes into which history has translated it. Note, however, that this translation cannot be made in direct and simplistic terms, such as attributing world war to individual aggressiveness. Buddhism needs sociology, and sociology Buddhism, in order to make this translation credible, comprehensible —and liberative.

Chapter 5

INDIAN BUDDHIST SOCIAL THEORY AND ENGAGEMENT

To WHAT EXTENT has the Buddhism we have received in the West brought with it a social theory and tradition of social engagement that is valid and serviceable for us today? In this chapter we will look at the social theory and forms of social engagement that evolved in Indian Buddhism, and consider its value for contemporary engaged Buddhists. It is worth repeating that, whatever the cultural packaging, the existential core of Buddhism, the heart of Dharma, speaks to the perennial human condition. It is transcultural. Primarily it is not about how to understand society and change it, but how to transcend the underlying unease and anguish we characteristically experience as individuals. Nevertheless, the Buddhist teachings of personal liberation have social ramifications. To experience the world differently implies behaving differently. In short, wisdom implies compassion. The social implications of core Buddhist teachings are inevitably colored by the social culture in which they arise and to which they refer. It is therefore necessary to appreciate and separate the intent—coming from the core teaching—from the particular diagnoses and prescriptions offered in and for a specific society.

Indian Buddhism arguably offers an expression of social engagement that was less refracted by strong cultural pressures and co-opted by the power elite than was the case elsewhere, including later Theravada developments in Southeast Asia. Indian culture tended to define itself transcendentally rather than in social and political terms, and there was little racial or national consciousness to color religion. Spiritual values were held to be universal. Different religious beliefs were assumed to be different manifestations of universal law, or dharma, and this belief encouraged religious tolerance. Indian Buddhist social teaching and practice therefore tended to be a relatively direct expression of the Dharma, whether in the bodhisattva ideal conveyed in the Mahayana texts, in the sutras of the Pali canon, in the welfare policies of the great emperor Ashoka, or in the great Mahayana philosopher Nagarjuna's *Jewel Garland of Royal Counsels*. These social teachings and practices have particular value in offering historical evidence of Buddhist social perspectives.

Indian Buddhism *did* recognize the relevance of political and economic concerns within its overarching project of spiritual awakening. In this I believe it was in advance of much of contemporary Western Buddhism. That it did so is to some extent explained by the striking economic revolution taking place on the plain of the Ganges at the time of the Buddha. The traditional communal system was being undermined by bigger private landholdings, by the expansion of trade stimulated by their productive surplus, and by the growth of cities. The rural communitarian "republics" were being absorbed into city-based monarchical states. It was, in every respect, a time of profound change and new growth.

The monastic community had a direct interest in receiving the protection and patronage of the new monarchs, and in the rising class of *gahapatis*, or householders, from which most of their lay support came. These householders, who appear often in the the sutras, constituted a landholding class of key importance. The Buddha came from an old aristocratic family, valued the political and financial support of kings and merchants, and was in touch with all levels of society. The sutras show that he was socially aware, politically astute, and had some grasp of the rudimentary economics of his time. On many occasions he argued the central principle of any socially engaged Buddhism, namely that public well-being depends ultimately upon individual personality transformation.

There are numerous passages in the *Mahavagga* and *Catukkanipata* of the Anguttara Nikaya urging followers of Buddha "to live for the welfare of the many." There is also hard-headed advice in the *Sigalovada Sutta* attuned to the interests of the householders, who are urged to work hard, accumulate wealth, and expand their property. There is also an awareness of the effects of economic conditions on social behavior and stability, as in this statement in the *Cakkavatti Sihanada Sutta,* from the Digha Nikaya: "Thus—from provision not being made for the poor—poverty, stealing, violence, murder, lying, evil speaking and immorality become widespread." The value of welfare and social incentives over punishment is a common feature of Indian Buddhist social theory, clearly expressed in the *Kutadanta Sutta:*

> Now there is one method to adopt to put a thorough end to this disorder. Whoever there may be in this royal realm who devote themselves to cattle rearing and agriculture, to them let His Majesty give food and seed corn. Whoever there may be who devote themselves to trade, to them let

His Majesty give capital. Whoever there may be who devote themselves to the government service, to them let his Majesty give wages and food. Then those men, each following his own business, will no longer harass the realm; His Majesty's revenue will go up; the country will be quiet and at peace; and the people will be pleased and happy, and with their children in their arms will dwell with open doors.

The Dhammaraja Ideal

The Buddha envisaged spiritually informed monarchs as the means of promoting the above policies. Such a dhammaraja would work in tandem with the monastic community responsible for the higher work of spiritual liberation. The chariot of state would thus run upon the two wheels, power and righteousness, with the authority of the ruler legitimized by the monastic sangha (the Buddhist community). The latter were the king's influential advisers and thus, in a sense, were power-sharers. Just as rulers sometimes intervened to purge the sangha of malpractices and even of heresies, so also was the sangha sometimes instrumental in the deposition of unrighteous monarchs. On this pattern great Buddhist civilizations were established in Sri Lanka, Siam, Burma, Cambodia, and Indonesia.

The most celebrated dhammaraja is undoubtedly the Indian emperor Ashoka (third century B.C.E.). Perhaps the world's most powerful ruler at the time, his achievements and pronouncements have been influential up to the present day. Ashoka's policies and exhortations to his subjects are carved in rock as a series of edicts. Robert Thurman, the renowned scholar and translator, has identified in these engraved edicts the "operative principles of the politics of enlightenment." In his essay "The Politics of Enlightenment" he enumerates these principles as follows:

1. Individual transcendentalism
2. Nonviolence
3. Emphasis on education and on religious pluralism
4. Compassionate welfare policies
5. Political decentralization

The first of these principles, individual transcendentalism, asserts that both personal and public well-being depend on working to transform one's own personality. This is the foundation of the politics of enlightenment. Thus Rock Edict XIII proclaims: "It is difficult to achieve happiness, either in this world or the next, except by intense love of dharma, intense self-examination, intense obedience, intense fear of sin, and intense enthusiasm."

As for nonviolence, after his conversion to Buddhism Ashoka renounced war as an instrument of policy and called upon his neighbors to follow his example. Rock Edict IV claimed that the emperor's inculcation of the spirit of nonviolence among his subjects "has increased beyond anything observed in many hundreds of years abstention from killing animals and from cruelty to living beings." Ashoka did, however, find it necessary to retain the death penalty in extreme cases, though he also introduced an appeals procedure.

With respect to the third principle, involving education and religious pluralism, Ashoka distinguished between, on the one hand, dharma as transcendent truth and universal morality, and on the other, the several specific religions through which it was variously expressed in his realm. These included Buddhism, to which he was personally dedicated. (Note that here and throughout this book, *Dharma* denotes the Buddhist teachings, whereas as *dharma* refers to universal morality and law.) In Rock Edicts VII and XII Ashoka "wishes members of all faiths to live everywhere in his kingdom. For they all seek mastery of the senses and purity of mind.... Growth in the qualities essential to religion in men of all faiths may take many forms, but its root is in guarding one's speech to avoid extolling one's own faith and disparaging the faith of others improperly, or, when the occasion is appropriate, immoderately. The faiths of others all deserve to be honored for one reason or another. By honoring them, one exalts one's own faith and at the same time performs a service to the faith of others.... The objective of these measures is the promotion of each man's particular faith and the glorification of the dharma."

In pursuance of compassionate welfare policies, Ashoka established medical and veterinary services, built rest houses and hospices for the poor and sick, introduced programs of public works and agricultural improvement, and appointed public welfare officers. Regarding the last of these principles, political decentralization, Ashoka, while exercising strong personal authority, nevertheless delegated considerable autonomy to his provincial governors, relying on the loyalty of his subjects to check any misuse of such local power.

Ashoka's policies often have been appropriated by modern revisionists who take them out of their original context and submerge their spiritual significance beneath a radical humanism. For example, professor of Indian philosophy N. V. Banerjee, in *Buddhism and Marxism: A Study in Humanism,* asserts that it is "evident that Buddhism was full of suggestions the implementation of which could transform even a kingdom into a sort of socialist state with a more or less humanistic foundation." A sharply contrasting assessment of Ashoka's reign is offered by Indian history scholar A. L. Basham in "Asoka and Buddhism: A

Reexamination": "Carried away by his new faith, [Ashoka] increasingly lost touch with reality until ultimately he was dethroned and the great Mauryan empire broke up, largely as the result of his intensely moral but thoroughly unrealistic convictions." In any case, the fact remains that while Buddhism was comparatively insignificant in the two centuries before Ashoka, after his reign it began to flourish extensively. Whatever substance his policies achieved, it is certain that Ashoka created a powerful myth that is still influential for a socially engaged Buddhism.

A less well-known Buddhist social model can be found in the advice given by Nagarjuna, the greatest of the Indian Mahayana sages and scholars, to his friend King Udayi of south central India, some five centuries after Ashoka. Nagarjuna's *Jewel Garland of Royal Counsels* is arguably more significant for engaged Buddhism than is Ashoka's reign, in that Nagarjuna's social perspectives are those of one of the most insightful personalities in the history of world religions. Moreover, Nagarjuna writes out of the supposedly "mystical," apolitical Mahayana tradition of Buddhism. Nagarjuna's *Counsels* are also valuable in that some two-thirds of the text is taken up with clarifying what Thurman calls the first principle of Buddhist social ethics, individualist transcendentalism—that is to say, the primacy of individual personality transcendence.

Nagarjuna urges the ruler and his officials to strive to awaken to a selfless understanding of society and its needs. In "Guidelines for Buddhist Social Activism Based on Nagarjuna's *Jewel Garland of Royal Counsels,*" Thurman recounts that "the bodhisattva man of action can and must be responsible for intuitive wisdom, and so Nagarjuna presents the king with a quintessence of the methods for developing the wisdom basis of effective social action."

Next Nagarjuna introduces the nonviolent principle in social activism, namely, as Thurman's describes, "revulsion from lusts, restraint of aggressions, vanity of possessions and power." Violence begets violence, so Nagarjuna condemns capital punishment and advocates the rehabilitative treatment of prisoners: "Just as unworthy sons are punished out of a wish to make them worthy, so punishment should be enforced with compassion and not from hatred or concern with wealth. Once you have examined the fierce murderers and judged them correctly, you should banish them without killing or torturing them."

Since in Nagarjuna's view the goal of society is to provide favorable conditions for each person to evolve toward awakening to his or her true nature, education to that end must be the most important function of government. This is not, however, a call for mass Buddhist indoctrination. Nagarjuna, like Ashoka, recognizes the validity of different routes to selfless enlightenment and he, also, uses *dharma* to signify spiritual truth in general, and not specifically the Buddhist path to its realization. He repeatedly argues that belief systems, dogmatic views, closed convictions, and fanatic ideologies, far from being the answer to anything, are themselves sicknesses that require remedy.

Finally, Nagarjuna advocates much the same kind of welfare state as did Ashoka, and with the same concern for animals as for human beings. Nagarjuna counsels: "Cause the blind, the sick, the humble, the unprotected, the destitute, and the crippled, all equally to attain food and drink without omission."

For many centuries in India and Southeast Asia there was a persistent ideal for Buddhist political rulers to establish in their realms a Buddhist culture and network of social institutions. Thus, in Japan, four centuries after Nagarjuna and almost a millennium after Ashoka, when Prince Shotoka proclaimed Buddhism as the state religion, he not only made provisions for a monastic sangha but also established a hospital, a dispensary, and an asylum for orphans and old people. In very general terms, the dhammaraja ideal prefigures the call for a spiritually informed social revolution made in this book.

In *The Social Dimensions of Early Buddhism,* Buddhist scholar Uma Chakravarti argues that early Buddhism advocated a central role for political leaders:

> The existing political system…had to be transformed into one in which kingship would be an instrument of social and political change. The new political system would be based on charismatic kingship, in which the [king] was morally responsible for the elimination of destitution and the creation of a new socio-political order.… Thus the [king] was the counterpart in the social world of the [spiritual teacher].… The two together would reorder human existence.

In my view this is a typical "modernist" reading of the evidence; the role of the lay ruler was more marginal than this to the Buddha's central spiritual project. In practice, he did not give a high priority to advocating the dhammaraja role, and some of his royal patrons were far removed from it. To state that he was aiming at "a new sociopolitical order" is an extravagant claim. Indeed, he censured underlings who criticized those above their social station as guilty of "wrongful envy."

In today's world of socially engaged Buddhism, there has been a prominent contemporary advocate of the *dhammaraja* model. Thai activist and Theravada monk Ajahn Buddhadasa argues for a political ideal that harks back to Ashoka's benevolent paternalism. In the closing pages of one of the essays in his book *Dhammic Socialism,* Ajahn Buddhadasa declares:

> I favor a Buddhist social democracy which is composed of *dhamma* and managed by a "dictator" whose character exemplifies the ten royal virtues

[of] generosity, morality, liberality, uprightness, gentleness, self-restraint, non-anger, non-hurtfulness, forbearance, and non-opposition…. In some cases this form of Buddhist dictatorial socialism can solve the world's problems better than any other form of government. In particular, small countries like Thailand should have democracy in the form of a dictatorial dhammic socialism.

However, he continues: "The character of the ruler is the crucial factor." Furthermore, a "ruling class of some kind is absolutely necessary; however, it should be defined by its function rather than by birth…. This kind of government, an enlightened ruling class…is in fact the kind of socialism which can save the world."

Apart from this one anachronistic feature of a Platonic dictator, Ajahn Buddhadasa's "dhammic socialism" does in fact present much the same social ideals and perspectives as this book. He has, moreover, been a major inspiration in the development of a socially engaged Buddhism in Thailand and beyond (see chapter 15).

Social Theory and Analysis

There remains the question of social analysis and social theory in early Buddhism, for it seems to be confined to social policy prescriptions.

Sociology, particularly an understanding of the dynamics of social structures, is a product of Western modernity, and no older than the nineteenth century. The West provided optimum conditions for the development of a science of society. The Greeks moved from mythologizing the social world to objectifying it in political speculation and historiography. And Judaism and Christianity were prophetic, history-centered religions alive with dualistic struggle—good versus evil, God versus the devil, contrasting with India's impersonal *avidya* (ignorance). Subsequently this strained dualism translated into the struggle to push back the frontiers of knowledge and to create new sciences, of society and of the mind. Economic, social, and political revolutions provided forceful lessons in social dynamics and an urgent need for societal understanding.

Comparatively speaking, East Asia seems to have provided less fertile ground for the birth of a comprehensive social theory, in part because the relatively fixed and hierarchical social relationships were accepted as having much the same changeless inevitability as natural phenomena. However in India at the time of the earliest Buddhist scriptures, there was greater fluidity in the social structure. There is an interesting account of the evolution of society in the *Agganna Sutta*, which was popular and widespread. This sutra traces the appearance of private property to greed combined with increased production, followed by the election of rulers to protect property and other rights and to prevent anarchy. It has a strikingly Hobbesian flavor, and, like seventeenth-century Western political theory in general, it understands society as an aggregation of individuals out of whose conflicting personal needs laws and institutions are in due course contracted. Although in the *Agganna Sutta* there is no awareness of social structure in the modern sense, it is noteworthy that personal delusion and delusive social phenomena are codependent and evolve together.

In conclusion, early Buddhism—in effect, Indian Buddhism—does provide contemporary Buddhist social theory and engagement with some modest but encouraging scriptural credentials and exemplars. However, any temptation to read ancient Buddhist social philosophy as a literal prescription for our own times should be resisted. While there are many passages in the sutras that offer legitimate pointers for a socially engaged Buddhism, we must be careful not to read them out of context, and to view them in relation to their overall soteriological purport.

Chapter 6

INSTITUTIONALIZED DELUSION:

TOWARD A BUDDHIST SOCIAL THEORY

FOR MANY PEOPLE today Buddhism appears as a quietistic creed bereft of any social awareness. This will continue to be so until it is culturally unwrapped and socially actualized. This is urgently necessary because socially engaged Buddhism offers an essential critique of the Western ideal of political and economic liberation. And because the Western ideal fails to reach to our very deepest liberative need, what it has achieved is flawed, restricted, contradictory, and problematic. We have all the resources needed to promote planetary well-being, yet somehow at every turn "the system" frustrates us. It is not enough for Buddhism and other spiritualities to explain the existential roots of the system. They have to explain how it came into being, what it is, and how it can be changed—and do so in ways that engage with contemporary social science. The key question here is how the Buddhist theory of the person translates into a theory of society. How does the existential struggle *to be* express itself in the typical structures and processes of societies and in their cultural norms and values?

Establishing a definitive relationship between individual and society, between human agency and social system, is clearly central to the development of both engaged Buddhism and sociology. While Buddhism, as a premodern spirituality, lacks a credible social theory, contemporary social theory lacks an in-depth understanding of what it is that moves the self—the ultimate "maker of history." In this chapter I offer a Buddhist social theory that draws on, and can contribute to, both disciplines.

For Buddhism the prime mover of history and society is the person, this fathom-long body, this bundle of consciousness struggling to affirm its existence, its reality, as securely and absolutely as possible. For the Buddha this human predicament was to be found in three characteristics of being-in-the-world:

insubstantiality, transience, and our ultimate inability to evade them, which is experienced as *dukkha* (suffering). Suffering flares—or smolders—as three "fires." The first fire is characterized by acquisitiveness, clinging, attachment, and identification with belongingness and belongings. The second fire includes rancor, rage, or quiet desperation, which may be repressed, turned inward in guilt, or projected outward in aggression. And the third fire is that of delusion— our ignorance as to the root origin of our sense of lack, our unease, and the behaviors by which we struggle to compensate for it. We are characteristically unaware that we are being impelled by anything, since we are ourselves the impulsion, and the impulsion is what imparts our sense of self-identity.

As we saw in chapter 4, the behavioral expressions of the fires and their meanings are interactively inherited, negotiated, and evolved. Through this interactive creation of meaning with others, persons—with their self-affirming life-worlds—are socially constructed. Thus cultures are evolved, social structures are elaborated, and history is made, but conditioned always by the meanings inherited from previous generations. Collective karmic momentum ensures continuity: The past validates the present.

Culture is a complex of meanings, a mentality, by which people manage to live, as expressed in their values and norms, their approved kinds of behavior and ways of life. Culture legitimates and society facilitates behaviors by which we endeavor to fill our sense of lack. And, further, they amplify and intensify these behaviors (as in the legitimization of the blood lusts of mass murder and pillage). History has provided a societal downdraft for the fires more inflaming than could ever have been imagined in the Buddha's time. Society also channels and regulates them so that they do not destabilize the social order or threaten dominant groups. Thus, in precapitalist societies entrepreneurial wealth creation was considered recklessly antisocial. Certain levels and kinds of wealth were appropriate as marks of status differentiating various ranks of society. Wealth creation was regulated to support hierarchy and stability. It would have been unimaginable to the medieval mind that it could become the driving force of society and the ultimate measure of value.

Ethical codes, rules of law, codes of honor, religious precepts and taboos, *raisons d'état,* and market imperatives all have variously acted as social legitimators and regulators. History, myth, and literature abound with tragedies where an individual or group has invoked some universal principle against the values that were believed to sustain the integrity of their culture and society. In the most poignant cases they have been reluctantly executed by otherwise humane realists faced with truths too socially disruptive to be tolerated.

The Emperor Has No Clothes

Culture and society evolve out of the need to facilitate and sustain collective and personal identities. The objectification of cultural values and social structures confirms "I" and "us." "Society" is thus reified—it is conceived as a solid thing that is spoken of as if it had a life of its own. But ultimately there is nowhere else it can exist except in the minds of its members as a shared mentality. For example, political authority can evaporate overnight when it loses enough credibility in the heads of enough citizens, as was illustrated by the dramatically sudden collapse of some of the communist regimes. When, through meditative practice, there is no longer the root need to affirm *this* self by solidifying all of *that,* then *that* displays the "emptiness" explained earlier.

So, for the mystical militant, the spiritually informed activist, "society" appears fluid, contingent, and ungraspable; there is an unobstructed openness toward all of its members and a relaxed, unthreatening way of "winning hearts and minds." This is readily sensed in spiritually informed change agents such as Mahatma Gandhi, Martin Luther King, and Nelson Mandela or in Buddhist contemporaries such as the Dalai Lama, Thich Nhat Hanh of Vietnam, Ajahn Maha Gosananda of Cambodia, and Aung San Suu Kyi of Burma. But even for people working for change in their communities who would not regard themselves as "spiritually informed," some quiet reflection about the ultimate insubstantiality of "the system" can be very empowering.

The emperor has no clothes, as the old story runs. And yet, the emperor certainly has. Society exists only in the mind, but most minds badly need to experience its reassuring sense of solidity "out there." And if, contrariwise, they want to change it and yet feel they are "beating their heads against a brick wall," they are commonly reassured by the possession of an equally solid ideology. Yet the objectification of society is nothing more than objectification. For example, the "market economy" is a set of subjectively agreed meanings, a game that has historically evolved. But "market forces" and the "laws of economics" are experienced as forces of nature, and the economy is something that can "get out of control." Of course, the sense of solidity of all established orders is maintained by tangible vested interests, but the deepest investment in it is the root emotional one. Both radicals and conservatives typically share that kind of investment. Social structures are also reinforced by the power of continuity. "How it is" is ingrained over time, which, given long enough, may make it difficult to imagine how it might be otherwise.

Furthermore, mentalities are physically objectified and embodied in the materiel of a society, such as its wealth and its weaponry. These, in turn, condition mentality and can take on a life of their own, so that their ultimate origins in mentality are forgotten. Such is the case with the very existence of nuclear missiles in the world, and also the existence of a well-developed arms industry that can supply assault rifles to youngsters for the price of a basket of groceries.

An informed Buddhist radicalism engenders three essential freedoms. The first is freedom from a sense of powerlessness under the weight of "the system." The second is freedom from the need for ideology in order to sustain empowerment. This is freedom from *our* entrenched belief system and from the lust for achievement. And the third freedom is to experience without illusions the power of the social order and yet be able to keep on working in good heart for a better world. It means to have no illusions about, say, the effectiveness of nonviolent protest in any situation. This is the higher third, beyond pessimism and optimism. It is to accept that this is how things are, and all that has to be done is to carry on the work, even if unsure whether it is being done in the most effective way. And it may mean accepting that at times "nothing" in fact can be done, and to do that well too—like dying. Thus, in his novel *The Crack-Up,* F. Scott Fitzgerald wrote: "The test of a first rate intelligence is the ability to hold two opposed ideas in the mind at the same time and still retain the ability to function. One should, for example, be able to see that things are hopeless and yet be determined to make them otherwise."

It is meditative practice that can clear the mind from self-reservation and support the selfless action of the passionate moderate, the radical conservative, the temperate extremist, the reasonable revolutionary—people who take up this or that position, but who do not *need* to do so. This may come from the empowering sense of acceptance of a still mind. Or it may come, as Buddhist author Christopher Ives describes in *Zen Awakening and Society,* from wearing out the urgent, questing self by battering away at questions like those that the Japanese Zen activist Hisamatsu Shin'ichi gave to his students: "Right now, if nothing you can do is of any avail, what do you do?"

Our discussion has moved from theory to practice, and from intellection to gut realization. For the ultimate value of theory lies only in its actualization. How can we experience and act in society—which exists as no more than the sum of its members and yet as more than that—at both the level of individual agency *and* social system?

Antithetical Bonding

The objective otherness of "society" helps to define the identity of "the individual." However, the principal social and historical means of self-affirmation is what I shall term *antithetical bonding.* This I propose as the main building block of a Buddhist social theory.

We discussed in the first chapter how the individual seeks the self-affirming assurance of membership in some kind of group or collectivity. This sense of belongingness can be established by a shared ideology and by the shared identity-transference of the collectivity to a leader—its hero. It was Freud who first identified the phenomenon of transference to explain the typically sheeplike behavior of people in groups, and it has been comprehensively developed by Alfred Adler, Carl Jung, Erich Fromm, and Ernest Becker. Identification with a superman who becomes a myth in his (or her) own lifetime helps relieve the followers of their individual sense of frailty, anxiety, and inadequacy.

A collective belongingness identity is more deeply established and exalted by subordinating another group or competing with it. Thus bonding tends to be *antithetical*. Acquisitiveness, aggression, and the whole complex of self-affirming compulsions require "others" if they are to satisfy the visceral appetite for being top dog; this appetite is satisfied better still if the others can be put down in some way. Thus collectivities commonly require another collectivity to oppress, exploit, and victimize. After all, as Ernest Becker said, "Somebody has to pay for the way things are." In *The Immortalist* Alan Harrington elaborates on this need to assert self as superior:

> If those weird individuals with beards and funny hats are acceptable, then what about my claim to superiority? Can someone like that be my equal in God's eyes? Does he, that one, dare to hope to live forever too—and perhaps crowd me out? I don't like it. All I know is, if he's right, I'm wrong. So different and funny-looking. I think he's trying to fool the gods with his sly ways. Let's show him up. He's not very strong. For a start, see what he'll do when I poke him.

It requires only a relatively insignificant stimulus to trigger this response to a deep existential need. This has been indicated by a number of classic experiments like that reported by Sherif and Sherif, in their book *Groups in Harmony and Tension*. This involved two groups of twelve boys each, all from a similar social background. The experiment was set up so that each of the two groups lived, worked, and played separately. It was not long before each group developed its own leadership and hierarchical structure together with its own sanctions against deviant behavior within the group. Intergroup contact enhanced in-group solidarity and friendship, on the one hand. However, on the other, it also very readily—and for no ostensible reason—led to out-group hostility, with name calling and even fights between the two groups. Even post-experimental efforts to break down this hostility met with strong resistance.

Much of contemporary armed ethnic conflict grotesquely illustrates how, when the existential supports of social structures begin to break down, fear and rage tear through decades of socialization and are projected onto neighbors, friends, and colleagues, often with unspeakable cruelty. For example, the apparent differences between Croats and Serbs had been steadily diminishing since the 1960s. And yet, within months, a common secular, humanistic outlook was abandoned, and opposing identities were conjured up by recalling ancient ethnic and religious antagonisms. For fifty years both peoples had spoken a common language, Serbo-Croatian, but it was not long before Zagreb and Belgrade linguists began insisting that each spoke a distinct language, and that it was necessary to purge impure derivations that had crept in from the alien tongue.

Once in motion both the bonding and the conflict tend to intensify; all other goals and values are subordinated to the ascendancy of one's own group; differences between the groups are exaggerated; and what they may have in common is ignored or denied. The middle ground disappears and the process seems to take on a life of its own, in which those involved find themselves trapped in "imperatives." Thus, as President George W. Bush declared about the war against terrorism, "Those who aren't with us are against us."

Whether within the group or by one group over another, the very activity of ordering and controlling, of bending others to our will, and even rejoicing in their vulnerability, fear, and pain has about it a gratuitous lust, a bloody-minded need that goes beyond what is functionally necessary or socially and morally sanctioned. This is very evident in certain insecure and rigid types of personality, but it is an impulse that appears to exist in most of us. This lust for power and control is a matter of common experience in police forces, prisons, and armies, where it is given some functional and moral license, but it also occurs quite commonly in everyday superior/subordinate relationships, as in parent and child, boss and worker, landlord and tenant. Always there is the tendency to merge into the role, and so avoid exposing our vulnerable humanity, as well as the urge to exploit it beyond any functional requirement.

The self tends to feel greater assurance and gratification by obeying authority—any authority—than by disobeying, even when there is nothing to fear from disobedience. There have been some classic social psychology experiments whose outcomes direct our attention to a hunger deep within the psyche to explain behaviors otherwise inexplicable in terms of the objective situations in which they occur. They also help to explain the recurrent hellishness of human history.

In one of these experiments, which took place in 1961, Stanley Milgram, a young psychologist at Yale, discovered how easily ordinary citizens could become perpetrators of evil. Volunteers were asked to take part in an experiment to test people's ability to learn. They were then told by the man in a white coat to administer electric shocks to a stranger behind a screen when he failed to perform a simple memory task. To Milgram's horror, two-thirds of the volunteers were ready to administer potentially lethal doses of electricity.

Another famous experiment was that conducted by Philip Zimbardo at Stanford University in 1971, when volunteer students were split into "guards" and "inmates" in a makeshift underground jail. The experiment had to be abandoned within days, as the guards began violently assaulting the inmates and several of the prisoners had nervous breakdowns.

Collectivities of antithetical bonding are found one within another, in hierarchical subordination, uneasy parallelism, and other kinds of relationship. Complex patterns may display combinations of bonding principles, for example ideological, ethnic, or patriarchal. Consensus and stability are balanced against conflict and flux. These different elements of social organization fit together loosely, subject to a contingency of outcomes and the accidental, open-ended nature of unfolding history. Tracing the boundaries and development of collectivities, and mapping their antithetical bondings is, I believe, an important undertaking for a comprehensive Buddhist social theory. But it must be a careful, teasing-out process, avoiding any tendency to categorization and reification. Buddhism is essentially a tool of inquiry and an ideological solvent, open to untidy complexity and suspicious of fixed conclusions.

Hunger—Existential and Physical

The foregoing sketch of a Buddhist theory of society must be qualified by the fact that most people for most of history were predominantly engaged in an objectively motivated struggle to keep alive and raise the next generation. Societies only begin "to make history" when they have achieved a certain level of subsistence and attain a production surplus that enables a flourishing ruling class to raid other societies and develop the arts of civilization. This making of history—the evolution of civilization—involves the establishment of a new, emergent self-consciousness, the recognition of personhood, the development of abstract thinking, and the objectification of body and nature. With the dawning of civilization, objective *and* subjective developments introduce an existential awareness—an *egoic era,* as transpersonal philosopher Ken Wilber calls it. Thus, as soon as history begins to be made, it begins to be made out of an existentially aware human condition.

Individuals and societies are motivated by both the objective necessities of survival and the subjective, existential need to affirm self-identity. At times it is difficult to distinguish between the two impetuses.

Physical survival is itself a first requirement for affirming the self. And, of course, physical survival needs continue to be major motivators for much of the world's population. But even the most materially deprived social group, living on the edge of subsistence, is sustained by some kind of culture that gives meaning to its existence and provides a sense of identity.

Even if we were to suppose that material necessity has for the most part governed human behavior, the question would still remain as to why that behavior has been so consistently and outrageously bloody-minded. Why has history not predominantly been about conflict resolution and the flowering of egalitarian and cooperative commonwealths? Such things are not beyond the possibility of human nature, as infrequent and short-lived episodes bear witness. Throughout history radicals and visionaries, like John Ball, leader of the great 1381 peasant revolt, have demanded an answer. Jean Froissart, a French historian of the period, recorded the angry pleadings of one of Ball's sermons:

> What have we deserved that we should be kept enslaved? We are all descended from one father and mother, Adam and Eve. What reasons can they give to show that they are greater lords than we, save by making us toil and labor, so that they can spend? They are clothed in velvet and soft leather furred with ermine, while we wear coarse cloth; they have their wines, spices and good bread, while we have the drawings of chaff and drink water. They have handsome houses and manors, and we the pain and travail, the rain and the wind, in the fields.

The rich and powerful, having made provision for their physical needs, are *still* driven by an insatiable existential hunger. They have frequently put their material security at risk by squeezing the poor into rebellion and by making hazardous wars on slight pretexts, all in the name of honor and glory. They have dangerously depleted their wealth in great monuments and pomp. For most of human history this "psychic greed" (or existential need) has been the prime mover working beneath and beyond Marx's "historical materialism." Clearly the phenomenon of social class exploitation is inexplicable solely on economic grounds and only becomes understandable when viewed from a perspective broader than that of Marxian economics.

I have argued that the Buddhist explanation of the human condition can be extended into a social theory by drawing upon phenomenology and other developments in sociology and social psychology. This Buddhist social theory, as I have suggested, must embrace the complex interrelationship of individual and societal conditioning, as well as the both the physical and existential hungers that drive the "making of history." It is a large and exciting field that is as yet barely explored.

Ideology

The Buddha observed that "the world in general grasps after systems, and is imprisoned by dogmas and ideologies," though the wise "do not go along with that system-grasping, that mental obstinacy and dogmatic bias" (Samyutta Nikaya XII, 15).

By *ideology* I mean a collectively held body of ideas that affirms the identity of the group that believes them at least as much as it provides a comprehensive explanation of society or some other phenomenon. Ideologies are an intellection that we make of reality in order to fill our sense of existential lack, and typically they powerfully reinforce the process of antithetical bonding. Traditional ideologies rested upon the authority of a sage and the weight of tradition, while modern ones tend to be rationally validated, such as Marx's "scientific socialism" or "free market" capitalism. The Buddhist sociology I am proposing in this book contrasts with conventional sociology in its interpretation of ideology, in that sociology explains ideology primarily in terms of conflicting social groupings: Here as elsewhere the human condition itself is the ghost in the sociological machine.

It is ideology that legitimizes the killing fields of history. The following description, from Norman Davies' *Heart of Europe: A Short History of Poland,* of the two great murderous ideologies of "the terrible twentieth century" at work together in Poland, graphically recalls the sharp end of ideology:

> The [Nazi] Gestapo followed *racial guide-lines,* consigning some two million Polish Jews to closed *reservaten* or ghettoes.... In the Extraordinary Pacification Campaign of 1940 some 15,000 Polish priests, teachers and political leaders were transported to Dachau or shot in the Palmiry Forest. The first experiments were made in euthanasia, in the selection of children for racial breeding, in slave labor schemes, and in gas chambers.

The communist secret police followed guidelines based on their own idea of *class analysis,* assigning some 2 million people associated with the professions or with prewar state employment to forcible deportation in the terrible railway convoys of 1939–40. At least one half were dead within a year of their arrest.

Ideology has a number of markers or characteristics that we can identify throughout its varied forms. First, ideology solidifies the objectivity of mere ideas into subjectively freighted articles of faith shaped to serve the believer's aspiration. Inconsistencies are smoothed out in seamless certainty. Thus for many Buddhists the various orders of cause-and-effect presented in the canonical literature are conflated into one—karma, which is then given a moralistic, puni-tive, and judgmental weight as the flywheel of popular Buddhist metaphysics.

Secondly, any questioning of authoritative texts and personalities is discour-aged except perhaps at a superficial level—including among the rank and file of "the movement," who can get very resentful about anyone rocking the boat. The publications of ideological movements consequently tend to have a repetitive, formulaic quality about them, no matter the subject. Their main purpose is to confirm the faithful in their beliefs and loyalties and to attract new supporters. Since ideology is about clinging to ideas *for all one's worth,* reason is subordinated to dogma, experience to self-righteousness, and evidence to belief. Ideological movements thus fracture readily into hostile and fiercely irreconcilable sects.

Thirdly, ideology fixates on one or more key issues or ideas (such as patri-archy, the class struggle, the market) that then become universal organizing prin-ciples. Everything else is subordinated, marginalized, ignored, or angrily denied.

Fourthly, ideologies are commonly embodied in movements, and character-istically these have a proselytizing mission. Such movements provide their mem-bers with more or less totally new "identi-kits"—a whole life-world of activities, friends, and lifestyles.

Finally, ideologues take themselves *very* seriously. Conversely, a sense of irony, a little playful humor about oneself and about one's beliefs and affiliations, does suggest a person who is not too badly hung up on any of these. As Oscar Wilde reminds us, "Life is too important a thing ever to be taken seriously."

One can locate various worldviews or perspectives on a continuum, with the most subjective at one end and the most objective on the other; ideologies are at the subjective end, while what I call *theories* are at the other. Theories are con-tingent and open-ended. They are explanations of phenomena that are *relatively* free of investigator bias, and that continue to be the subject of ongoing investi-gation and dialogue. Though the big theories, especially in the social and men-tal sciences, tend to be more freighted with ego-investment, even where contending scholars are well dug in, dialogue continues, with accepted stan-dards regarding impartiality and the understanding that new evidence may over-turn even well-rooted positions. Within the same subject field there may be an ideology-theory continuum, as in Marxism, with hard-line propagandists at one end and authoritative scholars at the other. Theory undermines ideology. His-torical revisionism, for example, has deconstructed grand ideological narratives about the making of nations.

After his great awakening the Buddha was reluctant to teach his newfound wisdom for fear of being misunderstood. At the end of his life Marx is reputed to have said, "At least I am not a Marxist." Ideologies have frequently been shaped from the theories of creative sages and thinkers—like the Buddha, Christ, or Marx. Ideology is the distortion of theory to reinforce ego identity—often in very subtle ways. Latter-day followers, struggling in the world to give effect to the message of the founder, find strength and security in solidifying it in dogma. Nietzsche, in "On Truth and Lie in the Extra Moral Sense," puts it splendidly:

> What, then, is truth? A mobile army of metaphors, metonyms, and anthropomorphisms—in short, a sum of human relations which have been enhanced, transposed, embellished poetically and rhetorically, and which after long use seem firm, canonical and obligatory to people; truths are illusions about which one has forgotten that this is what they are: metaphors which are worn out and without sensuous power; coins which have lost their pictures and now matter only as metal, no longer as coins.

"Soft" Ideology

The end of communism and the discrediting of the whole collectivist tradition was prematurely proclaimed as "the end of ideology" (and of history and much else) by triumphalist champions of neoliberal modernity. What then gained greater credence were our most prominent contemporary "post-ideological ideologies," which I call *soft ideologies*. Soft ideologies have their own special character. Like all ideologies, they seek to explain the world in which we live. And they tend to be reductive in that their perspective hinges on a single principle that is consistently and universally employed. Soft ideologies, however, have a more rational and objective, rather than emotional and subjective, basis. Examples are market ideology and techno-rationality.

The market is a useful economic device that, in market ideology, becomes a universal organizing principle. In public debate to deny its absoluteness is to run the risk of not being taken seriously. Anything that hinders its free operation is seen as a threat to social well-being. It is applied as a universal nostrum to every wretched country driven to seek the help of the free market ideologues who effectively control the global economy. It is treated as if it were a fact and force of nature, yet even the most "free" of markets is sustained by a normative and legislative framework allegedly designed to provide entrepreneurs with a "level playing field."

Techno-rationality is a manifestation of scientism. Scientism is an ideology that elevates the scientific method into a universally applicable, allegedly value-free, self-justifying methodology. Techno-rationality dismisses political philosophy as value-laden ideology. It assumes that if the appropriate information is collected and is subject to cost-benefit analysis and similar processes, the optimum policies will emerge. In fact within the paradigm of techno-rationality there are inevitably policy assumptions and an underlying political philosophy at work. Such "rationality" almost invariably favors the moneyed and influential.

Soft ideologies do not provide the same hard-edged, mass self-identity as do as fascism, communism, or religious fundamentalism. Nevertheless they are strongly owned as universal truths, embodying assumptions by which contemporary modernity is lived out.

Buddhism As Ideology

By now some readers may be ready to complain that this book fixates on our sense of lack as being ultimately the universal problem, that it presents enlightenment as the panacea, and that it juxtaposes the two as God and the devil. And, indeed, virtually every Buddhist starts out as something of a Buddhist ideologue, for whom "Buddhism" is an idea that makes self and world more understandable, and that provides assurance, consolation, and self-identity. This helps to get started! However, here are plenty of warnings in the scriptures about getting stuck there for the rest of one's life, such as this admonition from the *Vimalakirti Sutra:*

> He who is attached to anything, even to liberation, is not interested in the Dharma but is interested in the taint of desire.... The Dharma is not a secure refuge. He who enjoys a secure refuge is not interested in the Dharma but is interested in a secure refuge.... The Dharma is not a society. He who seeks to associate through the Dharma is not interested in the Dharma, but is interested in association.

Similarly, the Zen master Sengcan warned: "Do not search after the truth; only cease to cherish opinions." Buddhism is a religion of *ehi-passika,* come and see, come and experiment for yourself. In the following much-quoted passage from the *Kalama Sutra,* as rendered by prominent American meditation teacher Joseph Goldstein in "Tasting the Strawberry: Theravada Buddhism—Path of Awareness," the Buddha is said to have advised:

> Don't believe anyone. Don't believe me. Don't believe the teachers. Don't believe books and traditions. Rather, look to your own experience. Look within, and see what it is that is conducive to the growth of understanding, wisdom, compassion and love. Those things should be cultivated. Then look to your experience to see what it is that leads to greater greed, hatred and delusion. Those things should be abandoned.

Buddhism provides a rational, experience-based diagnosis of the human disease and proposes a course of treatment including instructions, teacher, fellowship, faith in the eventual cure, and many other resources. In the Buddha's analogy, this course of treatment is a raft for crossing the river of suffering. When you get to the other side, you no longer need the raft. The beliefs, the meditation, the rituals, remain the same but there is no impulse to identify with them any longer. The big idea, "enlightenment," is also seen as attachment to a delusion. When the attachment is dropped, the mirage vanishes; there is nothing to gain…. Similarly, the ethical precepts are to be adhered to as guidelines for behavior. But to the extent that we experience at-oneness with others, our conduct toward them is as naturally ethical as is the conduct of our left hand toward our right hand. Ajahn Chah, the famous Thai meditation master, observed in *A Taste of Freedom* that "some people develop goodness and cling to it…or they develop knowledge and cling to that."

There is thus an inherent tension within Buddhism, between Buddhism as a theory, a method, that can lead to the dissolution of self-identification with Buddhism and anything else; and Buddhism as an ideology, a metaphysic, an identification of self with Buddhism. Instead of our sense of lack being seen as simply illusory, lack is filled by Buddhism.

Avoiding Ideological Traps in Engaged Buddhism

The following reminders, when thinking, speaking, writing, and acting, may be helpful in steering clear of the enticements of ideology, and are particularly important for effective social engagement.

Most importantly: Be on guard against the seductive mindsets of greed, aversion, and delusion. Beware of the triumphalist itch: Your truth will be more acceptable if you don't rub people's noses in it.

Second, when presenting your version of the truth, try to avoid slanting it with your own wishful overlay. George Orwell warned about our "subjective contamination" of reality. "One cannot get away from one's subjective feelings," he wrote, "but at least one can know what they are and make allowances for them" so as to avoid falling into "a sort of masturbation fantasy in which the world of facts hardly matters." When presenting what you hope are objective conclusions from particular experiences or research, it may be appropriate to add some information about your assumptions, background, feelings, prejudices, and anything else that might help readers or listeners form their own opinions of the validity of your findings. Taking people into your confidence in this way will increase your credibility.

Ideology is about answers in search of questions and questions in search of problems. It is not unknown to end up with the wrong answer to the wrong question to the wrong problem. It is therefore not necessarily a sign of weakness to avoid coming up with firm conclusions. The evidence may not justify *any* conclusions. It may be best simply to present the dilemma and warn about the danger of jumping to conclusions.

Finally, beware of the edginess of ideologically inspired communication, which easily tips over into waspish and provoking language. Taking a jab at an adversary is a self-indulgence that will usually turn out to be counterproductive. Ideology fixates on things; it reifies. The process of communication is equally important. How something is written, said, or done—and by whom, when, and where—may say more than the particulars of its content.

Ideology skews our vision and creates barriers and antagonisms between different social groups. Exposing its roots and explaining its implications is surely a major task of a socially engaged Buddhism. We need to begin with ourselves and include our own organizations and systems of belief, as well as those movements for radical change with which we choose to associate ourselves.

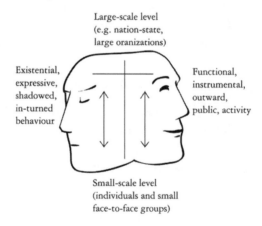

The Janus Syndrome

Important to establishing a Buddhist social theory is a phenomenon that I term the *Janus syndrome*. The Roman god Janus is usually represented with two bearded heads conjoined back to back so that he can look in two directions at the same time. The Janus syndrome draws attention to the two aspects of the response of the human to what discomfits it: the objective, instrumental activity and the subjective, expressive behavior of individuals, organizations, and states.

Expressive behaviors attempt to build and defend a strong sense of self, through belongingness identity, through "standing out," through power and possession—and, in short, through the whole delusive and ultimately frustrating *expressive project* to mask or fill our sense of existential lack described so far in this book. Expressive behavior is manifested through such instrumental activities as getting on in a career, competing successfully with a new product, and winning a war, and includes the systems, institutions, and cultures developed to support these activities. Instrumental activities are *socializations* of individual expressive behaviors in that they channel them so as to support the integrity, survival, and well-being of a society, organization, group, or individual.

Groups, organizations, and cultures, strongly fortified in the antithetical bonding described in this chapter, manifest a corporate expressive behavior in their struggles to survive, prosper, dominate, related in each case (and often in very complex, paradoxical, and ambiguous ways) to their overt instrumental functions. Thus, a forestry service does not only manage forests, and a transportation authority does not only build highways. They also exist in order to survive and prosper as corporate entities. At the corporate as well as the individual level, expressive behavior is usually not explicitly sensed even within the organization.

Even when the instrumental fire *could* burn with a clear, benevolent flame, in fact there is usually a lot of expressive smoke obscuring it. It is difficult for the "I" just to do what the situation needs. Also (or even instead) I tend to do what *I* need, thereby obscuring and spoiling the situation. The left-hand face of Janus reveals the expressive dance of delusion. And the right-hand side reflects its instrumental outcomes. The Buddhist ideal society is a benign, single-faced one, in which behavior is an authentic, at-one response to the needs and possibilities of situations.

Professionalism is an illuminating example of the Janus syndrome. Instrumentally, professionalism is about good and reliable standards of service to a client, given expertly and impartially, and free of profiteering. Expressively, and particularly in the high-prestige professions like medicine and law, ego gets a huge multiple reinforcement that it can feed on. There will, however, be some— "the professionals who cast no shadow"—who have no need of these reinforcements and find them irrelevant. Action is solely out of awareness of need and opportunity, unspoiled by identity hunger.

The Janus syndrome can also be seen in one's behavior in committees, teams, and other small work groups. Instrumentally, there are agendas, goals, and objective problems to be resolved, and these are the overt subjects of group activity on which the members feel they are focusing their attention. But the other side of this instrumental functioning is the expressive drive—the hidden personal agendas of emotional business that each person brings to the meeting. Much time in the meeting may be taken up in satisfying, frustrating, or otherwise processing the participants' emotional needs, but in only partial awareness and through the medium of "the business."

Note that in the Janus diagram, the double face is divided into upper and lower parts, referring to large-scale and small-scale activity respectively. The distinction and the interrelationship are significant. Short-term, small-scale expressive behavior (bottom left) builds up, more or less blindly, to the long-term, large-scale instrumental consequences in the top right quadrant of the diagram. Historical events, for example, are the result of many different wills, but are not necessarily willed by any individual. Small events, whose expressive origins are generally below the level of awareness, and whose instrumental implications may only be appreciated with hindsight, can accumulate into unimaginable follies. Buddhists will recognize here the karmic parallels in the unfolding of a person's life as well as in the unfolding of history.

Human affairs, whether of individuals, organizations, or states, tend to be reactive, piecemeal, and short-term in character—what Charles Lindblom, in *The Policy Making Process,* called *disjointed incrementalism,* or "the science of muddling through." Much of this may be rationalized so that people *feel* they are in control of events (or their own actions). There is a powerful myth of rational, calculative planning and control carried over into social affairs from technology. For "high egoic" modern man it is an *essential* myth. Someone surely has to be in control, and it isn't God any longer... There have, of course, been many examples of grand design in social engineering, latterly supported by the ultimate rationality of the computer, but all have foundered more or less badly on the rocks of social reality.

The Janus syndrome is a warning of the need, when we come to examine social problems, to turn our attention to the existential roots of society, that is, to the characteristically deluded and driven response of individuals to their human condition—the *expressive project.* In each case it is necessary to trace how this is manifested in group, organizational, and other subcultures; how it cumulates in social impact over time; and how it is expressed in overt social functions, instrumentalities, and norms, in the conventional and reassuring "normalcy" that both blinds us to the reality of the everyday world and makes it tolerable. I hope that this preliminary sketch of the Janus syndrome and the other forms of "institutionalized delusion" explored in this chapter will encourage further investigation and development of a comprehensive Buddhist social theory.

Chapter 7

BUDDHISM AND MODERNITY

OVER THE 2,500 YEARS since the Buddha started to turn the wheel of the Dharma, the three fires of acquisitiveness, ill-will, and existential ignorance have been supercharged at the societal level to an extent that would certainly be pathological in any individual. In the late nineteenth century Nietzsche commented on this state: "Madness is something rare in individuals but in groups, parties, peoples, ages, it is the rule." Following the Second World War, the novelist and social critic Arthur Koestler expressed a similar sentiment: "If one looks with a cold eye at the mess man has made of his history, it is difficult to avoid the conclusion that he has been afflicted by some built-in mental disorder which drives him towards self-destruction." And we hear another expression of this echoed in the words of Stephen Daedalus in James Joyce's *Ulysses:* "History is a nightmare from which I am trying to awake."

The history of the human race is indeed grand folly when viewed against the potential of humanity to have made it otherwise. Yet, though the whole may seem a folly, it is a folly that has been relieved by many instances of active compassion, self-denying endeavor, boundless humanity, and steadfast moral integrity—most of it unrecorded. The potential to transcend this madness and live compassionately and kindly is a potential that exists in all human beings, and to which all the world's spiritualities bear witness. Furthermore, we can see this potential beginning to be actualized in a number of varied liberative social currents that have gathered strength over the past two hundred years, such as the establishment of universal suffrage, civil rights, adequate livelihood and representative government throughout many parts of the world.

If Buddhism is to come of age in the twenty-first century it must surely offer its own distinctive understanding and response to what has been happening since the Buddha first turned the wheel of the Dharma and proclaimed that "all is burning." There are intimations of a Buddhist-style critique in Nietzsche's complaint that historians never wrote about the things that made history interesting: ignorance, anger, passion, and folly.

Modernity is the increasingly global social culture that had its beginnings in Western Europe in the sixteenth century and extends throughout the world to the present. This is the culture within which Buddhism must necessarily make its future and with which it must interact. Some understanding of modernity is therefore essential for any informed discussion of a "social face" of Buddhism. How inimical is this culture to the Buddhist project? And what particular opportunities does it present?

Characteristic features of modernity include an all-pervasive individualism, expressed politically as liberalism and economically as capitalism. These three traits—individualism, liberalism, and capitalism—have made possible the immense wealth and technology that pour forth an ever-accelerating output of goods and services. The impact of these forces on our finite ecosphere provides the most tangible argument for modernity's unsustainability. The nation-state remains the main geographical foundation and political power-container of modernity, though increasingly challenged by transnational corporate power and its global agencies. Modernity has another important feature, however, and that is the emancipatory thrust of the liberative social currents I mentioned at the beginning of this chapter. The past several centuries have brought with them a number of revolutionary movements that provided citizens unprecedented liberties and a "fair" share of the various benefits of modernity.

The breakdown of premodern society in Europe some five hundred years ago exposed the self to a hitherto unknown degree of insecurity—and freedom. That freedom empowered, collectively and individually, the gratification of an ever widening and more ambitious range of desires. This outer liberative project promotes an intense individualism that is modernity's flight from the terrifying sense of our human frailty. It is the latest historic attempt to fill that nagging something that appears to be lacking in us.

Objectively, this liberative dynamic is aimed at reducing some of the pain and inconvenience of human life, and making it, in English philosopher Thomas Hobbes's words, less "nasty, brutish, and short." There is here an authentic liberation from many ills. After five hundred years it is still flawed, contradictory, restricted, and unsustainable, but it has undoubted achievements. Science and technology are capable of controlling disease and famine, and organizational and communication systems are capable of applying these benefits on a global scale. It is now possible and practicable to provide all human beings with the necessities of life and free them from the grosser and remediable afflictions—and yet we find ourselves somehow unable to do so. It will only be possible through a very different social and economic system. Yet history suggests that this in turn would require the cultivation of a radically new kind of human sensibility.

The Buddha taught how the quality of life could be revolutionized through inner liberation. That, I believe, still remains the ultimate imperative. However, as we have seen, the Buddha was by no means unconcerned about material well-being, though the capacity to promote this 2,500 years ago was minimal. Buddhism and kindred spiritualities thus now assume an additional and *social* significance, where inner liberation becomes the ultimate precondition for a universal and sustainable outer liberation. Buddhism is a humanism, yet is much more than a humanism; it is the means for the full actualization of humanism, for the unselfrestricted flow of our humanity. Socially engaged Buddhism holds the promise of making a new kind of human history.

Subjectively, modernity's liberative quest is able to affirm a powerful sense of self, together with the mutually affirming belongingness of exciting new collectivities, whether a company of merchant adventurers, a revolutionary movement, a resurgent nation-state—or a prestigious brand name. And in the seemingly limitless expansion of human powers, driven by a restless spirit of inquiry, there are always expectations for tomorrow. Modernity conditions us to the external "fix" (including trying to fix up an objectified self), yet with each new gratification the existential hunger remains. Consumers now enjoy an endless range of conveniences, comforts, and consolations, but no one would claim that this has brought them greater wisdom or peace of mind. Insecurity and anxiety have actually been deepened by the limitless search for self-fulfillment.

Capitalism

Capitalism is a system of wealth creation that is also a historic response to existential lack. It makes public virtues of the ancient Buddhist "fires" of acquisitiveness and aggressiveness by maximizing the freedom of individuals and groups to aggressively pursue wealth as an ultimate social virtue, and by legitimizing the immense power this wealth has vested in the few over the many. At least for most people in the rich countries, the violence of modern corporate capitalism is relatively restrained, masked, and refined as compared with its nineteenth-century antecedents. It is in the poor countries of the world that its harshness is most grossly evident.

The characteristics of this economic and social system have been summarized by two Western Buddhists writing out of a lifetime's experience. David Brandon, who worked for many years to alleviate homelessness in Britain, wrote in *Zen and the Art of Helping* of social structures and institutions that reward and encourage greed, selfishness and exploitation rather than love, sharing and compassion.... People who are relatively successful at accumulating goods and social position wish to ensure that they remain successful.... Both in intended and unintended ways they erect barriers of education, finance and law to protect their property and interests.... These structures and their protective institutions continue to exacerbate and amplify basic human inequalities in housing, healthcare, education and income.... Certain people's lifestyles become dependent on the deprivation of the many.

Similarly, in "Buddhism and the Coming Revolution" American Zen Buddhist and poet Gary Snyder asserts that "the 'free world' has become economically dependent on a fantastic stimulation of greed which cannot be fulfilled, sexual desire which cannot be satiated, and hate which has no outlet except against oneself, the persons one is supposed to love, or the revolutionary aspirations of pitiful, poverty-stricken marginal societies like Cuba and Vietnam." In some cases frustrated "revolutionary aspirations" now find expression in terrorism, and hate finds a new outlet in "the war against terrorism."

It is characteristic of modernity that self-aggrandizement has proved to be the main incentive to wealth creation. *How can I use my money and talents to best enrich myself?* With the failure of altruistic alternatives this is the bottom line that presently determines the social use of wealth.

Emancipation

Anthony Giddens, a leading sociologist, has defined *emancipatory politics* in his book *Modernity and Self Identity: Self and Society in the Late Modern Age* as

a generic outlook concerned above all with liberating individuals and groups from constraints which adversely affect their life chances. Emancipatory politics involves two main elements: the effort to shed shackles of the past...the dogmatic imperatives of tradition and religion...thereby permitting a transformative attitude towards the future; and the aim of overcoming the illegitimate domination of some individuals or groups by others.

He refers to divisions of economic and social class, divisions of ethnicity and gender, divisions between ruling and subordinate groups, and divisions between rich and poor nations. "But in all cases," Giddens asserts, "the objective of emancipatory politics is either to release underprivileged groups from their unhappy condition, or to eliminate the relative differences between them." This is achieved "by reducing or eliminating exploitation, inequality and oppression."

Modernity has launched a succession of emancipatory movements, all of which remain unfinished business—religious, political, economic, national, colonial, ethnic, and feminist. The two biggest and least resolved freedoms (and responsibilities) are economic and ecological. Whereas political freedom has substantially evolved, the economy is marked by oppressive inequalities of wealth, income, and opportunity, and ecological politics is marked by a refusal to acknowledge the consequences of ecologically unsustainable and health-endangering practices and policies.

All these emancipatory movements are aimed at enlarging the freedom and autonomy of individuals and groups. They are part of the larger, outer liberative picture in that they are intended to remedy various kinds of objective affliction (or at least inconvenience) experienced by the individual. However, these movements tend to be flawed by the subjective motivation that is also at work. From that perspective these are all *also* endeavors subtly motivated by their apparent power to fill our sense of lack. Thus emancipatory movements readily fall prey to ideology, intolerance, and confrontation as collective gratifications that disfigure their ideals. The problem of creating a society free of war, poverty, tyranny, and ecological devastation is insoluble on its own terms.

W. H. Auden, after describing how superbly equipped for "The Quest'" was the human expedition, sadly concludes:

In theory they were sound on Expectation,
Had there been situations to be in;
Unluckily they were their situation.

The Need for the Inner Work

The relationship between the objective utilitarian aspect and the subjective existential aspect of the response of the human animal to whatever discomfits it I have called the *Janus syndrome*. In response to any discomfiture, the self tries to remove the cause. Thirsty? Then drink! And modernity has vastly increased the range of discomfitures that have been or can be eliminated (this can be regarded as *outer liberation* from the experience of suffering). But the self, which at bottom is so fragile and fearful in its selfhood, is commonly not satisfied simply to remove the cause of the discomfiture. An inner void still hungers to be filled. So something extra is demanded that is functionally unnecessary and often counterproductive. Thus a need may be functionally satisfied—we are no longer physically thirsty—but our sense of lack may still need slaking. So we proceed to get drunk…or at least order a Coke.

Liberation from our sense of lack is impossible as long as we evade accepting it's ultimately ego-created nature and instead go on trying to fill the imagined hole by top-loading our lives and the world with ego-affirming behavior that is needless, ineffective, and destructive. Our need for security is insatiable—until we tumble to the fact that it is that need itself that is the problem. In short, without an inner liberation all the outer liberations of modernity will never be enough to satisfy our deepest yearning.

Furthermore, the outer liberative thrust will be flawed so long as it is not informed by the radically different sensibility that is inner liberation—a mutuality that alone will make it possible to achieve the emancipatory dream of a truly democratic global commonwealth. Essential to Buddhism is the understanding that unless there is significant transformation in the ways we relate to ourselves and others, we will continue to develop social and cultural structures that manifest and reinforce the futile struggle to escape from our sense of lack by taking refuge in acquisitive and aggressive behaviors. Only some kind of psychospiritual conviction, training, and insight goes deep enough to support the necessary radical social shift. It is not an enlightened society of saints I have in mind, but only a significant enough number of committed people working to create a social climate that will help everyone to be more human. I call this a *radical culture of awakening*. It means relating positively and warmly to others and working with them unselfishly and fearlessly. It means understanding and diminishing the urge to secure ourselves, to put down others, to escape into negativity and passivity, to repress or to be carried away by our feelings, and to deceive ourselves and others in the many-layered "games" of trying to live a life. It means the development of a strong and fearless *awareness identity* instead of the delusive kinds of identity examined in the opening chapter. The Thai Buddhist activist Sulak Sivaraksa, in his book *Siamese Resurgence,* writes:

> First of all one has to be calm and impartial so that one can find out what sort of a person one is. On the whole one does not know or admit that one is lustful or greedy, although one would like to become rich at the expense of others. If one lacks that negative quality, one is normally ambitious and would like to play with power—in the name of social justice or serving the poor. Beyond this one is fairly ignorant about oneself as well as about the world in which one would normally dare to be involved and claim that one would solve those worldly problems.

The reader may know at least one or two truly good-hearted people who are kind and compassionate and yet strong and fearless enough in themselves as not to need in any sense to put their shadows over others. Imagine what it would be like if the average man or woman were thus—if there were enough of such people not just to modify the inhuman effects of so much in our social structures and institutions but to evolve whole new lifestyle cultures and forms of social organization. These new norms and institutions would in turn support and nurture profound personal change, instead of frustrating and distorting it.

However, all this is far from how the average social activist tends to view religion and spirituality. Religion is seen as more a problem than a solution. It is associated with ideological control, obscurantist authoritarianism, and the moral legitimization of an unjust social order. It is charged with preaching humility as a virtue, and suffering as something to be borne with patience in expectation of reward in the hereafter. (In reality, nowadays, matters are sufficiently reversed so that it is neither religion (as Marx claimed) nor revolution (as French philosopher and mystic Simone Weil claimed) that are the opiate of the people—but consumerism.)

Contemplative spirituality, whether Eastern or Western, Buddhist or Quaker, is viewed from the secular social perspective as largely irrelevant or even as escapist, irresponsible, and otherworldly. Since many of the spiritually inclined believe that social phenomena have, at best, no significant relevance, this separation of spirituality from active social concern is mutually confirming. From either standpoint the mystical militancy I advocate appears to be bizarre hybrid or suspect paradox. Clearly there is a lot of work to be done here.

I shall take up this agenda for a *radical culture of awakening* again toward the end of the book. In brief, I believe that Buddhism and other ancient inner liberation teachings must wholeheartedly come to terms with modernity's liberation project and, through social engagement, promote the convergence of these two great emancipatory movements of humankind. This is a view strongly advocated by the Dalai Lama, in numerous statements like the following, from *Universal Responsibility and the Good Heart:*

It is quite obvious that without material progress we will lack many material comforts. In the meantime, without inner peace material things alone are not sufficient. There are many signs which indicate that material progress alone is not sufficient for men. There is something lacking. Therefore, the only way is to combine the two.

High Modernity

In 1958–59 the microchip was invented, and integrated circuit technology led to the foundation of new high-technology industries. This was the beginning of a new industrial revolution. The foundations were also laid for a shift of resources toward the service sector and the development of a whole new culture of manipulative consumerism. Over the next several decades, a globalizing transnational capitalism became increasingly dominant. And there were the beginnings of widespread concern about "the environment." Some social theorists identify this period as *high modernity*, which, at least in Euro-America, is the first culture in which the evidence of the past is no longer strongly experienced in the present. High modernity is how people live in the most materially developed parts of the planet. It originated in what has been termed a Golden Age of Modernity (approximately 1947–73), but this book is concerned with its development in the second half of the twentieth century and its acceleration into the twenty-first. There are also good reasons for calling this period the *age of anxiety*.

In this chapter I shall be concerned with high modernity as a *social culture*, that is, as a complex of meanings, a collective mentality whereby people manage to live together as expressed in their values and norms, and their approved kinds of behavior and ways of life. An effective Western Buddhism must comprehend and address the changes wrought by high modernity in personality, lifestyle, and values. (In the later chapters of the book I shall examine high modernity in terms of transnational "free market" capitalism, consumerism, and globalization.)

Over much of the world, however, the culture of modernity is experienced only by relatively small elites. To a large extent traditional cultures remain embedded in the place, time, and belongingness reminiscent of premodernity. The impact of modernity is felt mainly in intrusive globalization—aggressive consumerism, low-wage industrialization, the undermining of traditional agriculture and crafts, and the mass media assault on indigenous cultures. In short, modernity affects the lives of most people in economic and political (and often military) ways rather than, as yet, in cultural terms. The situation is well described by American Buddhist monk and activist Santikaro Bhikkhu, writing of Thailand in "Socially Engaged Buddhism and Modernity":

> In Siam we are struggling to find a viable way of life as "traditional" and "modern" forces collide, entwine, blend and keep changing. There are many non-modern elements in this culture. For one, the political system is still based on personal contacts and relationships. The formal, important democratic system is a veneer, often a fraud. The foundations of

traditional societies—ways of life, values and Buddhism—are being pulled out from under people. Maybe this is what scholars mean by "modernity," but it is not much of a conscious issue among Buddhists here.

The electronic and economic "global village" should not be confused with the prospects for a global culture. The crude determinism that once forecast a universal Coca-Cola culture now lacks credibility, for we have clearly seen, for example, in the Balkans, that national, regional, and local identities have a resilience and even a resurgent, nation-building power. Civic nationality offers a creative challenge to engaged Buddhists, as an alternative to both militant ethnic nationalism and postimperial globalization.

The Disembedded Self

In premodernity social culture was embedded in traditional, time-honored ways of doing, feeling, and thinking. It was shaped by the needs of a particular society. The cultures of other societies were felt to be alien, and the local subcultures of specific communities within a society were also quite strongly differentiated from one another.

Modernity is marked by a social culture that is increasingly disembedded from tradition and locality. This disembeddedness is caused by the increased speed—and shorter time—in which information, people, materials, and energy can move between communities and societies and dissolve their localism. New technologies have "emptied time" and "emptied space." For example, a rapidly changing place can become so disembedded of reassuring and affirming meanings—in terms of the recollections of its inhabitants or the expectations of its visitors—that the experience of it can become quite alienating. It may feel a "nonplace" and perhaps convey so many conflicting impressions that these do not hang together to create any sense of identity.

In high modernity, change is so rapid, and successive innovations so radical, that all phenomena become increasingly disembedded, not only from place but from a sense of historical continuity. What is traditional never has time to solidify as such, and now grows ever more distant, preserved only as "heritage." With the global advance of modernity, more and more people feel disembedded, like this Indonesian intellectual, quoted by Robert Bellah in *Beyond Belief: Essays on Religion in a Post-Traditional World*: "The image of one's self, the answer to who am I, and who I want to be, has become blurred and fractured. Questions like: to whom or to what to be loyal, after whom to model oneself, which pattern of behavior to adopt or adjust to, have all lost their obvious answers, and no new satisfactory ones are readily available."

The premodern community required of its members that they conform to its traditions and honorably undertake what it expected of them. Those traditions were well-tried and reliable means of sustaining the cohesion and continuity of the community and securing the rights and well-being of its members (within the limits of the social structure). Conformity was required because the community was a relatively fragile thing in the face of God, nature, and the vicissitudes of human affairs. Even in the middle of the twentieth century in the most economically developed societies, most people still lived according to certain traditional expectations: school and learning a trade or acquiring a profession; courtship, marriage, and children; a career or steady employment for 100,000 hours from one's teens to sixties; and two weeks' holiday each year.

High modern society has no expectations of its members other than that they should not make a nuisance of themselves by breaking the law and that they should not willingly become a financial burden on society. The only kind of significant public belongingness universally available is the nation-state or, more intensely, nationality. For the rest, it is up to citizens to "get a life," as the saying goes—to earn a living and to figure out for themselves what life is about and what they should be doing with it. Getting a life has therefore to be accomplished through personal experience, available education and information, and whatever role models and social fashions may be attractive—for the process is, of course, still more or less socially conditioned. Nevertheless, the unprecedented degree of personal freedom requires an ongoing process of choices in the light of unfolding experience. This process is termed *reflexivity*. It is so central to the making of self-identity that high modernity is sometimes termed *reflexive modernity*. The choices that are made become integrated into a lifestyle, which provides an ongoing narrative of self-identity, and which is subject to periodic revision.

The construction of self-identity through lifestyle has been nicely illustrated by Helen Wilkinson and Melanie Howard in their book *Tomorrow's Women,* in which they offer portraits of five modern women: Networking Naomi, New Age Angela, Mannish Mel, Back-to-Basics Barbara, and Frustrated Fran. Peter Berger, in *The Homeless Mind,* has drawn attention to a further characteristic of reflexivity:

> Modern consciousness is…peculiarly aware, tense, "rationalizing." It follows that this reflectiveness pertains not only to the outside world but also to the subjectivity of the individual and especially to his identity. Not only the world but the self becomes an object of deliberate attention and sometimes anguished scrutiny…. Subjectivity acquires previously unconceived "depths."

This might be described as modernity's Hamlet syndrome.

Postmodernism: A Culture of Liberation?

Postmodernism is the latest intellectual episode in the long struggle to affirm the self and somehow fill its sense of lack.

As the solidity and permanence of a social reality in flux and fragmentation felt less and less dependable, and as the sense of lack deepened, a number of thinkers began to question how it was any longer possible to give life meaning. The anguish of Christian philosopher Søren Kierkegaard, one of the earliest thinkers to contemplate this question, is particularly striking.

Postmodernism, the dominant intellectual current in high modernity, originates in this disembedded reality of fragmented appearances. It finds all claims to absolute authority and universal applicability no longer convincing, and deconstructs them back to their subjective origins in time and place. It is thus understandable that it thinks itself *post*modern. However, as a cultural movement I see it rather as a culmination of what has gone before—a kind of intellectual end-of-the-road for modernity. It is, moreover, integral to high modernity as a whole, the social structures and processes of which are much more obviously a culmination of modernity rather than anything qualitatively and radically different—a true postmodernity. For postmodernism, all beliefs are reduced to contingent social products. Thus several parallel interpretations of a country's history may be—and have been—written from the points of view of different social classes, ethnic groups, and other interests. Each has its own validity, but none can claim to be exclusively true, or the final word. (Extreme "constructivists" claim that all ideas can be reduced to representations of specific interests, such as sexism, racism, colonialism, or speciesism, and that their claims to universality constitute a bid for power and dominance.)

This cultural relativism had specific origins within general changes in modern cultural experience that have loosened the grip of hard ideology. In the United States, in the climate of the 1960s, the emancipatory upsurge of the "underprivileged"—blacks, women, the poor, Catholics, Jews—led to the realization for many in the mainstream that the history of the United States was far more than the "established version" seen through the eyes of the dominant white, Anglo-Saxon, Protestant, middle-class patriarchy. Similarly, with globalization, the deconstruction of Western colonialist narratives meant that other world cultures, however small and obscure, could claim that their version of world history was equally valid.

Postmodernism therefore rejects what it variously terms "universalism," "foundationalism," "essentialism," and "grand narratives" (like liberalism and Marxism), and instead emphasizes "deconstruction" and "decentering." For postmodernists, any notion of historical progress is a meaning read into history by those who feel affirmed by it. Yet it is difficult to imagine how an avowed postmodernist could deny postmodernism itself as being some kind of *progress* beyond the "grand narratives" of the past.

Some two thousand years ago Buddhism, Advaita Vedanta, and Taoism understood the Sanskrit term *maya* as the delusive "reality" we experience when we do not recognize the true insubstantiality and impermanence of existence. The five-hundred-year search of modernity to find an objectivist anchorage for the self has led, step by reluctant step, toward a similar conclusion. Because it has led to the eventual convergence of these ancient spiritual traditions with modernity, the fragmentation and relativism of postmodernism is a welcome step. Welcome also, as a contribution to the ongoing emancipatory thrust of modernity, is the deconstruction of its hard ideologies, and of sexism, racism, and other mentalities of dominance and exclusion. However, as we shall see, there is one more step to be taken, and that is the most crucial and difficult of all. As I have remarked elsewhere in this book, Buddhism itself—and particularly as a Western import—also needs to be deconstructed as part of its own liberative agenda. With a light touch, its mythic, cultural, institutional, dogmatic, and political packaging needs to be distinguished from its perennial diagnosis of and prescription for our human condition. And the subtle Western meanings imparted to Buddhism require similar treatment.

Although postmodernism is, from a Buddhist point of view, a promising development in the intellectual history of modernity, its relativism creates a disturbing and destabilizing moral deficit. This is particularly evident in the phenomenon of "political correctness"(PC), which in some quarters has become a veritable ideology, and which is the only form in which postmodernist thinking has become familiar outside academia.

In its most extreme form PC maintains that since there are no all-inclusive ethical and cultural values, then those held by each social group—and, indeed, by each individual—are all equally valid. This is a perspective that is undoubtedly liberating but that, given a populist spin, can be oppressive. It becomes unforgivable to be "judgmental" about any group or individual no matter what the reason or the evidence. (However, in practice this seems to apply only to the oppressed and disadvantaged; white, male, middle-class, and Eurocentric interests are all fair game.) For example, oppressive and degrading conditions, applying, say, to women, in some cultures are to be respected as having as much validity as contrary practices in other cultures; attempts to intervene may be branded as smacking of Eurocentric postcolonialism. To suggest that there may be some among the poor who are feckless and irresponsible in their lifestyle is to draw accusations of supporting policies of social exclusion. To claim that there might be some universal standards of excellence that can be applied to commercialized junk culture or to the questionable literary achievements of some small, come-lately culture is to invite charges of elitism.   Fortunately a number of thinkers are at last beginning to question the stultifying dominance of postmodernist ideology and what one critic, secularist Muslim scholar Ibn Warraq, has called its "intellectual terrorism."

So much for the pros and cons of political correctness. We are now in a position to make some general assessment of postmodernism. Anthony Giddens, in *Modernity and Self-Identity*, remarks that "in fact, for writers in a poststructuralist vein, the self effectively ceases to exist; the only subject is a decentered subject, which finds its identity in the fragments of language and discourse." Similarly, for the postmodernist philosopher Richard Rorty, the self is a bundle of "quasi-selves."

But this view of the subject—the self—is but a mirror image of the fragmented object. True to the history of modernity, postmodernism itself remains inherently "objectivist." It offers an arm's-length picture of reality *out there* in terms of language and image; a flat, two-dimensional picture that has no place for passion or spirituality—as is evidenced by its "minimalist" fiction. Postmodernists decline to take the search inward, and to deconstruct the self (or, rather, *their selves,* for this is a very personal matter). On the contrary, they produce an anaesthetized reality in which the suffering in the world is reduced to the meaning in the "text" and the collage of images, and the anguish of lack is evaded in the play of cool irony.

Similarly, cognitive scientists also have concluded that there is simply no one inside the brain, no one there to make decisions and experience experiences. However Francisco Varela, one of the most distinguished among them, remarked in an interview in *Inquiring Mind* that, while many cognitive scientists have come to understand the egolessness of self, few apply this understanding to themselves personally. They close the door of the lab and go right back to their normal, self-absorbed life. In general it appears that the scholars and scientists of high modernity now widely accept Buddhist egolessness, but have been unable to come to terms with it on a personal, emotional level. Is this the final giant step to be taken from high modernity to *Dharmic modernity*?

The contrast between contemporary postmodernists and those heroic nihilists who were the forerunners of postmodernism (from Kierkegaard to the Existentialists) is striking and instructive. For these earlier thinkers, the self was exposed in dread to a meaningless world. However, the consequence for them was not, in fact, nihilism—meaninglessness, nothingness—but a *dread* of nihilism. It is the clinging to despair as the shadow of hope and the evasion of nothingness that is the problem, not nothingness itself (in which the present self has also vanished). When we let go of the self-pity and narcissism of despair, what appears as meaning*less* becomes simply meaning-*free*. We see that all along we have been trapped in our own circularity of the fear of fear, a trap from which it *is* possible simply to walk out. But before we can do so, some skillful meditative nurturing commonly is required. Otherwise despair can be dangerous: It can lead to profound depression in the loss of whatever precarious self-identity may have been built up.

What is necessary is to deconstruct the sense of self *also,* as well as the reality with which it endeavors to fill its lack. When we let go of the neediness to create the world in the image of the self, we let go into a world unshadowed by that neediness. We are then freed to develop and apply explicatory theories lightly and contingently, without having to identify with them and solidify them as reality itself. And our ethical values no longer need to sustain *me* and *mine,* however subtly. Like the jewels in Indra's net, each of us is both autonomous and yet at the same time dependent upon and at one with all others. We are able to respond to others with the compassion of an unobstructed mutuality, a transcendental humanism. We experience the world as meaning-free, yet that very freedom enables us to employ meaning in response to situations instead of in response to self-need.

Postmodernism identifies "grand theories" as social products. However, once we have begun to see, at the level of the person as prime mover, how and why they are produced we can begin to empty them of freighted ego and use them as lightweight tools, subject always to continual ideological audit lest they become sticky again with existential appropriation. The moral relativism of postmodernism carries us into an impasse from which modernity will find no ultimate escape unless it can at last confront the self—and the magnificent folly that the self has spent five hundred years creating.

Anxiety and Opportunity

Notwithstanding the worldwide increase in depression—claimed to be reaching epidemic proportions—high modernity is not as yet a nihilistic culture. Creeping anxiety mixed with narcissism would be nearer the mark. The signals are ambiguous, for at the same time there is an increased emphasis on the self and on the actualization of its potential.

Peter Berger, Brigitte Berger, and Hansfried Kellner, authors of *The Homeless Mind,* argue that:

> Modernity has accomplished many far-reaching transformations, but this has not changed the finitude, fragility and mortality of the human condition. What it has done is to seriously weaken those definitions of

reality which previously made that human condition easier to bear. This has produced an anguish all its own, and one that we are inclined to think adds additional urgency and weight to other discontents. Individualism, as freedom from all that obstructs our personal search for something to fill our sense of lack, has surely run into a cul-de-sac, like so much else in high modernity. We have already seen how postmodernism deconstructs the world into elusive fragments that "decontextualize" the self. What next? How far will we go in our shrinking and inturning of self-identity? In high modernity how much potential does the person have to cultivate an authentic inner liberation, thereby enabling the outer liberative project to be resumed in a very different way?

In addition to postmodernism's view of the self as fragmented and "constructed," there is in the culture of high modernity another influential perspective of the self, which focuses on *narcissism*. First articulated as a defining characteristic of contemporary culture in the work of social commentators Richard Sennett and Christopher Lasch, *narcissism* here means a total self-absorption and self-preoccupation. The whole experience of the world is interpreted in terms of self-need, to the extent that valid boundaries between the self and the external world become indistinguishable. Self-need becomes no longer objectifiable: The person *is* their self-need.

Sennett emphasizes that the alienation and impersonality of the public sphere and the decline of civil society have driven people in upon themselves and their personal lives. In his later writing he even refers to a "culture of survivalism." Today, impersonal experience seems meaningless and social complexity an unmanageable threat. By contrast, experience that seems to tell about the self, to help define it, develop it, or change it, has become an overwhelming concern. In *The Fall of Public Man,* Sennett observes that we have created an "intimate" society in which all social phenomena, no matter how impersonal in structure, are converted into matters of personality in order to have a meaning: events are viewed solely in terms of what they mean *to me* or *about me.*

This is reflected in much of contemporary culture. Public figures become media personalities and media personalities become public figures. Everything that can be is personalized and reduced to an ersatz intimacy. And consumer capitalism feeds on the yearning of the narcissist for a personally distinctive and socially attractive identity. Psychic and somatic self-improvement have become major preoccupations catered to by a whole range of new products, services, and experts. This is not to suggest, of course, that the cultivation of personal well-being is in itself a bad thing, but to draw attention to what the prevailing narcissistic character disorder (and the commercial response) makes of it. The narcissist's urgent search for intimacy is ultimately thwarted because he is unable to burden himself with commitment to another, and is anyway too self-absorbed to have much awareness of another's needs.

What are we to make of this condition of the individual in high modernity? Anthony Giddens takes a robust and optimistic view in his book *Modernity and Self-Identity: Self and Society in the Late Modern Age.* For him, the individual is no mere recipient of the afflictions of high modernity but an active and resourceful agent, thanks to the creative dynamism of reflexivity. While he does concede the alienating effect of disembeddedness, Giddens emphasizes the wide range of opportunities for positive and collective social endeavor in contemporary society. He refers, for example, to the re-creation of the extended family: "Individuals are actively restructuring new forms of gender and kinship relations out of the detritus of pre-established forms of family life." He presents a balanced view that suggests that the portrait of the severely dysfunctional self-identity within modern society may have something of caricature about it. My own view is colored by my Buddhist belief in individuals as *potentially* self-reliant and self-starting in addressing their predicament, and as possessed of an innate authenticity.

At its most narcissistic the self is, according to Lasch, struggling very hard indeed to hold on to its selfhood. It tends to be "chronically bored, restlessly in search of instantaneous intimacy, of emotional titillation without involvement and dependence." Even Anthony Giddens recognizes the onerous weight of sustaining the self in high modernity: "The task of forging a distinct identity may deliver distinct psychological gains, but it is clearly also a burden. A self-identity has to be created and more or less continually re-ordered against the backdrop of the shifting experience of day-to-day life and the fragmenting tendencies of modern institutions."

Similarly, literary critic and author George Steiner, in *Grammars of Creation,* observes that "our thoughts and feelings find nothingness and the pressure of non-being difficult to sustain."

All this prompts a large question: Is this crisis of the self, this breakdown of self-identity, really welcomed by Buddhists, for whom the self is supposed to be an illusion? The Buddhist agenda is to make the burden to which Giddens and Steiner refer a spur to self-transcendence. The personal identity crisis of high modernity mirrors that of the individual who is ripe to finally resolve the question of self-identity because she "has tried everything"—just as modernity in the course of its history seems, existentially speaking, also to have tried everything. Stuck in that impasse a person is ready to take the next step and to explore whether the problem might not be lack itself but the struggle against the sense of lack.

In the following striking passage from *Modernity and Self-Identity*, Giddens, as a perceptive sociologist without a spiritual agenda, ends up pointing in much the same direction as does this book:

> It is arguable that the period of high modernity is one of fundamental transition—not just a continuity of modernity's endless dynamism, but the presaging of structural transformation of a more profound type. The expansion of internally referential systems reaches its outer limits; on a collective level, and in day to day life, *moral/existential questions thrust themselves back to center stage. Focusing around self-actualization,* although also stretching through to globalizing developments, such issues call for a restructuring of social institutions, and raise issues not just of a sociological but of a political nature. (Italics added.)

Buddhist practice is ultimately concerned with a personal re-embedding in time, space, and above all, with others—and hence with moral recovery. This happens when the self begins to observe that the burden of trying to sustain a separate and invulnerable selfhood is a source of frustration and anguish and has no inherent necessity. Subsequent liberation into a world of *suchness,* of factuality unshadowed by self-need, has been described as coming home. In particular we are freed to relate to others without either feeling threatened by them or hungry for intimacy. We feel at one with others and yet, no longer casting our shadow over them, can appreciate them in the light of their own distinctive individuality.

It would be a questionable academic exercise to try to compare the spiritual potential of high modernity with that of typical premodern cultures. However, it is arguable in the light of the foregoing discussion that, at least in terms of existential pressure and of reflexive response, high modernity has an unprecedented potential for spiritual inquiry.

Part 3

The Inner Work

Chapter 8

THE FACE OF
CONTEMPORARY SPIRITUALITY

BUDDHISM FUNCTIONS as a vital catalyst in the culture of existential awakening. However, although there is a widespread interest in Buddhist meditation, a strong and sustained commitment to Buddhist training is likely to remain very much a minority concern. It seems most unlikely that Buddhist influence in the West will take the form of mass movements proselytizing in the Christian or Islamic fashion. The very idea of *converting* someone to Buddhism seems strange to most Buddhists. Buddhism has affinities with current developments in many different fields, and its diverse and suggestive influence will doubtless increase. The following two quotations from Asian Buddhists resident in the West make much the same point, emphasizing that the strength of the influence of Buddhism in the West is in its support of the essence of all spiritual paths and practices rather than in its becoming another institutional ideology. The Dalai Lama has consistently maintained a similar viewpoint. Dr. Rewata Dhamma, a Theravada monk, in "Towards a Better Society: A Buddhist Perspective," writes:

> Amidst a plurality of ideologies, political and religious, it would be best if Buddhism did not draw attention to itself, in a missionary way, as yet another *-ism*. Its ideal has always been to encourage what is in conformity with the Eightfold Path in other faiths and systems. It has always primarily been not so much a religion in its own right as a system of effective practice, of use to the individual whether he or she professes to follow some other religion or none at all.

Similarly, Chögyam Trungpa, a Tibetan Buddhist teacher, when asked what he foresaw as the future of Buddhism in the West, replied: "It is scientific and practical, and so ideal for the Western Mind. If it becomes a Church it will be a failure; if it is spiritual practice it will have strong influence in all areas—arts, music, psychology."

This chapter reviews the wider spiritual context within which Buddhism exerts its influence, and particularly its relationship to Christianity. It also offers a Buddhist perspective on ecospirituality, the New Age movement, and other contemporary trends.

The Essential Role of Nondualistic Spirituality

The new discipline of transpersonal psychology embraces the schools of personal psychology—behavioral, analytic, and humanistic—but goes beyond them to embrace the *transpersonal,* or *spiritual* states of consciousness. Its concerns are thus very close to those of the spiritual traditions, and, indeed, a number of transpersonal psychologists are working on conceptual systems intended to bridge and integrate psychology and the spiritual quest.

Ken Wilber, one of the most influential—and controversial—of these "consciousness researchers," maintains that before individual consciousness can transcend itself, the person must evolve through a hierarchy of levels of consciousness. Of fundamental importance is the development of a healthy ego, in which the rational and the emotional, the conscious mind and the subconscious "shadow," the "top dog" and the "bottom dog," are integrated and in harmony. At this stage of development—the self has attained a substantial degree of integration of body, persona, ego, and shadow and has realized significant autonomy and authenticity. Beyond are the transpersonal realms of consciousness, where, as Wilber explains in *No Boundary: Eastern and Western Approaches to Personal Growth,* "We begin to touch on an awareness which transcends the individual and discloses to a person something which passes far beyond himself."

Whereas there are hierarchies where the upper dominates the lower, in natural hierarchies each level integrates and includes all the lower levels, and is qualitatively more than the sum of them, as with an ecological system and the different life forms comprising it. Ken Wilber, following Arthur Koestler, has given the name of *holarchies* to these natural hierarchies. And consciousness research suggests that the different levels of consciousness exist holarchically. Thus many scholars would maintain that the consciousness of the nondualistic sage subsumes and embraces the theistic dualism of the saint, which in turn subsumes the empirical dualism of the scientist.

This research is still at a comparatively early stage, and many of its findings are controversial and provisional. However, the idea of evolving levels of consciousness can provide a helpful preliminary understanding, so long as it does not become too schematic. There is now substantial agreement among many scholars about the resemblance of specific levels of consciousness attained in spiritual traditions widely separated in time and space—such as contemplative Christianity, Mahayana Buddhism, mystical Judaism, neo-Confucianism, Sufism, or Advaita Vedanta. Particularly noteworthy is the widespread recognition of a non-dualistic spirituality, with which this book is primarily concerned, in which self and other (and self and God) are one. These insights appear with the force of simple fact, and cannot be adequately communicated. Their appearance, profundity, and power to shape the adept's personality can be affected through long-established systems of training under a spiritual director (for example, a *roshi*, *guru*, *shaykh*, or *staretz*). Such perennial wisdom has been refracted through a diverse range of cultures. As William James observes in *Varieties of Religious Experience:* "The fact is that the mystical feeling of enlargement, union and emancipation has no specific intellectual content of its own. It is capable of forming matrimonial alliances with material furnished by the most diverse philosophies and theologies." And when, seventy years ago, theologian Rudolf Otto compared the descriptions of the Godhead by the medieval Christian mystic Meister Eckhart and of Brahman by the eighth-century C.E. Hindu mystic Shankara, he concluded that "the words of one read like a translation into Latin or German from the Sanskrit of the other, or vice versa."

The study of modernity and its history suggests the need for a spirituality that begins by inquiry into the nature of the self, that prime mover of history. When the self endeavors strongly to identify and define itself in terms of belief in some spiritual *other,* whether God or Nature, a whole uneasy dualism follows—reason against emotion, spirit against flesh, and, socially, a proneness to the bonding of the followers of the One True God against the rest of the world. Dualism, the gap between subject and object, is, as twentieth-century Indian mystic J. Krishnamurti remarked, the cause of all the misery of humankind. As Ken Wilber observes in *Up from Eden:* "In the orthodox religions of the West, the spheres of the Divine and the Human never evolved to the natural point where they became one.... Thus the *separation* of God and man was never overcome in a higher synthesis or transformation, either in theory or practice."

Through the practice of the nondualistic, inner-path spiritualities of esoteric religion it begins to dawn upon us that there is not the split we had assumed between who we are "in here" and the world "out there." There is only an undivided presence, readily accessible through meditation, that is manifested in the myriad phenomena of our experience, and that exists *only* as those transient and insubstantial phenomena. But if we get stuck with these *ideas,* then dualism makes a covert return, as absolute versus relative, spirit versus matter, the one versus the many, the sacred versus the profane, and so on. The embodiment of such a nondualistic consciousness is ultimately the only way to change the course of history—and in the context of modernity it implies the ultimate political and economic radicalism.

This book is based on one such nondualistic spirituality, Mahayana Buddhism. In the monotheistic "religions of the Book" the nondualism of the God within, the God who is everywhere, was marginalized as a suspect and esoteric "mysticism." In Judaism the Hasidic movement came into conflict with the God of the Covenant. Islam had outstanding mystics in Abu Yazid, Al-Hallaj, and others in its Sufi tradition, but the conflict between internalized and confrontational forms of religious experience was here particularly intense. The mystical teachings of Jesus, recorded in the (uncanonical) Gospel of Thomas, have been obscured both by the need to make the teachings popularly accessible and by subsequent institutional myth-making. Jesus' insight that "the Father and I are One," together with his teaching of personal liberation, were interpreted by the emergent church so that he became remote and more-than-human—the Son of God. Attention shifted from his teaching to the resurrection and other myths.

From the start of "high egoic" modernity in the sixteenth century there has been a steady decline in the Christian tradition of mystical, nondualistic spirituality, which has been sustained only in the margins of orthodoxy by small contemplative communities such as the Carmelites and the Quakers. Only comparatively recently have there been signs of reversal. Exoteric, institutional Catholicism and Protestantism both became preoccupied with punitive morality and dogmatic orthodoxy and became caricatures of inner spirituality, particularly at their nadir in the bleak "industrial Christianity" of the nineteenth century.

Contemporary religious philosopher Jacob Needleman has drawn attention to this "bizarre forgetting of the instrumental nature of religious forms" with the following analogy, from his book *The New Religions:*

> It is as though millions of people suffering from a painful disease were to gather to hear someone reading a textbook of medical treatment in which the means necessary to cure the disease were carefully spelled out. It is as though they were all to take great comfort from that book and in what they heard, going through their lives knowing that their disease could be cured, quoting passages to their friends, preaching the wonders of this great book, and returning to their congregation from time to time to hear more of the inspiring diagnosis and treatment read to them.... Perhaps for

some a troubling thought crosses their minds as their eyes close for the last time: Haven't I forgotten something? Something important? Haven't I forgotten actually to undergo treatment?

Traditional mythic religion presented an easy target for science-based Enlightenment rationalists, who would stand on public platforms, watch in hand, and defy God to strike them dead. Secularization inverts and reduces spirituality to being at best a handmaiden to social change and other major concerns of modernity. A little respectability can be borrowed by including a clergyman on the campaigning platform and a priest can be borrowed for a television program as the obvious specialist in morality. Spiritual witness is tamed to become a marginal attraction in the secular zoo. "Reductive modernism'" is the term used here for that movement which in effect secularizes religion from within.

Though in conventional Christianity there has been a dearth of emphasis on transformative, inner spirituality, there is in the tradition nevertheless a rich heritage of mystical, nondualistic spirituality. It stretches from the Gnostic Gospels and the Desert Fathers to contemporary figures like Thomas Merton, Martin Buber, and Paul Tillich. The closing lines of Tillich's book *The Courage to Be* reflects the orientation of many of these thinkers: "The courage to take the anxiety of meaninglessness upon oneself is the boundary line up to which the courage to be can go. Within it all forms of courage are reestablished in the power of the God above the God of theism. The courage to be is rooted in the God who appears when God has disappeared in the anxiety of doubt."

In recent decades the writings of Christian mystics have become fresh, meaningful, and relevant. For example, from 1961 onward Penguin Books has continually reprinted the classic, fourteenth-century work of Christian mysticism, *The Cloud of Unknowing*. More significant still has been the revival of the Christian contemplative tradition, drawing on Orthodox practices (like the mantric Jesus Prayer) and Eastern, especially Zen, meditation methods. William Johnston, in his book *The Mirror Mind* has referred to Christian interest in Eastern meditation methods as "a revolution in Christian spirituality," whereby "Christians who dialogue with Buddhists are discovering that levels of consciousness previously dormant are opening up to the presence of God." The literature of Buddhist-Christian dialogue and comparative study over the past fifty years has been rich and extensive. And I have the impression that many Western Buddhists—particularly the older ones—find inspiration and helpful pointers from the spiritual tradition within their own culture, and not only from fourteenth-century mystics like the much-quoted Meister Eckhart but also from contemporaries as wide-ranging as Simone Weil, T. S. Eliot, and Thomas Merton.

The questionable claim that all religions "meet at the top" is of less concern than the strong affinity in values, practices, and revelatory experience that undoubtedly exists between Buddhism and Christianity. This is well summarized in Christian theologian William Johnston's conclusions at the end of a Christian-Zen dialogue in Kyoto:

> An unbridgeable gulf appeared to separate those who believed in the soul, the Absolute and the objectivity of truth from those who spoke of Nirvana, Nothingness and the void.... Soon it became clear that what united us was not philosophy but religious experience. While in philosophical formulations we were poles apart, when it came to the discussion of values we were one. The value of deep meditation, of poverty, of humility, of the spirit of gratitude, of non-violence, and the love of peace—these were things in the discussion of which we had but one heart and soul. Indeed, it was amazing that such diverse philosophies should produce such similar experiences!

Religious scholar Ninian Smart has advocated "a certain outlook based on the complementarity of Buddhism and Christianity" and believes that the two religions share a common global destiny. In *Beyond Ideology* he writes: "The love which Christ self-emptyingly symbolizes, the compassionate non-violence which Buddhism expresses—these values are of even greater importance now than they were before such terrible means of destruction reposed in the hands of hard and confused men." In my own experience of interfaith work I have been impressed by the Christian regard for and interest in the Buddhist tradition of deep contemplation and, contrariwise, the Buddhist appreciation of the commitment to human liberation that has developed within most sections of world Christianity over the past fifty years. In their involvement in movements for peace and nonviolence, in their opposition to racism, poverty, and unemployment at home and abroad, and in the qualities that they have brought to this involvement, Christians have set an example that Buddhists are only slowly beginning to follow.

It is a staggering irony of history that the ancient mysticisms have achieved an unprecedented availability and interest in the midst of a rational modernity that has demythologized traditional institutional religion. Conventional religion is now being supplanted by the "spiritual supermarket" offering a variety of spiritual alternatives, ranging from the individualism of pick-and-mix New Age groups to so-called new religious movements that provide mass refuge from social atomism and anomie. The failure of even high modernity's cornucopia to fill the sense of lack has moved a small but significant minority to look more deeply. Sociologist Robert Bellah writes in *Beyond Belief* of the new "stress on inner authenticity and autonomy [which] can yet have the most profound social and moral consequences":

A great shift in the balance between elite and mass religiosity has taken place. The unexamined magical and religious conceptions of nonliterate and semiliterate strata, what used to make up the bulk of religious life in any society, has come more and more under conscious inspection and critical evaluation as levels of literacy and education reach unprecedented peaks. This has involved the erosion of numerous beliefs and practices, some formerly considered essential to orthodoxy, but many peripheral or of doubtful orthodoxy. On the other hand the old elite notion that religion involves a personal quest for meaning, that it must express the deepest dimensions of the self and in no way violate individual conscience, has been generalized as the dominant conception of religion in modern society.

The future shape of a nondualistic spirituality, theistic or otherwise, is still very much in question. Ken Wilber has argued that it will need to have some reassuringly familiar cultural resonance, like combining Christian symbolism with meditative practice. Buddhism, however, also makes strong claims. It does not present barriers of metaphysical and ethical dogma; it is based upon an experimental examination of human experience; it offers rationally explicable practices for opening to higher levels of consciousness; its different "traditions" have the underlying unity of an individual search based on personal responsibility for oneself: "Work out your salvation with diligence," said the Buddha. Present trends may lead to a spectrum of overlapping practices and networks for personal, inner search, with a strong ecosocial, nonviolent orientation, that may serve as the foundation for the creation of an authentic postmodern spirituality. However, a deepening ecological and social instability could tip the balance in favor of large, organized movements that provide a reassuring sense of belongingness, a charismatic leadership, and a common ideology. Already in Britain there are Buddhist movements such as the Friends of the Western Buddhist Order, Soka Gakkai, and the New Kadampa that have attracted much critical controversy.

Belief, Faith, Experience, and Internalization

With reference to the proposed "culture of awakening" it may be helpful to clarify four stages of spiritual unfolding.

The first and by far the most common is *belief.* Religious belief is a mental construct powered by the emotional need to find meaning and make sense of life, and hence firmly to situate the self in an assured identity. It focuses on the beyond, a God who is totally Other, salvation, enlightenment, the promise of immortality, and so on. It can be a particularly potent kind of ideology, binding members in a self-affirming need to convert others. On the other hand, any spiritual search does commonly begin with belief. We listen to the speakers, read the books, and decide that some particular spiritual persuasion "makes sense."

The believer may fortify herself more emphatically in her belief when doubts arise. Or, if belief does not appear to be delivering its promise, she may abandon it. But sometimes, when belief relaxes its ego-grip, space opens in which *faith* can grow. Faith somehow intuits what is beyond belief, yet has no assurance, no direct experience, of what it might be. In the person of faith dogmatic and pros-elytizing fervor diminish. In its place there is more likely to be a wry smile and a shrug of the shoulders. In contrast to the strenuous conviction of belief one finds oneself in a limbo of doubt, and yet one is moved to remain faithful. This state of mind sustains strong spiritual practice, which may well open the way to the third stage, *experience.* Nevertheless, the person of faith who has clarity of understanding joined to a mature, ethical strength of character may have more wisdom to offer than one who has experienced spiritual "openings" but has yet to integrate these insights into his or her life and character.

Spiritual experience, a direct, immediate apprehension of the divine or numi-nous, can strike anyone at any time—even unbelievers. When it knocked Paul of Tarsus off his donkey he was obliged to adopt a culturally relevant belief system in order to make sense of the experience. At the fourth level, *internalization,* insight has become embodied in the personality, which now has access at will to transpersonal levels of consciousness.

Fundamentalism and Mythic-Exoteric Religion

Exoteric here refers to a dualistic religious belief or faith in a God "out there." It may be accompanied by a belief in the literal truth of myths, like the biblical creation story. In contemporary, nondualistic spirituality myths help to focus, exem-plify, and inspire practice. They are in Buddhist parlance *upaya,* or "skillful means," rather than objective truths. Thus in contemporary Christianity the resurrection has been a source of contention between literalists for whom it is an actual and affirming event and those who understand it as a metaphor that may be the subject of profound contemplation. Anthropologically speaking, myths may express common themes across different cultures (like the risen god), but for believers they are ethnocentric: only their God is the true God. And so, in the typical monotheistic religion there is a Holy Father who is the creator of the universe; a God who is totally "other," mediated by saints, priests, and scripture. This deity is the object of petitionary prayer from devotees who alone receive the promise of eternal life.

Exoteric religion covers a wide spectrum of adherents across the culture of high modernity. There are followers of faith (as described earlier) as well as of belief. The former are not impelled so strongly by the *need* to believe and to uphold this against that. In this sense there are people of all faiths who are able to make a positive contribution to our nondualistic culture of awakening. They are free to heal divisions rather than being driven to affirm them.

In all three of the great monotheistic religions there have been opposing pulls between the reassertion of traditional belief and demythologizing modernism. A number of radical bishops created public scandal in the 1960s by proclaiming "the death of God." Modernity pulled religion *up* from myth and magic and *down* from mysticism to a flatland of rationality. It is an uncomfortable and unsustainable position, but it has the potential of gravitation toward a nondualistic spirituality and the recovery of the contemplative tradition. This radical postdogmatic Christian theology originated a hundred and fifty years ago with Kierkegaard, and with theologians such as Rudolf Bultman and Paul Tillich it acquired a modern existentialist flavor. Dietrich Bonhoeffer, a hero of the anti-Nazi resistance, sought to "live before God as if God did not exist"—the Christian equivalent of the Zen Buddhist injunction, "If you meet the Buddha on the road, kill him!" This tradition has now broadened out, with movements of agnostic spirituality like Don Cupitt's "Sea of Faith." Here, clearly, are major contributions to postmodernity's culture of awakening.

The opposite pull, of mythic reaffirmation, has been much more powerful, and is indeed the most tangible mass response to the root anxiety generated by the culture of high modernity, both by those inside it (as with American fundamentalism) and by those threatened by it (notably in Islamic cultures). It is most emphatically expressed in Protestant fundamentalist mythology, full of proselytizing fervor, and usually with a strongly authoritarian and patriarchal spin. In milder forms evangelical fundamentalism is also flooding into mainstream churches. Fundamentalism veers off into extreme cultic manifestations, Christian and otherwise. These attract—and trap—personalities with low self-esteem and little self-direction who are drawn to strong authority figures and group belongingness.

Gatherings of true believers are sometimes marked by trance states and the mass enthusiasms of the God-possessed. Arguably these are in the main regressions to exclusively bodily and emotional levels of consciousness. However, the experience may jolt believers into a higher level of consciousness or, more usually, simply energize and affirm their existing belief that they are God's chosen instrument. These kinds of experiences can charge up existing personality dysfunctions, giving rise to the "spiritualized ego" of the charismatic religious leader (Jung's "spiritual inflation"). And when God "opens the eyes" of a true believer already laden with guilt and repression, the consequence can be a moralizing crusade against sin. These are the origins of the irrational and intolerant mass movements claiming to be the "moral majority"—a social pathology that is inherent in high modernity's precarious individualism and cultural disembeddedness. Contemporary nondualistic spirituality in fact has more in common with the rationality still dominant in the political and business establishments, the universities, and the media than it has with this mass religiosity.

The Contribution of Ecospirituality

The gathering ecological crisis, together with the social afflictions of industrial capitalism, have given a new impetus to the long Romantic tradition. This crisis has challenged mechanistic rationality with alternative and increasingly influential perspectives in areas ranging from spirituality to economics. These amount to a whole new paradigm, that is to say, a distinct mindset of values, assumptions, feelings, and behaviors. In this new Romanticism, holistic and organismic perceptions of reality are set against reductive and mechanistic ones; the intuitive against the rational; the feminine against the masculine; the fluid and dynamic against the fixed and the static; network against hierarchy; the responsive against the imposed; process thinking against structural-functionalism. The Creation Spirituality of Matthew Fox, for instance, emphasizes immanence over transcendence. The new age movement exalts the merits of premodern cultures, past and present, and denies or ignores those of high modernity. The eco-Romantics celebrate nature over industrialism.

This new organismic paradigm implies a level of consciousness that is essential for the development of the radical postmodernity envisaged in this book. Unfortunately to *believe in* the conceptual formulation is easier, and more common, than to internalize it as a higher level of consciousness *that is holarchically inclusive of the lower levels,* and that integrates each of the opposing pairs mentioned above in a higher third. It draws on both masculine and feminine qualities. It employs rationality to create objects whose beauty transcends rationality. It goes beyond network and hierarchy to holarchy. It honors culture as well as nature. It spirals up through premodern organismic perceptions to integrate them in a culture of postmodernity, instead of nostalgically hankering after replication. However the more typical new age vision accepts the conceptual formulation of the new paradigm but remains stuck at the lower, rational, level of consciousness. So it incorporates the new concepts into the old ideological dualisms of this against that, our righteousness against their ignorance. Back to antithetical bonding again! Yes, these concepts do *represent* a higher level of consciousness, but if we deploy them at the old level of consciousness we disable ourselves. Cultural historian Morris Berman emphasizes the importance of the "ability to tolerate ambiguity." In "Metapolitick," he writes that "installing a new paradigm in place of the old one, nailing down a new belief system as fast as the old one crumbles, will surely prove, a hundred years hence, to have been a big mistake. We did that before; why do it again?" Or, as pioneering psychiatrist and phenomenologist Ronald Laing puts it, "It was all a machine yesterday; it is something like a hologram today. Who knows what intellectual rattle we shall be shaking tomorrow to calm the dread of the emptiness of our understanding."

In its dualistic perversion the new paradigm is sold as nature versus the culture of modernity. To appreciate and remedy its disabling one-sidedness it is necessary to examine its understanding of "nature" and its typical claims, like this by famed *The Tao of Physics* author Fritjof Capra: "The Western version of mystical awareness, or version of Buddhism and Taoism, will be ecological awareness." Nature is identified with the "spiritual" as the ultimate, wholesome good, a purer reality that is threatened by the corruptions of modernity. History is seen as a downhill path from an idealized state in the distant past in which humans lived as part of nature.

Ironically, this eco-Romanticism is in fact well anchored in modernity. Premoderns were too much *in* nature and *of* nature to be *aware* that they were. Only with modernity, from the Renaissance onward, does the sense of dualism between culture and nature arise. First there was the struggle to "tame brute nature." Afterward there was the reaction against industrialism, and nature became "sublime."

It is understandable to attribute spiritually transforming experiences of the beauty of nature to nature itself (immanence). Yet in fact this overwhelming experience occurs when the meddling self has withdrawn (has been transcended), and the beauty floods in without being dulled by the shadow of our neediness. As Zen master Dogen Zenji observed, only "when the self retreats do the ten thousand things advance." To open to nature it is necessary to open fully to the self that is the experiencer of nature, to "cleanse the windows of perception."

Deep ecology is a highly influential ecospirituality that stands over and against environmentalism (a benevolent form of anthropocentrism that casts humankind in the role of a paternalistic lord of creation who protects and conserves nature only on his own terms and from his own standpoint). The starting point of deep ecology is a biocentric egalitarianism: All life forms have equal value and all are equally worthy of respect. As deep ecologist and activist John Seed puts it, *Homo sapiens* is no more than a "plain member" of "the council of all beings."

Yet such ecocentrism is surely as much a half-truth as is anthropocentrism. The relationship of modern men and women to nature is paradoxical. They are flesh-and-blood of nature, and yet their consciousness sets them apart: Nature is something they contemplate, and with which they consciously interact. This paradox remains an intractable challenge for deep ecology. For human beings *are,* under the conditions present in ecosystem, substantially omnipotent—*and know that they are.* Thoreau declared that "the pine is no more lumber than man is, and to be made into boards and houses is no more its true and highest use than the truest use of man is to be cut down and made into manure." The pine, however, is unable to pontificate about what it thinks its own "truest and highest use" might be. Human beings do have to make difficult and complex decisions at all levels. What of circumstances where, at least in the short-term, a swollen and poverty stricken population is compelled to plunder its environment? The ethical guideline proposed by leading deep ecologists Arne Naess and George Sessions was that "humans have no right to reduce the richness and variety [of the biotic community] except to satisfy vital needs."

Here again we have the pull of two truths, and the need for a serviceable truth—a higher third—that embodies and yet transcends both. And here again we must train ourselves to be aware when making decisions of what in fact may be no more than a projection upon nature or humankind of our deep emotional self-needs. Naess underlines the need for the trained internalization of an ecological ethic, so that it moves us spontaneously in an authentic shift of consciousness. As he is quoted in Bill Devall's *Simple in Means, Rich in Ends:*

> We need environmental ethics, but when people feel they unselflessly give up, even sacrifice, their interest in order to show love for nature, this is probably in the long run a treacherous basis for conservation. Through identification they may come to see their own interest served by conservation, through genuine self-love, love of a widened and deepened self.
>
> In short, deep ecology is ultimately about the cultivation of a consciousness in which, in Naess's words, "human beings will experience joy when other life forms experience joy, and sorrow when other life forms experience sorrow."

The outstanding contemporary American poet of deep ecology Gary Snyder brings it all nicely down to earth in *The Practice of the Wild,* maintaining that the "proper study of mankind" is what it means to be human.... Then we can be uniquely "human" with no sense of special privilege.... The Grizzlies or Whales or Rhesus monkeys or *Rattus* would infinitely prefer that humans (especially Euro-Americans) got to know *themselves* thoroughly before presuming to do Ursine or Cetacean research. When humans know themselves, the rest of nature is right there.

This, then, is the essential transition from eco-Romanticism through so-called nature mysticism to a serviceable ecologism.

New Age Spirituality

The New Age "movement" is extraordinarily diverse and eclectic, ranging from a shallow, commercialized narcissism resting on a fuzzy, consoling ideology to authentic transpersonal awareness. Although it traces its roots to premodern cultures and spiritual traditions, the New Age movement is clearly marked by many features that betray it as high modernity's own Romantic eruption of an alienated and disillusioned individualism. In our contemporary, democratic spiritual culture, each individual maintains his or her right to pick-and-mix from the range of decontextualized spiritual products available in the global supermarket, be it witchcraft, Taoism, Rosicrucianism, alchemy, fire-walking, occultism, theosophy, Transcendental Meditation, Kabbalah, neopaganism, Zen, Sufism, and so on, all of which are assumed to convey the same "inner reality." And all are reflected through the cultural prism of high modernity, with its assumptions, needs, and expectations.

In an article entitled "Buddhism and the New Age," British Buddhist author Visvapani critically observed that "one branch of the New Age discards countercultural orientations in favor of 'prosperity teachings' (money as energy, life and empowerment; poverty as self-hatred). As the Sanyassin slogan had it 'Jesus saves, Moses invests, Bhagwan spends.' This is spiritualized materialism masquerading as materialized spirituality." For the most part, however, what is sought after and commodified is novel and exotic experience, the more extreme and "ultimate" the better (like the Buddhist "enlightenment").

Typical New Age philosophy believes that the "outer personality," or "lower self," is limited and corrupted by materialism, whereas the inner being is pure and drawn toward love and spirit. All the spiritual traditions and practices are assumed to be essentially alike, and all, in the words of academic commentator Paul Heelas, "provide means to the same end, liberating the Self from the contaminated 'outer personality' ('ego' and 'lower self' to use more common New Age expressions).... This is what we are by virtue of the impact of the unnatural, notably capitalistic modernity." I wish to draw attention especially to that final sentence, to the Romantic leanings of the New Age (which it shares with utopian political radicalism). Although New Age ideology focuses exclusively upon the self, all its ills are supposedly due to the corruption of cultures alien to nature (ranging from impure food to aggressive masculinity). Apart from its concern for the environment and animal rights, and an implicit feminism, these ills are to be addressed solely at the level of personal consciousness. The self is naturally pure and its purity can be recovered by cultivating an at-oneness with all that is "natural" and by dropping out of high modernity, creating a reinvented premodern alternative lifestyle. There is even the customary Romantic millennarianism, this time the coming of the "Age of Aquarius," to be achieved solely by the spread of a new, enlightened consciousness.

Much of this superficially resembles perennial spirituality, particularly the need to open to a nondualistic level of consciousness. Unfortunately Romantic narcissism tends to draw seekers away from the disciplined work of self-disclosure indispensable to all paths of spiritual search. As critic Kate Thomas remarks in *The Destiny Challenge,* "The New Age entrepreneurs have demonstrated a preoccupation with nurturing the ego, not sublimating it.... New Age workshops and courses do not produce enlightenment, they predominantly produce fantasy, singularly resistant to self-discipline and self-analysis."

In fact, in the early stages of *any* spiritual discipline the self almost inevitably translates the spiritual agenda in terms of the self and the values of the culture that it inhabits. For example, in the consumerist West, some really big experience is expected for all the time, money, and energy that has been invested. At the beginning, self is so full of self that self cannot even see self. The delusion of the narcissistic self does sooner or later begin to become transparent, with persistence, time, and the promptings of an experienced teacher. Then real practice can begin. There are, of course, many new age explorers who stick with the instructions of one of the time-proven spiritual traditions, and quietly transcend the limitations of the new age, whose forms they may retain. In this sense the new age movement may be seen as a problematic but encouraging precursor to authentic spiritual renaissance.

Chapter 9

BEYOND MEDITATION

UNDER THE CONDITIONS of modernity, to what extent is a shift to a higher level of consciousness by a significant number of people a practicable proposition? And how might a socially informed Buddhism be the catalyst for a shift to some future culture in which a strong, nondualistic, inner-path spirituality has a prominent and influential social face? The present chapter continues this theme by reviewing the various enabling resources of psychospiritual practice, ancient and modern. It overlaps with the next chapter, which is about the cultural and social shaping of spiritual practice. "Beyond Meditation" reflects my concern with any overemphasis on sitting meditation, or, indeed, on that other fetish—"enlightenment." A similar concern is found in Kenneth Kraft's *Wheel of Engaged Buddhism*: "Although meditation may be indispensable neither it nor any other discipline can stand (or sit) alone. (Socially) engaged practice also entails development of character, cultivation of generosity and other virtues, refinement of ethical sensitivity, and the day-to-day activation of compassion."

Meditation and Mindfulness

Meditation is the historic foundation practice of Buddhism. It comprises two elements—*shamatha* (tranquillity) and *vipassana* (insight). With the former, conditions are created that allow the mind to become quiet, usually by bringing the concentration to bear on a single object, such as the rise and fall of the breath. In *vipassana* the mirrorlike mind can now be opened to reflect all that is discernible within. Thus the nature of our human condition is revealed to consciousness. A profound and wholehearted acceptance of the *thusness* of how things are liberates the spiritual adept from the struggle to sustain an alienated self against what had appeared to be a world of solid and enduring phenomena. Combined with other practices such as those reviewed below, meditation ripens a personality that eventually becomes the stable embodiment of such insights. This "enlightening" process requires a patient and lifelong practice.

Such meditation, both as sitting meditation and walking meditation, is typically the intensive practice of a monastic and hermetic religion. For the lay people of contemporary society this kind of monastic training is encapsulated in periodic retreats, ranging from a day or weekend to, exceptionally, several months. Such retreats usually embrace not only meditation, but also a range of traditional ritual "skillful means" to awakening, like chanting the liturgy, devotional practices, and the invocation of myth. These retreats are invaluable for refocusing a mode of experience that tends to become blurred and distorted in the intervening pull and push of everyday life.

The basic everyday life practice is an ancient form of meditation called *mindfulness,* or, more graphically, *bare awareness.* This practice walks, as it were, on two metaphorical legs (and, ideally, when the trainee is not walking on one he or she is trying to walk on the other). One leg is the continual attempt to give total attention, moment by moment, to what is being done now. In *The Miracle of Mindfulness,* Thich Nhat Hanh writes as follows of mindful tea drinking: "Allow yourself a good length of time to do this. Don't drink your tea like someone who gulps down a cup of coffee during a work break. Drink your tea slowly and reverently as if it were the axis on which the earth revolves—slowly, evenly, without rushing towards the future. Live the actual moment. For only this actual moment is life." The other leg of this practice is a scrupulous awareness of the rising and falling of the emotions as a physical sensation. In my experience, this is the more directly transformative practice and it is with this that I shall primarily be concerned in this chapter.

Awareness practice is learning to open up to the onslaught of raw emotional energy without either letting it discharge itself (as anger or self-pity, for example) or suppressing it (perhaps by trying to rationalize it or otherwise get it under control). This is not easy to describe, and harder still to do; it requires a lot of personal experimentation. Transpersonal psychologist John Welwood writes of an awareness practice that he calls *befriending emotion* which, "by neither suppressing emotions nor exploring the meaning in them, teaches us a way to feel their naked aliveness and contain their energy.... This approach to emotion is called *transmutation* in Vajrayana Buddhism as well as in other traditions." Some further explanation from teachers in different Buddhist traditions may help to get the measure of awareness practice. In the Theravada Buddhist tradition, Nyanaponika Mahathera writes that "by the methodical application of Bare

Attention…all the latent powers of a non-coercive approach will gradually unfold themselves with their beneficial results and their wide and unexpected implications." "Let yourself be in the emotion," wrote the Tibetan Buddhist teacher Chögyam Trungpa in *The Myth of Freedom*. "Go through it, give in to it, experience it…. Then the most powerful energies become absolutely workable rather than taking you over, because there is nothing to take over if you are not putting up any resistance." And Zen philosopher and author Hubert Benoit warns as follows: "If a humiliating circumstance turns up, offering me a marvelous chance of initiation, at once my imagination strives to conjure what appears to me to be in danger…. [I]t does everything to restore me to that habitual state of satisfied arrogance in which I find a transitory respite but also the certainty of further distress. In short, I constantly defend myself against that which offers to save me; I fight foot by foot to defend the very source of my unhappiness!"

Bare awareness is thus a practice of attentive yielding to and acceptance of the entire content of our experience in the body, in the emotions, which gradually dissolves our futile habit of conducting a kind of emotional lawsuit with everything that agitates us or threatens us in any way. Energy previously blocked in "controlling" ourselves or wasted in negative, self-centered discharge is thus purified of the various colors of driven feeling; it becomes available for appropriate and positive response (including compassionate, outgoing feelings) to situations we encounter.

The practice also requires a reconsidered lifestyle, especially in endeavoring to live within an ethical framework, socially as well as personally. Buddhist practice and lifestyle customarily involve practicing "forms" or disciplines that are challenging enough to evoke strong feelings and so expose them to awareness, but that should not, however, be so rigorous as to require heavy and insensitive control, with the danger of causing one to become a robot or a self-righteous ascetic. The self-denying, tightly ordered program of a monastery is an obvious example, but the pressures and tight deadlines of the modern working day balance with family life and obligations can provide for many people as much of "discipline" as they can handle.

Social Action As Mindfulness Practice

Dana paramita, the virtue of giving, is another important ingredient of traditional Buddhist mind-training. Its practice is double-edged: outwardly it is clearly beneficial; inwardly, giving is a potentially transformative meditation. Giving up something of mine is a self-diminution and preparation for the time the delusion of self may itself be yielded up. Zen Buddhist philosopher and teacher D. T. Suzuki, in "Knowledge and Innocence," characterizes *dana* as "anything going out of oneself, disseminating knowledge, helping people in difficulties of all kinds, creating arts, promoting industry or social welfare, sacrificing one's life for a worthy cause, and so on." The essence of dana is that it really is giving, and that this giving transcends the giver, receiver, and gift—and not a form of exchange through which "merit" or a sense of virtue is acquired. This particularly applies to dana as beneficent social action.

Social action typically provides plenty of opportunity for a disciplined awareness practice. We usually make a voluntary commitment of time and energy to some project and to the other people who are working on it. It is likely that much of the work will be tedious and not immediately rewarding—a round of fundraising, secretarial and committee work, leafleting on street corners, knocking on doors on dark, rainy nights to win support for a petition. Much indifference, hostility, and even abuse may be experienced, creating feelings of frustration, fear, and defeat. Not least, social action requires us to work in close fellowship with others, whom we may find awkward or disagreeable.

Moreover, if we are to be effective in our social action we have to be able to learn from hard experience even when it contradicts our deeply held assumptions and threatens that person who at the present time we feel we are. Peace work and similar kinds of campaigning are likely to feel most comfortable and self-confirming when we distance ourselves from those with whom we are trying to communicate. If we talk with them at all, then we talk *to* or *at* them and make sure we do most of the talking so as to retain control of the situation. Vulnerable communication in which we express our own feelings or receive someone else's is more threatening than cool, removed, rational discussion. And yet closeness, real dialogue, and shared feelings are the best ways of opening up genuine communication. And these are excellent opportunities, if only we can handle them, for cultivating the awareness practice and hence slowly becoming a person who can make effective, heartfelt response to the fear and resentment that can be aroused in people who are reminded about something upsetting.

And there are other ways, also, in which our awareness needs to be extended and informed. In "Non-Violence: Practicing Awareness," Thich Nhat Hanh reminds us that

society makes it difficult for us to be awake. I am sure you know this, but you keep forgetting: Forty thousand children in the Third World die every day of hunger, forty thousand of them. We know, but we keep forgetting because the kind of society in which we live makes us forgetful. That is why we need some exercise for mindfulness, for awareness. A number of Buddhists practice this—they refrain from eating a few times a week in order to be in communion with the Third World.

Self-awareness of emotional states is critical in every aspect of social engagement. How this awareness can help others as well as oneself is illustrated in the Samyutta Nikaya by a story about two traveling acrobats who perform hazardous feats on the end of a long bamboo pole. One said that their act would be accomplished safely if each watched and attended to the other. But the other and wiser one maintained that if each concentrated on doing his own part of the act safely and well he would thereby protect his friend as well as himself.

Consider the situation of a stormy group meeting where an important but contentious decision has to be made. Would it not be helpful to pause, to shut up for a while, to look inward at the turbulence of one's own seething indignation and see how this—and the angry feelings of others—makes it more difficult to find a sound and acceptable solution to the problem at hand? Social action can throw up many "white water" situations, when the emotional rapids become too turbulent for us to paddle our little awareness canoe skillfully enough, and it capsizes. We go over the top with our feelings, or screw them down with white-faced control, or slide into a wallow of self-pity, or otherwise forget where we are. Therefore it is best to learn in calmer waters. This means avoiding situations that cannot yet be ridden out without upset to self and without contributing negatively to what is happening. All mass nonviolent demonstrations tend to arouse powerful emotions that may threaten the success of the action, as well as upset the mindfulness practice of any militant mystics who happen to be involved! Organizations that imply the absolute virtue and truth of their own cause and the unmitigated falsehood and evil of their opponents are probably too common to be avoided, but it is usually best to steer clear of those that go out of their way to foster animosity and promote counterproductive adversarial situations.

A meditation practice directly related to social activism is the ancient *brahma-vihara* (sublime abidings) meditation. The meditator generates a spirit of loving kindness *(metta)* within which is directed successively to oneself, to a friend, to a stranger, and to an enemy. When he or she has become adept at this *metta-bhavana,* the meditation is extended successively to include the virtues of compassion *(karuna),* sympathetic joy *(mudita).* and equanimity *(upekkha).*

Teachers, Lay Practice, and Sangha

In all traditional inner-path training a major role is played by the teacher. The teacher is one who has "been up the mountain" of realization and can provide a reliable one-to-one guide to the hazards and pitfalls along the way. The role of the teacher differs in the different Buddhist traditions. In the strongly monastic Theravada, there is teaching for lay groups supplemented by individual advice, but no tradition of close, long-term, student-teacher commitment. At the other extreme is the guru of Tibetan Buddhism, with whom the disciple closely identifies. Generally speaking a spiritual teacher or director is best likened to a combination of tutor and athletic training coach.

Study, whether guided or on one's own, is another important resource for spiritual awakening. As Buddhism has taken root in the West, the value of study has at times been overshadowed by an emphasis on meditation, probably as a misinterpretation of Zen Buddhism. In high modernity Dharma study needs to be extended outward to be socially informed. As we shall see in the next chapter, on the opening of the "fourth eye" of social responsibility, a philosophy that is socially illiterate can lead to one that is socially unethical.

In the Mahayana tradition laypeople were encouraged to practice, and a few became respected and enlightened figures. Generally speaking, however, they were the exception to the rule in an essentially monastic religion. The historic role of laypeople has been to provide material support for the monastics, and to try to follow their example as best they are able. In return, the laity received teachings and guidance appropriate to their generally ill-educated condition and their necessary preoccupation with winning a livelihood and bringing up their families. By contrast, lay practitioners in many countries today are as well, or better, educated than typical monastics; they have leisure and other means for becoming knowledgeable about Buddhism through the extensive published literature; and many of them are dedicated practitioners of meditation, and of a Buddhist lifestyle.

In the Far East the growth in recent times of mass lay Buddhist movements has diminished the influence of the monastic tradition. These movements are charismatic and strongly filiative, and tend to focus on simple mantric practice and devotional fervor for their transformative effect. Western Buddhist monasticism has been mainly confined to the Theravada and to ethnic Buddhist communities, although there are increasingly numerous Zen monasteries in the West. But much more typical in the West is the "practice center," which primarily serves to support the meditation practice of its lay members and offer periodic meditation retreats. These centers usually comprise one or more teachers, a few permanent staff and long-term resident students, and a much larger body of affiliated, nonresident students.

In "Monks, Laity, and Sangha," Stephen Batchelor, a former monk with considerable experience of Buddhist communities, confirms the validity of Buddhist monasticism today, but at the same time concludes:

> It can no longer be taken for granted that as a monk one will automatically be serving a more valuable role [than as a lay person] in the preservation

of Buddhism and its *sangha*. Likewise the traditional notion that a monk is somehow intellectually and morally superior to the laity can no longer be accepted.... Whatever form it takes, an alternative *sangha* structure needs to arise in correlation with the present situation that is able to replace the traditional model of monastic domination and lay-monk polarity.

Nevertheless in both the West and in Asia there is evidence of the value of monastic communities supporting serious lay practice, and even Buddhist-inspired social activism, in a new kind of partnership. Much of that support is intangible, amounting to the very presence of monastics. As Batchelor observes, "Irrespective of one's intellectual opinions about monasticism, to actually encounter a monk has a definite psychological impact: in a believer he acts as a concrete affirmation of one's faith; in a non-believer he challenges an exclusive preoccupation with secular affairs and stirs unconscious tendencies to spirituality." Several social activists have testified to the value of the monastic community as a source of strength and replenishment for them. Thus, in *Siamese Resurgence,* Sulak Sivaraksa writes:

These meditation masters [and] monks who spend their lives in the forests, are very, very important for us and for our society. Even those of us who are in society must go back to these masters and look within. We must practice daily our meditation, our prayer. We must do it at least every morning, or every evening, or both. And those of us...who work in society and confront power and social injustice, we get beaten every now and again and we get tired often. At least annually we ought to retreat into the forests, into the monasteries, to sit at the feet of the masters, to gain our spiritual strength, in order to come out again to confront society.

For reasons of geographical convenience and, above all, the demanding preoccupations of lay life, most Westerners will only attend a practice center (monastic or otherwise) for a few weeks a year at most. So there remains the need for something resembling the best kind of Christian congregational community, which provides support on many levels to integrate one's spiritual commitment along with concerns of relationships, family, home, and career. It is unclear how far the hundreds of small, local Buddhist groups meet that need. Arguably much Western Buddhist practice, instead of embodying a counter-culture of personal and social awakening, tends to accommodate itself to the individualism, the decay of face-to-face community, the demands of relationships and nuclear family, and the devouring work-and-consumption ethos that characterize contemporary society. Indeed, Rita Gross, a pioneer of Buddhist feminism, has argued that "the lack of sufficient community, of genuine friendship, psychological comfort, and emotional nurturing within one's Buddhist *sangha* is one of the most pressing and vital issues facing American Buddhists."

The Contribution of Transpersonal Psychology

Transpersonal psychology is concerned with understanding and facilitating psychospiritual health and development across the whole spectrum of consciousness, personal as well as transpersonal. It thus provides an essential guide to a wide range of strategies for the personal changes—the inner liberation—with which this book is concerned. In this sense it would be more accurate to refer to a *psycho*-spiritual culture of awakening.

Humanistic therapy can enable us to become more integrated personalities, be more in touch with our feelings and our bodies, and have greater inner strength to take charge of our lives without dependency on authority or belongingness of one kind or another. It enables us to respect the autonomy of other people and to relate openly and caringly to them, and to encounter new experiences and challenges without rigid and defensive reactions. For the most part these ends are achieved by bringing into awareness buried emotions, traumas, and "unfinished business" relating, for example, to childhood griefs, sexual phobias, or destructive relationships, which distort and inhibit our perceptions and behaviors. The more profound changes require professional attention, but much can also be achieved by simple therapies like co-counseling. However, it is essential that therapy, like spirituality, be socially informed and involved in the work of cultural change, rather than simply facilitate personal adaptation to the status quo.

The relationship between the psychological and the spiritual, between therapy and spiritual practice, has been the subject of considerable discussion. Some years ago the linear view was popular in some quarters: that it is necessary to clear the ground for spiritual practice by first going into therapy intended to produce a rounded personality. Arguably this implies a misunderstanding of the character of spiritual training. There is a saying that the river gradually wears down the rough and jagged stones and by so doing it eventually carries them to the great sea; by contrast, those that are smooth to start with do not travel far. Visualizing the path of spiritual training as proceeding through a succession of stages can be misleading. The beginning prefigures the end, as well as simply preparing the way for it. A spirit of unwavering humility, for example, is cultivated from the very start, as the beginner learns to bow to the Buddha image, to the teacher, to food, and even to the meditation cushion. Spiritual practice is holistic and polychronic as much as it is sequential and linear. The practice is much more than the sum of its techniques. Proposals to substitute various religiously uninformed therapies for earlier stages of spiritual training are therefore questionable.

Jack Kornfield, a psychotherapist and highly regarded Western meditation teacher, reports in "Psychological Adjustment Is Not Liberation" that

in the course of spiritual practice, I have observed what we would call psychological transformation, in which people become increasingly aware of different motivation patterns, different kinds of attachment, and different images or relationships, in most profound ways. Through practice and through a sitting meditation discipline that is most central in Buddhism I have observed many people going through the kind of growth that also happens in psychotherapy.

He elaborates further in "Meditation: Aspects of Theory and Practice":

There is a kind of illumination in the meditation awareness process that's very much like doing therapy for oneself, simply by listening and paying attention. These insights and the acceptance that comes with a nonjudgmental awareness of our patterns promotes mental balance and understanding so it can lessen our neurotic identification and suffering.

Furthermore, Kornfield draws attention to the deep, penetrating observation obtainable in traditional meditation practice through its combination of stilling the discriminating mind in deep absorption *(samadhi)* sufficient to open up to clear and nonmanipulative contemplation *(vipassana)*. By contrast, in Western psychology he finds a

predominant emphasis on the qualities known in the Abhidhamma as analysis and investigation. This is true even in the best awareness traditions, like gestalt, where people pay very close attention in a mindful way to their inner process. Still there is a real neglect for the cutting power of *samadhi,* the stillness of the mind in meditation.... Thus a lot of psychological tools, which are similar to spiritual techniques, achieve different results because they do not penetrate the surface of the mind. They lack these other important aspects: concentration and tranquility and equanimity, which empower the awareness to cut the neurotic speed.

Nevertheless, traditional spiritual practice originated in cultures far removed from today's culture of reflexive individualism. And while Buddhist philosophy possesses extraordinary insight into the higher stages of the evolution of consciousness, it offers little understanding of the earlier, pre-egoic stages of personal development. These can originate traumas and neuroses that may be "bypassed" by spiritual practice and that may require therapy in order to sustain a balanced personal development. Thus, a person may have opened to profound spiritual insights yet still experience disastrous personal relationships, arising from some deep-seated problem that is inhibiting overall maturation.

In *A Path with Heart: A Guide through the Perils and Promises of the Spiritual Life,* Jack Kornfield likens the map of spiritual growth to a four-petaled lotus. The work needs to be done in all four areas of mind, emotions, body, and—in the widest sense—external relationships; when there is not balanced development in all four areas, the consequences can be serious. Similarly, transpersonal psychologist John Welwood maintains in *Awakening the Heart: Eastern and Western Approaches to Psychotherapy and the Healing Relationship* that

> if a person has not developed the ability to relate to others in a wholesome way, or is unable to acknowledge and express feelings, psychotherapy may be the first treatment of choice before he can even begin to consider meditation.... To attempt to skip over this area of our development in favor of some spiritual bliss beyond is asking for trouble.

Nowadays there appear to be many spiritual teachers like Jack Kornfield, who sends "quite a few of the people who come to my meditation retreats to therapists who I know are good and also have some spiritual understanding and perspective."

Two kinds of the above "spiritual bypassing" have received particular attention. Firstly there is little doubt that meditation and spiritual practice can have a regressive effect on people with a poorly developed sense of self-identity. Yet these are the people who are particularly likely to be drawn to the warm womb of a religious practice, gratefully embracing the "humility" and self-negation that justifies their inability to compete in an acquisitive world, yielding up their failed struggle to assert themselves to conformity to a quasi-monastic discipline, escaping into a group membership that itself makes no difficult psychosocial demands, and finding a lost super-parent in the omniscience of a bhikkhu, roshi, or guru. Such people readily offer themselves up as victims of the various cultic perversions of spirituality.

Another form of bypassing is the opposite of the above. Here a strong but still immature and acquisitive ego attempts, self-deludingly, to simulate and appropriate higher states of consciousness. This ego-charged, pseudo-spirituality has long been recognized in the ancient spiritual traditions, and Carl Jung coined the term "spiritual inflation" for it.

The common contemporary view is to see therapy and spiritual practice as complementary. Indeed, Jack Kornfield, in an essay in *Ken Wilber in Dialogue,* finds it increasingly difficult to separate the psychological from the spiritual, a separation he finds to be

an arbitrary division not actually found in the psyche. In fact, the beings I know who are the most spiritually mature among Western students in all the various [Buddhist] traditions are those in whom there has been a maturing and development of emotional, psychological, personal and historical, as well as universal, understanding. Such understanding has been tested for these persons repeatedly through the fire of relationships (thinking of relationships in the broadest sense): relationships to work, to community, to other individuals, and to their environments. In that sense there's no sense of separation between the psychological and the spiritual.

Moreover, the conditions that favor psychospiritual growth in one person may be ineffectual with another, and may have regressive effects in a third. Appropriate guidance or treatment may remain to some extent elusive, depending very much on the skill and empathy of the teacher or therapist. Robyn Skinner, a psychotherapist, testifies that "many who follow a sacred tradition change profoundly as regards their ordinary life adjustment...under the influence of some subtler and finer influence that begins to permeate and alter the entire organism." On the other hand Skinner has noticed that others who follow such traditions "become more closed, narrow, and intolerant, both of others and of their own hidden aspects. Of those I see professionally, this group is the most intractable and untreatable of all, for the knowledge derived from a religious tradition has been put to the service of perceptual defenses, of complacency, of narcissistic self-satisfaction, of comfort and security." But, contrariwise, there are those in psychotherapy, and particularly in group therapy, whom Skinner finds "can reach a point of simple openness, of awareness of themselves as part of mankind and of the universe, and of direct communion with others, more intensely than many following a traditional teaching, at least as far as one can judge by the statements and external behavior of each. *It does not last, of course, and cannot be pursued systematically,* but in the psychotherapeutic experience it is often there, sometimes in awe-inspiring fashion, and we have to make a place for this in our ideas." (Italics added.)

Finally, in terms of what we now know about human potential, what is accepted as normal begins to look like arrested development. Abraham Maslow observes in *Towards a Psychology of Being* that "what we call normality in psychology is really a psychopathology of the average, so undramatic and so widely spread that we don't even notice it." This applies no less to the arrested social development achieved by modernity, which makes the actualization of the transpersonal vision now so urgent. This is the argument of two pioneers of transpersonal psychology, Roger Walsh and Frances Vaughan, in *Paths Beyond Ego:*

> This actualization may be crucial for the survival of our planet and our species, for we have created a global situation which demands unprecedented psychological and social maturation. In the past we could consume without depletion, discard without pollution, multiply without overpopulation, and fight without fear of extinction. In other words, we could act out our immaturities whereas now we need to outgrow them. Our global crisis, like the transpersonal vision, calls us to grow up and wake up.

Chapter 10

SOCIAL AWARENESS:

OPENING THE FOURTH EYE

TRADITIONALLY *the opening of the third eye* refers to a spiritual awakening. But such an awakening cannot afford to be culture-blind and socially illiterate. Thus, to *open the fourth eye* is to be aware and knowledgeable of the social and cultural contexts of the Dharma—and particularly the ethical implications of those contexts. The opening of that fourth eye is the gift of modernity to the traditional spiritualities. For a pronounced cultural skew may be impervious to wisdom, compassion, knowledge, or even information—as with the ingrained misogyny of traditional religions. There have been many insightful sages whose social views have been naïve, pedestrian, crudely prejudiced, or just downright silly—and thus Carl Jung sometimes reads as no more than a prewar Swiss German bourgeois. Philosopher and champion of indigenous spirituality Laurens van der Post was as zealous and unquestioning a Thatcherite as any Colonel Blimp. And to his enthusiasm for Japanese imperial aggression the renowned Zen master Hakuun Yasutani even added anti-Semitism.

Spiritual traditions, like any other type of tradition, are invariably embedded culturally in time and place. Ancient spiritual teachings are embedded in cultures increasingly remote from and alien to our own. In this chapter, we will explore a number of questions about, and implications of, the social and cultural contextualization of the Dharma. For example: What are the characteristics evolved by different social cultures in response to the profound sense of precariousness of our human condition—and how has Buddhism been shaped by these characteristics? How might a distinction be made between essential, core elements in Buddhism and more culture-specific developments, between Dharma (the essential Way) and *yana* (the vehicle of its expression)? How might we safeguard the core of the Dharma while at the same time making it available in forms accessible and serviceable to contemporary society? And what would this imply for a wider culture of existential awakening?

Asian *Yanas*

Scholar of Indian and Buddhist philosophy Hajime Nakamura, in his landmark study *Ways of Thinking of Eastern Peoples: India, China, Tibet, Japan,* uses the cultural variants of Buddhism as pointers to the distinguishing features of its different host cultures. In the following discussion of the various yanas, or vehicles, in which Buddhism has evolved in its migration through different cultures, I rely substantially on his observations.

The traditional Indian culture that gave birth to Buddhism can be understood as responding to existential lack by emphasizing the illusory, insubstantial unreality—*maya*—of the material world, through which the individual transmigrates successive lifetimes in accordance with karmic destiny. Indian culture defined itself in terms of the transcendental realm. It tended to identify with myth and abstraction, and was vague about details of historiography, geography, and biography, in which it found little interest. It was, however, spiritually creative and prolific, and comparatively indifferent to institutionalization, spiritual hierarchy, and the alleged authority of lineage. The Buddha did not feel it necessary to nominate a successor, and advised those who came after him to "be lamps unto yourselves." Institutional ossification came later in the Theravada schools of Sri Lanka, Burma, and Thailand, but was always challenged by followers of the original tradition.

Compared with Indian culture, traditional Chinese and Japanese cultures are much more *membership* cultures. The sense of self was—and is—sustained by close identification with a tightly regulated, formalized, and hierarchical society, providing optimal security and predictability and minimal individuality. These are cultures of facticity. Geography, historiography, and biography flourished, with a concern for chronology and detail. In further developing the Indian Yogachara the Chinese took pains to emphasize *form*—substance—and to warn of the dangers of meditatively losing oneself in emptiness. "Though the two exist because of the One, do not cling to the One" was a common refrain. Everyday mind *is* the Way; practice *is* enlightenment. Granted this is taken from Indian Mahayana, but in fact this tradition did not survive in India and Southeast Asia, and was the one Indian school of thought to thrive north of the Himalayas.

In the Chinese and Japanese cultures there is relatively little interest in metaphysical speculation or purely logical inquiry, notwithstanding exceptions like Huayen Buddhism. And there is much reliance on the authority of tradition—

hence the importance of spiritual lineages. Searching public critique and debate is seen as disloyal and potentially disruptive, and therefore contradictions and inconsistencies tend not to be satisfactorily resolved. Chinese and Japanese Buddhism are thus cheerfully syncretic. And as we shall see later in this chapter, violation of the first Buddhist precept, against killing, was perpetrated without any sense of outrageous incongruity, particularly in Japan. The pragmatism of China is found in Japan as a capacity for imitation and adaptation, and a strong goal orientation. This latter was identified by Robert Bellah in *Tokugawa Religion: The Cultural Roots of Modern Japan* as the major characteristic of Japanese society, combined with a lack of interest in theoretical principles. This presumably helps to explain the highly purposive, combative struggle to attain enlightenment in the *koan* training of Rinzai Zen. Nakamura warned that this kind of orientation in religion "may easily degenerate into the sheer utilitarianism of profit-seeking activities, should it lose sight of the significance of the absolute." He might well have had in mind the internationally popular Japanese Soka Gakkai sect, which once achieved some notoriety for its practice of "chanting for a BMW" and other worldly goods.

As might be expected of this-worldly cultures there is little emphasis on karma and even less on rebirth. When asked what happens after death, Zen master Hakuin responded, "Why ask me?" "Because you're a Zen master," came the reply. "Yes," said Hakuin, "but not a dead one!" There is in most forms of Japanese and Chinese Buddhism a matter-of-fact acceptance of sex, saké, and whatever else comes naturally—"the passions are our buddha nature." There is also an emphasis on the problematic and situational nature of ethics, and in classic Zen koan training the questions relating to ethics are often addressed only at the end of the training curriculum.

Where in China family loyalty was the main social integrating force, in Japan one's loyalty was to one's lord and subsequently to the emperor as the head of the whole Japanese family. Rather than expressing universal values, religion was co-opted to serve the needs of Japanese culture, the requirements of the imperial political establishment, and an obsession with ethnic purity (a more extreme version of imperial Britain and its established church, incidentally). It was not that the doctrines were changed: Japanese Buddhist chants make reference to the vow to "save all beings"—not only Japanese ones. It was in interpretation and behavior that the cultural adaptation took place, which I will examine in more detail in the discussion of Japan's Imperial Way Buddhism that follows.

The fourth major Buddhist culture is that of Tibet. Tibetan culture shares some features with those of India and China, but has a strong, distinctive character of its own, with a rich life of lore and magic and a complex pantheon of deities. Tibetan Buddhism is elaborate, intricate, diverse, mythically abundant, and very culturally embedded, with strong emphasis on karma and rebirth. As Buddhism became established in Tibet, it evolved a tradition based on devout submission to a highly formalized and regulated monastic theocracy authenticated by spiritual lineage. Tibetan Buddhism was thrust into the West in the diaspora following the Chinese invasion, and together with Japanese Zen and the Theravada of Southeast Asia, is one of the three major traditions that have taken root among Westerners.

Imperial Way Buddhism

All of the Japanese cultural characteristics outlined above, and taken together, help to explain the extraordinary subordination of Buddhism—and especially Zen Buddhism—to Japanese militaristic imperialism. This *Imperial Way Buddhism,* as it was called, has been given prominence by Zen priest and professor of Asian studies Brian Victoria in his book *Zen at War.* It affords the most dramatic example of how a specific social culture can co-opt and pervert core Buddhist belief.

After the Meiji Restoration, which restored imperial rule in 1868, Japanese institutional Buddhism was faced with the prospect of going underground (like Christianity) or becoming a useful part of the new order. Certainly for the Zen sect the latter came naturally enough. For centuries Zen had been associated with samurai culture and its sense of militaristic allegiance.

Zen at War contains dozens of passages from leading Zen teachers including Shaku Soen, Sawaki Kodo, D. T. Suzuki, Hakuun Yasutani, and Harada Daiun. These displayed ingenious casuistry in presenting "emptiness" and other Mahayana concepts in ways that eliminate personal moral responsibility—such as killing, but doing so with "no mind." Victoria quotes D. T. Suzuki, from *Zen and Japanese Culture,* written in 1937:

> The art of swordsmanship distinguishes between the sword that kills and the sword that gives life. The one that is used by a technician cannot go any further than killing.... The case is altogether different with the one who is compelled to lift the sword. For it is not really he but the sword itself that does the killing. He had no desire to harm anybody, but the enemy appears and makes himself a victim. It is as though the sword automatically performs its function of justice, which is the function of mercy. The swordsman turns into an artist of the first grade, engaged in producing a work of genuine originality.

This is very typical of the Zen apologetics of this period, though, to give him his due, Suzuki did begin to take a different view by the time of Japan's entry into the Second World War. However, in the year that Suzuki's book appeared, a certain second lieutenant Tanaka put this kind of teaching into effect at the sack of Nanking by the Imperial Japanese Army—one of the great war crimes of the last century. He gave a demonstration to his troops on how to behead Chinese civilians—the "unruly heathen" to whom Suzuki and Shaku Soen referred. Tanaka's victims were lucky not to be used for mere bayonet practice, for clearly the lieutenant was "an artist of the first grade." Iris Chang reports the following eyewitness account in her book *The Rape of Nanking:*

"Heads should be cut off like this," he said, unsheathing his sword. He scooped water from a bucket with a dipper, then poured it over both sides of the blade. Swishing off the water he raised his sword in a long arc. Standing behind the prisoner, Tanaka steadied himself, legs spread apart, and cut off the man's head with a shout, "Yo!" The head flew more than a meter away. Blood spurted in two fountains from the body and sprayed into the hole. The scene was so appalling that I felt I couldn't breathe.

More recently, the Soto Zen sect, at least, has publicly expressed regret for its support of Japanese militarism. In the postwar period the Zen establishment has shifted to training businessmen for the "war" of international trade. In *Zen Awakening and Society,* a study of Zen ethics in the context of social engagement, Christopher Ives observes that "Zen Buddhists have recently begun to reflect critically on traditional Zen in Japan and to give more explicit attention to ethics and the various problems confronting humanity." He attributes this shift to the impact of Western thought, a dialogue with Christianity, and the shock of surrendering in the Second World War. One of the most penetrating critics of Buddhist complicity was Zen priest and university professor Ichikawa Hakugen. In books such as *The War Responsibility of Buddhists,* published in 1971, he condemned Zen (and his own) collaboration with fascism, and drew attention to the ethical pitfalls of Zen in relation to society. In this context Ives draws attention to another prominent Zen thinker, Hisamatsu Shin'ichi, who is an important figure in the development of a postwar, socially engaged Buddhism in Japan very different from Imperial Way Buddhism. Together with his students Hisamatsu summarized his standpoint in the following "Vow of Mankind"—a declaration of universal humanism, and a noteworthy contribution to the evolution of a Buddhism of modernity: Keeping calm and composed, let us awaken to our True Self, become fully compassionate humans, make full use of our gifts according to our respective missions in life, discern the agony both individual and social and its source, recognize the right direction in which history should proceed, and join hands as brothers and sisters without distinctions of race, nation or class. Let us, with compassion, vow to bring to realization humankind's deep desire for self-emancipation and construct a world in which everyone can truly and fully live.

Imperial Way Buddhism offers an instructive case study. It reveals the power of cultural and political co-option to pervert in practice core tenets of Buddhism. And Buddhism can be co-opted and secularized by the political left as well as the right (such as the Buddhist "modernism" that appeared in Southeast Asia in the period of postcolonial euphoria, with its secular, socialist gloss). Therefore a requirement for a Buddhism serviceable in the culture of high modernity is an adequate social theory and social ethic—keeping the fourth eye wide open. At the same time, such a Buddhism must be demonstrably rooted in perennial Dharma and adapted to modernity without any implicit denial of central tenets. This is the only sure way for Buddhism to achieve authentic social expression.

Core Dharma, Variable Dharma, and Corrupt Dharma

Some reference has already been made to *core Buddhism,* and we must next consider how it might be defined and distinguished from the different cultural manifestations of Buddhism, or *variable Dharma.*

No living belief system can exist outside a social culture. However, I believe it is possible to define a perennial and transcultural core Dharma. This would comprise the distinctive essentials of Buddhist teaching. To some extent it could and must be validated interculturally. That is to say, all or almost all Buddhist cultures would have incorporated these core beliefs, or at least without so much cultural refraction as to make them problematic.

A core Dharma, or essential aspect of Buddhism, would need to include the basic diagnosis of the human condition, the prescription of meditative practices, and the goal of existential awakening (i.e., enlightenment). Hence, in the traditional shorthand it would consist of the four noble truths (referring to the origins of dukkha—lack, angst, suffering—and its remedy); the three signs of being (impermanence, insubstantiality, and dukkha); the three fires of greed, aggressiveness, and existential delusion; dependent co-origination *(paticca samupada);* the expressions of mutual causality (from the *ida paccayata* of the Pali Canon to Huayen); the moral precepts; and the summary of the various constituents of Buddhist practice to be found in the noble eightfold path (these refer to understanding, intention, perseverance, mindfulness, concentration, the precepts, and appropriate speech and livelihood). Karma, in the canonical sense explained earlier in this book, also qualifies for inclusion—that is to say, as a psychological rather than a cosmological phenomenon. In the 1950s Christmas Humphreys, president of the Buddhist Society of London, formulated and publicized a core Dharma of such essential principles.

Beyond this core lies what I call *variable Dharma*. This includes beliefs and practices that some traditions add to the core but that are not, in the eyes of most Buddhists, inconsistent with it, or with one another. All the main Buddhist traditions share core Dharma but interpret it in a variety of ways. Thus Theravada and Mahayana may be seen as complementary or parallel, rather than contradictory, and refer to different levels of truth. Also within variable Dharma are differences of emphasis and perspective. Thus, Indian Madhyamika emphasizes "emptiness," whereas Chinese Huayen and Chan/Zen balance this more strongly with "form." To say that these variations have long been *tolerated* within Buddhism would be somewhat misleading. Rather they have long been accepted as the norm, representing different adaptations of the core Dharma to the needs of different cultures, and providing a wide range of "skilful means" *(upaya)* for understanding and practice.

Given the diversity of spiritual paths available to Western culture, Westerners can choose from a range of Buddhist traditions to suit all temperaments. The boundary between core Dharma and variable Dharma is, of course, ill-defined and controversial. Some Western Buddhists would not accept the teachings regarding rebirth as essential, and others are frankly agnostic.

Thirdly there is *corrupt Dharma*, which is typically the consequence of the cooption of Buddhism by a host culture that in some particular flatly contradicts core Dharma tenets. For example, until very recently Nichiren Buddhism and some of its derivatives have been marked by a paranoiac pugnacity, an exclusive self-righteousness, and an intolerant missionary zeal that led the Buddhist scholar Edward Conze to conclude that "it would be more appropriate to count it among the offshoots of nationalistic Shintoism."

The Dharma of Modernity

The above three distinctions may be helpful in coming to terms with the global portable Buddhism that now exists. We can next consider how Western modernity might embody Buddhism without eroding its core integrity.

As does Indian culture, the West has a tradition of transcendentalism and ethical universality, which can be traced back to the Greek Sophists and the Hebrew prophets. Western philosophy is readily able to separate universal truths as distinct from the material circumstances of life. However, in the grounded culture of the West, physicality could not be dismissed as illusory—*maya*. And so, except for the rare forms of nondual mysticism within the Christian and Jewish traditions, there developed the conflict between the sacred and the profane, God and the devil. This Augustinian tradition persisted through the Middle Ages until the Reformation translated it into the mind/body dualism of modernity.

Whereas traditional Indian culture sought to remedy existential lack by transcending it, in the West ever increasingly "free" individuals sought meaning in the development of the power of self over other, and in the *objective* investigation of the self. Meaning became increasingly elusive, precipitating existential crises in a world whose insubstantiality and transience was experienced ever more keenly. The stage was set for the attraction to Buddhism. In *The Awakening of the West* Stephen Batchelor observes that when Buddhism first appeared, "the Dharma was either obscured by the grid of reason or twisted by the dreams of romanticism. It required two World Wars, Hitler and Stalin, the threat of nuclear war and environmental destruction, and, in many cases, a hefty dose of LSD to render Europeans sufficiently humble to seek their lost spiritual center elsewhere." The Western individual was liberated from the inevitabilities of tradition into the freedom of reflexive modernity and a wide range of "meaning of life" choices.

While Westerners have generally felt at home with the universality and the (relative) individualism and egalitarianism of the Indian Buddhist tradition, nevertheless Theravada Buddhism has until recently garnered only a small following in America, probably on account of its austere and moralistic character. A home-grown variety known as the Insight Meditation movement has been preferred. In Britain, however, thanks to national temperament and the legacy of its empire in Southeast Asia, Theravada has put down strong roots. The pragmatism of Zen, its tricky intellectual fascination, its seeming freedom from the burden of explicit morality, its apparently anarchic outrageousness, and even its exquisite black-and-white aesthetics have all assured it a large Western following. This has ranged from the "Beat Zen" of Alan Watts and California to the "Square Zen" of Judge Christmas Humphreys and middle England. Finally, there has been some valuable scholarly inquiry into the exotic, devotional, and shamanic attractions of Tibetan Buddhism for the Western psyche—with the empowerments and potent teachings of celebrated gurus, and the fascination of tantric practices.

This is the preliminary picture; now let us examine the fundamentals.

The Transpersonal Double Bind

Whether from a personal or a global viewpoint, many people have come to the same conclusion as Einstein when he observed that "the world that we have made as a result of the level of thinking we have done thus far creates problems that we cannot solve at the same level as we created them." They may then seek to follow a spiritual path leading to a transpersonal level of consciousness. However, although they may be able to understand this level intellectually, they will still not yet have profoundly experienced it. They can only view it with their present kind of consciousness.

For example, in Buddhism, opening to a higher level—enlightenment or awakening—may be correctly understood as a dropping off of the self as presently experienced, a falling away of craving, and a living more in the present instead of in an imagined future or recreated past. However, the self cannot transcend itself by mere wishing and willing. So, in the first place, it is *this present self* that delusively imagines "enlightenment." Secondly, this self desires some ultimate and amazing experience *for this present self,* which *craves* inordinately for "Big E"—ego's ultimate acquisition. Thirdly, enlightenment is always just around the corner—the really big escape from the present. Hopefully sooner or later the aspirant becomes aware of this threefold irony. Then the only way forward is to appreciate the ridiculousness of the situation in which one aspires to be elsewhere than here, to accept defeat, and in place of disappointed belief to find sufficient faith to sustain patience, perseverance, and acceptance of whatever does or doesn't come up. This leaves space for the practice of meditation to work, and the self has gotten out of its own shadow.

High egoic modernity culturally reinforces this double bind in that the disembedded self hangs onto its selfhood with especial tenacity. And yet, at the same time, this very vulnerability can create a desperate resolution to resolve the "Great Matter" of human existence, of life and death and suffering. High modernity is potentially a spiritual pressure cooker.

These dilemmas are most graphically evident in the experience of the double bind in the North American heartland of Western Buddhism, where high modernity is perhaps at its highest. This particularly is an energetic, high-achieving culture of self-reliant success—a culture of hungry, speedy, self-indulgent individualism.

The goal of enlightenment as a single, stupendous, transformative, lifetime event was given undue prominence by D. T. Suzuki, the great Zen popularizer of the 1960s. In fact, his perspective was only that of the Rinzai sect of Zen, which uses the great goal of enlightenment to inspire the urgency to engage a kind of life-and-death struggle to precipitate awakening. A more typical Buddhist view is that of personality change over time, usually accompanied by insights of varying intensity. There is no doubt, however, that profound existential awakening—the essential soteriological project—is absolutely central to Buddhism, as the path of the Buddha, or "Enlightened One."

The early wave of enthusiasm for "getting enlightened" was followed by a disillusioned reaction in the America of the 1980s. This has commonly been attributed to a wave of sex scandals and other abuses of power by prominent and presumed "enlightened" teachers. Ethical probity now began to look more attractive than what was turning out for most to be a tiresomely long quest for enlightenment guided by teachers who had lost their students' confidence and respect. However, the full explanation for this disillusionment with the enlightenment project is, I believe, more complex. The heart of the disenchantment is exclusive reliance on meditation as a technology to produce sensational and speedy results. Such a practice is commonly pursued as a hobby, an optional extracurricular activity in a lifestyle that continues otherwise unchanged. If "nothing happens," perhaps after only months or maybe even a few years of effort, the result is a demoralizing sense of failure that is unforgivable in a high-achieving, self-validating culture. Some see the point of dedicated practice—possibly they caught a shocking glimpse of how self-obsessed we tend to be—and from then on their practice can seriously begin. The majority will give up: Buddhism has failed them. Interestingly, disillusionment can be mutual: Buddhist commentator B. Alan Wallace observes in "Tibetan Buddhism in the West: Is It Working?" that "a number of lamas generally regard Westerners—with many fine exceptions—as being impatient, superficial and fickle...so a few of the finest lamas are now refusing even to come to the West."

Traditionally meditation has been practiced as an integral part of ascetic, monastic subcultures, themselves embedded in cultures very different from the West. Western practitioners need to be alert to the assumptions and expectations of their culture, which can otherwise make it that more difficult to see through spirituality's classic double bind. Meditation is not a quick-fix technique; it does, to say the very least, benefit from a supportive context.

The American Dharma Revolution

Helen Tworkov, longtime editor of the Buddhist journal *Tricycle* and a well-informed observer of the American scene claims in her 1989 book, *Zen in America,* that

> the quest for enlightenment has been derided of late as the romantic and mythic aspiration of antiquated patriarchal monasticism, while ethics has become the rallying vision of householder Zen. To pursue the unknowable state of enlightenment is now often regarded as an obstacle to a practice that emphasizes "everyday Zen," a state of mindful attention in the midst of everyday life.

Her charge is that the centrality of awakening has begun to be marginalized or even denied in American Zen. I suspect that this applies also to some extent outside Zen and outside North America. The kind of Western Buddhism that has emerged from the so-called American Dharma Revolution has been dubbed (and caricatured) as *Congregational Buddhism*. Undoubtedly its greatest achievement has been the "coming out" of women from under the patriarchal weight of the earlier charismatic era. Congregational Buddhism tends to be a family affair, relaxing the tradition of monastic rigor but maintaining a strong moral tone (which sometimes extends to the moralizing undertones of political correctness). The teacher becomes a safe, predictable figure reporting to a controlling lay board that is in effect his or her employer. There is an openness to social and environmental engagement. There is also the influence of psychotherapeutic perspectives and at times even the offering of counseling resources. This is of positive value in that for many Westerners, and certainly in the early stages of the practice, the help they require is apparently more therapeutic than existential.

If the centrality of enlightenment is lost or downgraded, then Buddhism simply becomes another belief system or therapy—a secularized part of "the new paradigm," instead of something that subverts all paradigms and creatively challenges and disconcerts both personal identity and collective ideology. On the other hand, if the enlightenment project *is* retained as fundamental, then the kind of Buddhist practice and community outlined above *can* provide a vital, supportive context for a profound path of existential awakening.

Unpacking the Asian Import

The above "enlightenment question" has been exacerbated by cultural problems. How can the traditionally absolute authority of the teacher—and the traditional religious hierarchy—be questioned by the egalitarian, modern practitioner when that authority comes from a higher level of consciousness to which the practitioner at present can only aspire? Similarly, cannot the condemnations of the gender inequality of traditional patriarchy be understood as just the willful, unreconstructed ego asserting its claims yet again in the face of the ultimate truth that there is no male nor female?

On the other hand Western humanism, egalitarianism, and universalism are arguably vehicles that are highly consistent with core Dharma, and that represent an authentic evolution of cultural consciousness that should not be relinquished. Considerable progress has already been made in the sensitive embodiment of Western values on authority, gender, and social responsibility in the organization and norms of Buddhism in the West. The debate on these and similar issues continues, turning on the question of whether a particular belief or practice is essential Dharma or a disposable cultural option (ranging from the wearing of monastic robes to a literal belief in rebirth).

Under the leadership of second and later generation teachers the cultural externalities of Asian Buddhism are certain to be increasingly modified in Western terms. A better appreciation of the cultural contingency of the Asian traditions will assist this process, even though various culture-specific practices (like Zen koan practice and Tibetan visualization) will surely be retained and valued as "skillful means" to achieve awakening, as with the interactive koan-type questioning of John Crook's "Western Zen retreats" in Britain. Buddhism has been intensely pragmatic from the start. An Englishman named Dennis Lingwood (better known as Sangharakshita) opted for an *integrative* strategy, and in 1967 founded a "Western Buddhist Order" by selecting and adapting different Buddhist traditions around a core of essential Buddhism—and adding his own idiosyncratic stamp. "We may take different things from different forms of Buddhism," he writes in *New Currents in Western Buddhism,* "but we take them according to our actual spiritual needs, rather than in accordance with any preconceived intellectual ideas. We take whatever will help us grow under the conditions of Western life." The Friends of the Western Buddhist Order (FWBO) is now a flourishing worldwide movement with many innovative features. In American Zen there also have been several fruitful points of departure, such as Bernie Glassman's exploration through the Zen Peacemaker Order of various forms of social engagement as spiritual practice or Charlotte Joko Beck's informal Ordinary Mind School. Longer established, in both America and Britain, is the Order of Buddhist Contemplatives, founded by Jiyu-Kennett at Shasta Abbey in California—Soto Zen with a flavor of Christian monasticism.

More complex is the future of Tibetan Buddhism in the West, cut off from its homeland for half a century, yet deeply embedded in a culture that faces an uncertain future. It is still predominantly directed by Tibetans who are understandably reluctant to let Tibetan Buddhism be tinkered with to suit Western tastes. The first attempt in that direction was made by the highly influential Chögyam Trungpa, who wrote several outstanding books and founded the Shambhala Training project. Subsequently Pema Chödrön, an American nun and student of Trungpa, has produced a succession of popular books in the new "everyday Buddhism" genre. With titles like *Start Where You Are* and *When Things Fall Apart,* these aim to relate basic Mahayana teachings directly to readers' and students' daily life experience.

American Buddhist teacher Joanna Macy has developed "spiritual exercises for social activists," which she teaches in "despair and empowerment workshops." These facilitate, she explains in *Despair and Personal Power in the Nuclear Age,* "the psychological and spiritual work of dealing with our knowledge and feelings about the present planetary crisis in ways that release energy and vision for creative response." Macy's valuable resource books offer numerous exercises that include guided meditations, group interaction, dance, and ritual, together with much useful advice.

Such gradual modifications of Asian Buddhist religion contrast with more radical approaches. For example, the Insight Meditation movement in America and Britain has drawn on the meditative practices and core beliefs of Theravada Buddhism, but has relinquished its ritual, its monasticism, and other seemingly religious features. It has been described as Dharma without Buddhism—the peas without the pod. In his book *Buddhism without Beliefs* Stephen Batchelor acknowledges the strengths of "religious Buddhism," working though "hierarchic institutions that have weathered centuries of turmoil and change." However, he states:

> While such institutions may provide excellent settings for sustained training in meditation and reflection, it is questionable whether they alone can provide a sufficient basis for the creation of a contemporary culture of awakening. The democratic and agnostic imperatives of the secular world demand not another Buddhist Church but an individuated community, where creative imagination and social engagement are valued as highly as philosophic reflection and meditative attainment.

Batchelor therefore envisions "an existential, therapeutic, democratic, imaginative, anarchic, and *agnostic* Buddhism for the West."

Batchelor's vision for the future of Buddhism in the West recalls some of the strengths of the Quaker Society of Friends: "Instead of authoritarian, monolithic institutions, it could imagine a decentralized tapestry of small-scale, autonomous communities of awakening. Instead of a mystical religious movement ruled by autocratic leaders, it would foresee a deep agnostic, secular culture founded on friendships and governed by collaboration." Batchelor notes that, in the evolution of a Western Buddhism, "two broad themes are already beginning to emerge.... These are the distinctively contemporary ways in which Dharma practice is becoming *individuated,* on the one hand, and *socially engaged,* on the other." He emphasizes the Western emancipatory vision that "strives to create and maintain social and political structures that uphold the rights and optimize the creative possibilities of the individual." By *individuation* Batchelor means the "process of recovering personal authority through freeing ourselves from the constraints of collectively held belief systems.... In valuing imagination and diversity, such an individuated vision would ultimately empower each practitioner to create his or her own distinctive track within the field of dharma practice."

Batchelor's perspective relates strongly to the concerns of this book. Certainly it is highly consistent with modernity. Both themes—individuation and social engagement—are, however, vulnerable to secularization and reductionism, and in his concern with Buddhism as religious ideology, Batchelor has perhaps failed to take adequate account of this opposite threat. A contemporary Western Dharma will need to tread a mindful middle way between these two poles.

Social engagement all too readily co-opts Buddhism rather than vice versa. As to individuation, the various oriental Buddhist traditions have evolved an impressive and well-tried array of "skillful means" to lead to awakening—meditative practices, rituals, chants, visualizations, koans, empowerments, teacher-bonding, myths, and other devices that provide guidance and sustain faith and perseverance. It is from these traditions, I feel, rather than secular insights and techniques that Batchelor's individuals and small groups must primarily draw in developing "their own distinctive track within the field of dharma practice."

The parallel continuance of the Asian traditions—which will in any event be subject to gradual Westernization (and ossification)—therefore seems to be important. It is out of the creative tension between these and the various modernizing impulses that a Western Buddhism will be shaped. It will take a wiser Western culture, many decades beyond the present egoic modernity, to evolve its own distinctive but comparable Dharmic tradition. That, however, is no reason for not making a start.

Chapter 11

BUDDHIST MORALITY

THE CENTRAL IMPORTANCE of morality in the cultivation of wisdom and compassion has been acknowledged in all the main Buddhist traditions. "Refrain from evil; do good; do good for others" are the three *pure precepts* of Mahayana Buddhism. "Avoid evil; do as much good as possible; purify your intentions. This is the teaching of all the buddhas" is an expression of fundamental Zen teachings. And, recently, to the question, "What is a simple basic practice one should bear in mind if one finds it difficult to comprehend all the different levels of practice?" the Dalai Lama gave the following reply, published in *The Middle Way:* "I think in short that it's best, if you're able, to help others. If you're not able to do so, however, then at least do not harm others. This is the main practice." Since Buddhist social action is an expression of Buddhist morality, an understanding of the nature of Buddhist morality and how it is practiced is the foundation of a Buddhist social activism.

Morality and its attendant themes of guilt and retribution remain powerful considerations in the minds of "secularized" people. It is still as if there were tangible standards of good and evil available somewhere "out there," to be implemented by the will if only they can be found. The anxiety to appropriate them, or defy them, is also evident. Moral justification is an important prop in personal and collective identity building. Above all else, we need to be in the right.

Literalist theology did provide such notions as God-and-the-devil and other popular relativities-made-absolute. But our secular age has set itself adrift on a trackless ocean of relative truths of which, obliquely and unconsciously, it tries to make absolute values. It is assumed that these relative values are read into the objective situation by free and objective actors. Rather, they are *needed* to empower *me, us,* and *ours*—thus they become the *absolute good* of free enterprise, or feminism, or animal rights. These absolute values are the morally weighted polarities that we encountered in chapter 6, which fortify our identity through antithetical bonding. How can we look deep into the clinging need to assert *our* good, and loosen the hold of our need for an opposed evil? How can we experience more clearly the underlying moral ambiguity in most social problems, and become free to act solely on the terms of those problems, without the adulteration of personal and collective ego-need?

Evil-doing arises from existential ignorance of our oneness with all that is other, from the deluded experience of separateness, of alienation. "Evil," wrote Aldous Huxley in *Eyeless in Gaza,* "is the accentuation of division; good, whatever makes for unity with other lives and other beings. Pride, hatred, anger—the essentially evil sentiments; and essentially evil because they are all intensifications of the given reality of separateness, because they insist upon division and uniqueness, because they reject and deny other lives and beings."

Even those with the most seemingly altruistic of agendas get caught again and again in the egoic trap of fortifying self through one's sense of *difference* from the other. Our virtue is confirmed not only by putting down another's evil but also by practicing virtues upon others that confirm us at their expense. By becoming the recipient of our magnanimity they affirm their own weakness, inferiority, and inability to help themselves. In this way, others exist ultimately only for us, and their own intrinsic humanity is denied, even if unknowingly and for the best of motives. David Brandon, in *Zen and the Art of Helping,* reminds us that "respect is seeing the Buddha Nature in another person. It means perceiving the superficiality of positions of moral superiority. The other person is as good as you. However untidy, unhygienic, poor, illiterate, and bloody-minded he may seem, he is worthy of respect. He also has autonomy and purpose. He is another form of nature." An important aspect of Buddhist service and activism is, therefore, the acceptance that our moral motivation is likely to be a mix of both the authentic fellow-feeling of our buddha nature and, at the same time, an alienating self-need.

The emphasis in Buddhist morality is on the cultivation of a personality that cannot but be moral, rather than focusing upon the morality of particular choices and acts. But it is not the will that can create such a personality, no more than I can pick myself up from the ground by my own collar. It is to the training that the will must be applied, from which virtue will naturally flow. "Hit the horse, not the cart," as the Zen saying puts it. The exercise of the will is, of course, needed by all of us from time to time in order to avoid doing harm to others or ourselves; the impulse to act wrongly is blocked short of action, but, if possible, there should be an open, nonjudgmental awareness of the feeling that has flared. This requires much practice, as we shall see below. Willing virtue into one's life is a notoriously unsatisfactory way of bringing about changes in behavior.

Whether we fail or succeed, either way we lose. The ego and the superego live in fear of one another; when ego is indulged there is guilt; when ego is repressed there is a nagging feeling of self-deception arising from knowing that one's "saintliness" was not genuinely obtained. The saintliness achieved by willpower alone is obsessed by evil and depends for its existence on evil. (Fiercely determine *not* to think of a rhinoceros and what then is the first thing to spring to mind?) Consumed by *not* being angry or *not* having sexual feelings, we are tossed endlessly on a sea of mutually punishing relativities.

The authentic moral personality emerges through the ripening of wisdom/compassion. This ripening takes place through a system of spiritual training that *includes the practice of morality as a part of the practice of mindful awareness.* Through trying to conform to the moral precepts, we incite an emotional revolt. Without either suppressing that revolt or being possessed and carried away by it, we open ourselves in full awareness to containment of that upsurge. By thus willingly enduring it we contribute to our overall practice of mindfulness, which is essential to the training system through which fundamental personality change occurs.

Clearly, in many cases our use of the will has an objective necessity in enabling us to avoid hurting others or self, as noted earlier. In other words we may by no means have evolved to the stage of spontaneously feeling at one with people who have harmed us, but in such situations we try to follow the moral precepts and to act as if we did, yet without deceiving ourselves as to our real feelings. We need as far as possible to find a middle way in this use of the will, lest it strengthen ego instead of being a means by which ego is gentled, becomes more pliant and less stiff-necked and opinionated. After some time in the practice it becomes possible to make spontaneous decisions that previously would have required a tremendously strenuous exercise of will: The ripe fruit can be plucked whereas previously it was as if the whole tree would have to be uprooted.

In short, the cultivation of morality in Buddhism (and not least in decisions and behavior relating to social action) is double-edged and paradoxical. By (subjectively) serving the extinguishment of the delusive self, in "doing *my* practice," at the same time we serve others (objectively), and vice versa, until this supposed dualism merges in the unity of self and other. As found in the Digha Nikaya (I, 124): "From the observing of the moralities comes wisdom and from the observing of wisdom comes morality.... It is just as if one should wash one hand with the other...exactly so is morality washed round with wisdom and wisdom with morality." In other words, one does not become a truly moral person without having practiced being one. But neither does one practice morality solely out of a concern eventually to become a moral person.

The Precepts and Their Social Implications

The Buddhist precepts are general guidelines for ethical behavior and training, which I will elaborate on in the following paragraphs. They are in no sense commandments, since there is no Other doing the commanding. What is expected is a sincere effort to uphold the precepts, but the power of karmic momentum is appreciated, and the ripening of an intrinsically moral personality takes time. One does one's best, acknowledges and forgives failure, and resolves to try to do better in the future. Thus Christopher Titmuss, a British meditation teacher, prefers the term *ethical foundations* to *precepts,* and formulates each as in: *"I endeavor to practice to be free from killing and violence."* In *Zen Dawn in the West* American Zen master Philip Kapleau explains the significance of the precepts as revealing

> how a deeply enlightened, fully perfected person, with no sense of self-and-other, behaves. Such a person does not imitate the precepts; they imitate him. Until you reach that point, however, you would do well to observe the precepts, for unless your mind is free of the disturbance that heedless behavior produces, you will never come to awakening. That is why the precepts are the foundation of spiritual training.

Nevertheless, it is recognized that literal interpretation may, in a particular situation, violate the spirit and intention of a precept. This *situational* character of ethical choice is examined below.

On the face of it, Buddhist prescriptive morality may seem unremarkable; it is much like the moral codes offered by all the world's great religions. Various codifications exist, according to the different schools of Buddhism. Here we will examine the five basic precepts that are universally included in the various traditions' codes of conduct.

The first precept is to cultivate freedom from the urge to violence and killing, "to avoid the killing of living beings and abstain from it. Without stick or sword, conscientious, full of sympathy, [to be] anxious for the welfare of all living things" (Anguttara Nikaya X, 176). This precept raises important situational questions addressed later in this chapter.

The second precept, which is sometimes rendered as "not to take what is not given" is hardly less central to the theme of social action. Its original formulation refers to a much less complex society than the acquisitive, industrial society about which social theorist Pierre-Joseph Proudhon could argue that "property is theft." Some present-day Buddhists have maintained that this precept is about more than petty theft and good table manners, that the fact of possession does not necessarily imply any moral right to possession, and that the piling up of possessions well beyond modest personal needs is a denial of the precept. More controversially, it has been argued that the accumulation of personal wealth through the appropriation of the time and energy of others who work for us either directly or indirectly is also something that violates the second precept.

This question is a very pointed one today when the human and ecological effects of acquisitive industrial materialism are so profound and pervasive. It is also sharpened as never before by the fact that we now have developed the resources to be able to provide basic food, clothing, and shelter for all the world's peoples, and have the means to evolve a nonacquisitive *dana-paramita* (perfection-of-giving) Good Society. Given a sufficient change of heart by a sufficient number of people, this ideal is a practical possibility. Although the question of personal need, consumption, and acquisition needs to be posed in the above poignant context for each of us to answer, in practical terms, for him- or herself, how profound our response can be depends on numerous factors in our personal situation—ranging from our strength of character to the number of our personal dependents. As with all the precepts, we can only keep gently but firmly pushing ourselves to do our best—even if it's only to shift our investments to a socially responsible growth fund that will not fatten them on armaments manufacture and the grosser kinds of Third World exploitation. It is best to weed even the edges and corners of a lifestyle as far as we are able, since weeds tend to spread.

The third precept refers to sexual ethics. For Zen master Robert Aitken, this precept is about abstention from "boorish misuse of sex" or, as Christopher Titmuss puts it, from "sexually exploitive activities." While for certain Buddhist monastics this precept prohibits sexual activity entirely (although Japanese and some American Zen monks do marry), for lay practitioners the third precept is about conscious and responsible engagement of our sexuality.

The fourth precept enjoins us to abstain from lies and abusive speech. The "unrighteous practices" in speech are set out in the Majjhima Nikaya (I, 41) as lying, slander, spreading dissension, and idle and malicious gossip. The wise man speaks only at the right time and in accordance with known facts, "accompanied by arguments moderate and full of sense." There is more than folk homily here. In many organizations, whether families or large institutions, communication is warped by heavy-handed authority and consequent resentments; the climate becomes clouded by a restless ill-will that feeds upon itself through petty slander, rumor, and gossip. This becomes compulsive, and it is difficult to resist being drawn into an insidious and corrosive daily experience of this kind of communication.

Here again an ancient moral precept has been hugely amplified by contemporary social developments. Increasingly we live in an "information society" where it is now commonplace for information to be withheld or otherwise manipulated for one's interests by those who have the power to do so.

The last of the five precepts refers to abstention from drugs and intoxicants, since these reduce the level of awareness and self-responsibility and are karmically addictive.

A Buddhist morality that stops short—as it often does without assiduous effort—at our personal circle of family, friends, acquaintances, and workmates may have been adequate for a bygone village society, but if it is to be fully helpful today and command respect, then our moral awareness surely must extend as far as the world brought to us through the newspaper and the television screen. The Buddhist ethic is an ethic of *intention*. But the implications of what we do in our global society are complex and far-reaching. To act responsibly we need to be well-informed. For example, about the precept to abstain from violence and killing, Sulak Sivaraksa argues in *Siamese Convergence* that:

> Unless the monk knows how to deal with the first precept in the modern world, he simply loses his role. For the last 2500 years Buddhism has had a corpus of writings explaining what is meant by killing. You must have the intention to kill, you must use a weapon or you must order someone to kill, and that is called the act of killing. But now you have all the new machinery of killing, you have the multinational corporations dealing with killing, and they are linked to banks, and the first precept on killing relates to the second precept on stealing, and so on. Unless you understand the complexities you simply cannot apply Buddhism meaningfully as an example for the younger generation.

The precepts are neither internal commandments nor external legislation to provide a Buddhist "party line"; they are delicate instruments for subtle investigation within and without. If this is kept in mind the formulation of the precepts in contemporary terms provides a valuable set of prompts for maintaining a fully open awareness. The fourteen precepts that follow constitute the spiritual discipline of the Tiep Hien Order, which was founded during the Vietnam war as an instrument of "engaged Buddhism." They grew out of the experience of the Order members—nuns, monks, and laypeople—in cultivating an inner serenity that sustained their antiwar demonstrations, social projects, and resistance to all forms of violence and repression, from whatever direction they came. Many of the Order members lost their lives, and others, like Thich Nhat Hanh, were forced into exile. These precepts offer valuable guidelines for a Buddhist social activism.

1. One should not be idolatrous about or bound to any doctrine, any theory, any ideology, including Buddhist ones. Buddhist systems of thought must be guiding means and not absolute truth.

2. Do not think the knowledge you presently possess is changeless absolute truth. Avoid being narrow-minded and bound to present views. One has to learn and practice the open way of nonattachment from views in order to be open to receive the viewpoints of others. Truth is to be found only in life and not in conceptual knowledge. One should be ready to learn during one's whole life and to observe life in oneself and in the world at all times.

3. Do not force others, including children, by any means whatsoever to adopt our view, whether by authority, threat, money, propaganda, or even education. However, one should, through compassionate dialogue, help others to renounce fanaticism and narrowness.

4. One should not avoid contact with sufferings or close one's eyes before sufferings. One should not lose awareness of the existence of suffering in the life of the world. Find ways to come to those who are suffering by all means such as personal contact and visits, images, sound. By such means one should awaken oneself and others to the reality of suffering in the world.

5. Do not accumulate wealth while millions are hungry. Do not take as the aim of your life fame, profit, wealth, or sensual pleasure. One should live simply and share one's time, energy, and material resources with those who are in need.

6. Do not maintain anger or hatred. As soon as anger and hatred arise, practice the meditation on compassion in order to encompass with love the persons who have caused anger and hatred. Learn to look at other beings with the eyes of compassion.

7. One should not lose oneself in dispersion and in one's surroundings. Learn to practice breathing in order to regain control of body and mind, to practice mindfulness and to develop concentration and wisdom.

8. Do not utter words that can create discord and cause the community to break. All efforts should be made to reconcile and resolve all conflicts however small they may be.

9. Do not say untruthful things for the sake of personal interest or to impress people. Do not utter words that cause division and hatred. Do not spread news that you do not know to be certain. Do not criticize or condemn things that you are unsure of. Always speak truthfully and constructively. Have the courage to speak out about situations of injustice, even when it may threaten your own safety.

10. One should not use the Buddhist community for personal gain or profit or transform one's community into a political party. One's religious community, however, should take a clear stand against oppression and injustice and should strive to change the situation without engaging in partisan conflicts.

11. Do not live with a vocation that is harmful to humans and nature. Do not invest in companies that deprive others of their chance to life. Select a vocation that helps to realize your idea of compassion.

12. Do not kill. Do not let others kill. Find whatever means possible to protect life and prevent war.

13. Possess nothing that should belong to others. Respect the property of others but prevent others from enriching themselves from human suffering.

14. Sexual expression should not happen without love and commitment. In sexual relationships one must be aware of future suffering it may cause to others. To preserve the happiness of others, respect the rights and commitments of others.

The Situational Morality of Uncertainty, Humility, and Courage

At a personal level there appear to be three kinds of obstacles to practicing the Buddhist moral precepts.

First, it is necessary to summon up the necessary willpower and determination in order to affirm the precepts in practice, always bearing in mind the previously discussed limitations on the use of the will. Without some strong moral commitment, some energy and determination, it is impossible to get started.

Secondly, there is the difficulty of cultivating a fully open awareness of the kick-back of emotion, of resentment, that occurs when the will is used to thwart desire, as when we have to push ourselves to get on with unrewarding work in order to meet a commitment previously made to others. This mindfulness is a self-awareness, but it is also awareness of the feelings of others.

Thirdly, there is the difficulty of moral choice, of knowing how to apply the precepts in complex and ambiguous situations. Just as in keeping to them there is a danger of making too heavy a use of the will, so in interpreting their meanings there is a danger of clinging to a narrow and superficial literalism. In many situations the precepts provide the questions, not the answers. We may have too little information to make a realistic decision or even know what really is the problem, or what will be the outcome of this or that decision. And what if a greater good may come from a lesser evil? What if by upholding one precept in a small way we break another in a big way? Is that not a self-serving virtue that refuses to see the large and inconvenient evils that follow from it? What if the merits of alternative choices seem equally balanced? If I misled the huntsman as to which way the fox ran, will the fox ravage another hen coop tonight? Is it possible that my animosity toward the fox-hunting is class-consciousness masquerading as pity for foxes? And is that animosity something that arises as a sense of ill will at my discomfort at being me, inside my skin, which needs to find a morally justifiable outlet? This is not to imply that cruelty to foxes is an irrelevant matter or that "it's all in our heads," but just to recall that reality is both subjectively and objectively defined, and we must not forget old two-faced Janus.

Moral perplexity is more commonly experienced nowadays not, I suggest, so much because moral precepts are less observed, but because it is more difficult to interpret them in the ambiguous, obscure, and interconnected situations in which we increasingly find ourselves. And the very fact that we live in a "high egoic" era of human consciousness has increased our sense of choice while making it more difficult to choose. Perplexity has the merit of honesty, and is less simplistic than the quick fix of instant and presumed righteousness that is the usual public response. The latter tends to give moral weight to the self-affirming polarization of people, systems, and ideas—the antithetical bonding to which I referred in chapter 6.

In my experience a question that commonly disturbs Buddhists interested in embarking on radical social action is how they can *know* that their decisions are authentic responses to situations of need rather than motivated by delusive self-need. For it has dawned upon them that they do not act out their lives with the clear, selfless objectivity that they once thought they did.

It is necessary to work for as much inner and outer clarity as possible. Inner clarity may be increased by awareness, meditation, and retreat situations that encourage these. These tend to clear, cool, and purify our perspective and give some space for *right view* to show itself because we are less full of "my" wanting. With greater inner/outer clarity it is a common experience that we begin to ask new questions and seek less partisan, self-confirming answers. Over and beyond what additional inner and outer clarity we may be able to bring to bear upon a particular moral decision, however, we can appreciate that the very fact of being a Buddhist is acknowledgment of ignorance of one's deepest motivations and the delusive nature of one's experience of the world.

The following statement by philosopher and novelist Iris Murdoch, from *The Sovereignty of the Good,* sheds light on the ways in which self-need and personal will obscure true moral vision and action:

What we really are seems much more like an obscure system of energy out of which choices and visible acts of will emerge at intervals in ways which are often unclear and often dependent on the condition of the system in between the moments of choice.... The chief enemy of excellence in morality (and also in art) is personal fantasy: the tissue of self-aggrandizing and consoling wishes and dreams which prevents one from seeing what is there outside one. Rilke said of Cezanne that he did not paint "I like it," he painted "There it is." This is not easy, and requires, in art or morals, a discipline.... What I have called fantasy, the proliferation of blinding, self-centered aims and images, is itself a powerful system of energy, and most of what is called "will" or "willing" belongs to this system. What counteracts the system is attention to reality, inspired by, consisting of, love.... Freedom is not strictly the exercise of the will, but rather the experience of accurate vision which, when this becomes appropriate, occasions action.

Without making a virtue of ignorance, it is important to acknowledge it, and be open to the awareness that in a particular situation we may not be focusing upon the real problem let alone the real solution. Yet my ignorance is a threat to my need to know "where I stand." Zen trainees are urged to keep an unblocked, "don't know" mind, which resembles what Keats described as Shakespeare's "negative capability"—"being in uncertainties, mysteries, doubts, without any irritable searching after fact and reason." Unfortunately the creative use of ignorance, or *not-knowing,* is no more understood in our society than is the humility and patience that go with it. And yet it is out of that place that it is so often necessary to act (or forbear) and to do our best, appropriately and morally, "according to our lights."

It may be helpful to conclude this chapter with two examples of situational morality at work. The first is the case of abortion, around which strong opposing and defending ideologies are gathered, and which is no less of a dilemma for a religion that is both profoundly compassionate and that counsels against all killing. The three statements by Buddhists in the West that I have encountered on this topic all come to similar conclusions. After reviewing the pros and cons, they acknowledge the complexity of life and the difficulty of living as a human being without taking life in some form or another, and they accept that abortion is a profound moral dilemma to which there is no clear-cut solution. All agree with the (Shin/Pure Land) Buddhist Churches of America Social Issues Committee statement that "although others may be involved in the decision-making, it is the woman carrying the fetus, and no one else, who must in the end make this most difficult decision and live with it for the rest of her life. As Buddhists we can only encourage her to make a decision that is both thoughtful and compassionate." In response to the question of how such a decision can be made, Zen master Philip Kapleau, in *Zen Dawn in the West,* counsels:

> If your mind is free of fear and of narrow selfish concerns, you will know what course of action to take. Put yourself deeply into zazen [meditation]—look into your own heart-mind, reflecting carefully on all aspects of your life situation and on the repercussions your actions might have on your family and on society as a whole. Once the upper levels of mind, which weigh and analyze, have come to rest, the "right" course of action will become clear. And when such action is accompanied by a feeling of inner peace, you may be sure you have not gone astray.

Our third testimony is from Zen master Robert Aitken, who in *The Mind of Clover: Essays in Zen Buddhist Ethics* writes:

> Sitting in on sharing meetings in the Diamond Sangha, our Zen Buddhist society in Hawaii, I get the impression that when a woman is sensitive to her feelings, she is conscious that abortion is killing a part of herself and terminating the ancient process, begun anew within herself, of bringing life into being. Thus she is likely to feel acutely miserable after making a decision to have an abortion. This is a time for compassion for the woman, and for her to be compassionate with herself and for her unborn child. If I am consulted, and we explore the options carefully and I learn that the decision is definite, I encourage her to go through the act with the consciousness of a mother who holds her dying child in her arms, lovingly nurturing it as it passes from life. Sorrow and suffering from the nature of samsara [the transitory world of phenomena], the flow of life and death, and the decision to prevent birth is made on balance with other elements of suffering. Once the decision is made, there is no blame, but rather acknowledgment that sadness pervades the whole universe, and this bit of life goes with our deepest love.

An episode from the life of Anglican priest and peace activist Michael Scott provides a second example of situational morality, and this suffering through of one's own ignorance with the moral courage needed to respond positively to the demands of the situation. Scott was in many ways an outstanding exemplar of spiritual activism. Early in life he had become convinced of the value of Gandhian nonviolent civil disobedience, and he later became a rigorous and effective practitioner of that discipline. However, when the Second World

War broke out, he experienced a profound dilemma. David Astor, in his obituary for Scott, explains:

> He felt bound to resist the Nazis physically (unlike Gandhi who advised the Czechs against doing so); on the other hand, he did not feel able to kill in the name of Jesus. He resisted the usual compromise of being a non-combatant chaplain and joined the Royal Air Force to train as a rear-gunner. This does not mean any loss of devotion to Christianity; he simply could not see its application to stopping the Nazis. It was an example of his scrupulous self-questioning.

Astor recalls that Scott once said that he "belonged to the Religion of Doubt." In this he had much in common with theologian Dietrich Bonhoeffer whose pacifism was also put to the test by the Nazi movement. After much suffering through profound inner conflict and doubt, Bonhoeffer joined the plot to blow up Hitler and other Nazi leaders in hope of bringing the war to an early close. The attempt miscarried, Bonhoeffer was arrested, and he was eventually executed only a few days before the end of the war.

I suggest that to experience these kinds of situations as moral dilemmas, as spiritual paradoxes, to suffer them through in the humility of uncertainly, helplessness, and despair, and to nevertheless find the moral courage to act, may be evidence of a riper spiritual maturity than a ready certitude of what's right and what's wrong.

PART 4

ACTION

Chapter 12

PEACEWORK AND SOCIAL JUSTICE

WILLFUL VIOLENCE is the explosion of anger, resentment, greed, defensiveness, and the whole gamut of alienated passions, volcanic and oceanic. Institutionally embodied, and in its karmic momentum on the stage of history, it has created unimaginable suffering.

Violence can bring quick results, is understood by all, and gratifyingly and sensationally discharges frustration, bitterness, and sublimated aggression. Although for the oppressed, violence may seem a justifiable means to an end, it habitually corrupts the peaceful ends to which the violent may sincerely aspire, as well as profoundly affecting the whole character of the perpetrators' undertaking. The objectification and depersonalization of other people that is inevitably involved in doing them violence not only tends to dehumanize and brutalize the violent but also becomes ingrained and institutionalized in coercive and insensitive policies and organizational forms. In the kind of people they have become, the formerly oppressed resemble more and more their former oppressors. And my violence provokes your violence in an ever-spiraling culture of aggression that becomes difficult to root out. In his book *Violence: Reflections from a Christian Perspective* Jacques Ellul, a perceptive Christian social theorist, likewise questions the efficacy of violence as a means of social change:

My study of politics and sociology have convinced me that violence is an altogether superficial thing; that is, it can produce apparent, superficial changes, rough facsimiles of change. But it never affects the roots of injustice—social structures, the bases of an economic system, the foundations of society. Violence is not the appropriate means for a revolution in depth.

Beyond the impulse toward violence, however, we also ordinarily experience at least *some* sense of the buddha nature—of fellow-feeling, pity, and empathy, which inclines us to helpfulness and harmlessness, peacefulness and harmony. In the great religions are many saints who have perfected such compassion, and moral guidelines for those who aspire to cultivate that higher level of consciousness.

The Buddhist first precept, against taking life, is also commonly interpreted as a precept of nonviolence, of nonharming or "harmlessness." And since this precept is about the most fundamental relationship of self to others, all the other precepts may be read as particular applications of it. It is noteworthy that distinction is made in Buddhism between different degrees of willfulness, of volition, that may move us to violence. For example, killing by a conscripted soldier under orders, or killing in self-defense, carry a label of diminished responsibility.

Buddhism has a comparatively good historical record in holding to the precept against killing. There appear not to have been any Buddhist wars of religion aimed at forcible conversion, and there have been a great many examples of positive religious toleration even of aggressive missionary religions. On the other hand, China was freed from Mongol rule in 1368 by an uprising spearheaded by Buddhist "freedom fighters" of the White Lotus Society. The long association of Japanese Zen Buddhism with military prowess and aggressive imperialism has already been noted, and Buddhist scholar Trevor Ling has argued that Southeast Asian Buddhist kingdoms were as militarily aggressive and self-seeking as any others.

In the perennial favorite *What the Buddha Taught* Walpola Rahula argues that "according to Buddhism there is nothing that can be called a 'just war'— which is only a false term coined and put into circulation to justify and excuse hatred, cruelty, violence and massacre." However, in *Zen and the Taming of the Bull* Rahula describes a war of national independence in Sri Lanka in the second century B.C.E. that was conducted under the slogan "Not for kingdom, but for Buddhism," and he concludes that "to fight against a foreign invader for national independence became an established Buddhist tradition, since freedom was essential to the spiritual as well as material progress of the community." And in recent years in Sri Lanka there has been substantial support in the Buddhist sangha for the government's efforts to eradicate the Tamil "Tigers" who claim a homeland in the northern part of the island. It is arguable, however, that this is not a defensive war but an extremely bloody and destructive Sinhalese-Tamil struggle for territory. Athuraliya Rathana, secretary of the (Sri Lankan) National Sangha Council, is quoted in "In Defense of the Dharma: Just-War Ideology in Buddhist Sri Lanka" as making the controversial claim that "there are many stories in the canon that depict the Buddha as an advocate of force and violence if there is a just cause."

In the previous chapter I maintained that the moral precepts must be applied situationally, rather than literally, if they are not sometimes to be violated in spirit and intent. This certainly applies to the first precept, though the above example does illustrate the slippery slope to which this can lead. I used the example of abortion in the last chapter, and many possible situations come to mind, in both personal and public life, wherein a lesser killing may be the means of avoiding a greater killing. These range from exterminating disease-bearing insects to shooting an armed murderer running amok in a crowded street.

Sometimes we are obliged by circumstance to seek the middle way between, on one hand, killing the precept with a self-righteous literalism that violates its intention, and, on the other hand, bending the precept to accommodate too many hurtful means and too many questionable and self-serving ends. This requires a meditative insight into self-driven predilection and its picture of the situation; it necessitates penetrating through the top layer of prejudice and ideology to the underlying thrust of need and fear (including the need to be in the right), and gently disarming this rigid complex with calm awareness. Opening fully to the racking quandary of relative choices can best reveal what must be done. In complex situations a higher third may open up beyond the either/or trap, recasting the conflict in terms of larger realities and exposing an ultimately beneficial course of action. In "Two *Teishos:* The First Precept" Robert Aitken expresses this transcendental middle way: "'No killing' refers in some sense to prohibition, but basically it is a positive exhortation to be in touch with true nature, where negative and positive, right and wrong, birth and death, are simply concepts that we seek to use appropriately according to circumstance."

Structural and Cultural Violence

Beneath all expressions of violence there is a spirit of coerciveness, which is pervasive in virtually all cultures. Short of the overt violence of threat, imprisonment, and torture (increasingly routine in many countries), the sense of coercion is never far below the surface in most social sectors, in the workplace and school, on the streets, in politics, in government and the law, and in constant reminders in the news media. This coercion, and the periodic clenched violence, are fueled by the violent and coercive itch in all of us, which easily erupts in hot-righteous ill-will. Austrian psychoanalyst Wilhelm Reich observed that "there is not a single individual who does not bear the elements of fascist feeling and thinking in his structure."

It is the task of Buddhist meditative practice to expose for each of us the roots of coerciveness and violence within ourselves, and the task of Buddhist activism and social psychology to point to the dynamic mutual reinforcement of this ill will and the social conditions that are sustained by it. We need to be both well informed of, and sensitive to, the attitude of often very subtle rejection and discrimination with which we relate to the various kinds of "put down" people in our society, including (often especially if we are men) the other half of the human race, the mentally and physically handicapped, people of other ethnic cultures, and those who suffer from the many different kinds of poverty and powerlessness.

As we've explored previously, to be fully meaningful, compassion has to be socially informed and socially effective. We are no longer living in the comparatively simple societies in which the great world religions were conceived. The help we may personally give to another individual and the example we try to set through our own conduct are essential and may be all that we can give, but they will fall short of fully effective helping. This requires working to change the social institutions and structures that affirm coerciveness and indifference and maintain their karmic momentum. Again, it is the Buddhist recognition of the power of conditioning—including social conditioning—that points to the importance of a radical and transformative social activism.

At the same time, the results of legislation (structural change) in support of the rights of women and ethnic minorities—when it is not accompanied by a widespread change of heart and reflected in new social norms and attitudes (cultural change)—are disappointing, and evidence, once again, that legal and institutional changes are only superficially transformative. This is not to say they are not important. They are essential concommitants to any turnabout in how people feel. But that turnabout cannot be legislated into existence.

Johan Galtung, a pioneer in peacemaking theory, distinguished ingrained coerciveness from *direct* violence. He recognized that ingrained coerciveness is sanctioned by most societies in *structural* and *cultural* forms of *covert* violence.

Structural violence is inherent in the everyday working of social systems. For example, a level of poverty tolerated as economically "normal" causes many of the poor to have significantly higher risks of cancer, heart disease, depression, premature death, and so on. The International Monetary Fund, dominated by the United States, could be considered structurally a "terrorist organization." It regularly coerces poor debtor countries with threats of withholding further aid unless they adopt draconian domestic policies with respect to social programs and welfare services. These have been shown to have predictably "violent" impacts upon the poor, including increased child mortality and reduced life expectancy.

Cultural violence includes racism, sexism, homophobia, and the devaluation of particular groups and cultures. It may justify and inform both structural and direct violence—including the violent resistance of oppressed groups like the Chechens and the Palestinians.

The most extensive and pervasive example of cultural violence is undoubtedly that of sexism. Consciousness-raising through the women's movement has enabled many women to become aware of how much their dignity is denied in subjection to innumerable forms of discrimination—whether thoughtless, selfish, patronizing, or overtly contemptuous. Twenty years ago the sixty Buddhist scholars, monks, and lay people, for whom James Hughes drafted *A Green Buddhist Declaration,* maintained that: A Buddhist analysis of patriarchy points to the interdependence of social power and spiritual oppression, in that the organized power of men over women is rooted both in threat of violence, the greed to maintain privilege, and a subtle form of ego-ignorance, male chauvinism.... We see [the subordination of women] as part of the more general problem of objectification and commodification of human beings, alienating subject and object.

Virtually everywhere, women have to bear a triple burden of child care, domestic labor, and paid work outside the home, usually with less recompense than men. Overall, they still have to undertake inferior work for less pay and with poorer promotion prospects. In many respects they remain second-class citizens. In the mass media they are publicly paraded as sexual objects, and are subjected to apparently widespread sexual harassment at work and to increasing violence and the fear of violence in the streets and even in their own homes. The fact that, until quite recently, all but a few women were socially conditioned to accept their "inferior" status indicates the depth to which this pervasive form of cultural violence is ingrained.

Further, we can see reaction to cultural violence vividly in the terrorist attack on New York and Washington in September 2001. In the final analysis these are desperate acts of direct violence in response to decades of systematic structural and cultural violence inflicted by the United States government and business interests upon the peoples of the Middle East and beyond. Time after time popular leaders throughout the world who wanted the wealth of the land to be shared by those who worked it have been ousted and replaced by tyrants who would ensure unbridled "freedom" for the transnational corporations. Activist and author William Blum, in *Rogue State: A Guide to the World's Only Superpower,* states that since 1945 the United States has attempted to overthrow some forty foreign governments, has crushed some thirty freedom movements around the world, and has killed millions and reduced millions more to the kind of despair that breeds terrorism. When structural and cultural violence are challenged by direct violence, the response, as in this case, is likely to be retaliatory direct violence on a massive scale. This, in turn, deepens the bitterness and desperation of the wretched of the earth, creating a global culture of terrorism and counterterrorism—a blind antithetical bonding of rage and hysteria. At time of writing we are witnessing a most tragic vindication of the Buddha's famous warning: "Hatred is never appeased by hatred in this world; by love alone is hatred appeased. This is an eternal law" (Dhammapada, 5). Love in this context amounts to a radical reversal of United States world policies, and notably a commitment to a just peace in the Middle East in place of the present counterterrorism.

Several prominent engaged Buddhists have emphasized that understanding and responding to structural and cultural violence is at the core of Buddhist social and ecological engagement. To see only the violence of those who, in desperation, answer intolerable institutional coercion with overt violence is to become party to the hypocrisy of established power.

If structural and cultural violence is a core issue for engaged Buddhists it is also an extremely challenging one. Donald Rothberg, a leading member of the Buddhist Peace Fellowship, in "The Parking Lot Sutra," identifies no fewer than ten reasons why it is hard to respond to structural violence. He emphasizes its hidden, taken-for-granted character, which can make working for institutional change a long haul, often lonely and difficult.

Creative Nonviolence

There are three different kinds of thinking about nonviolence that can be broadly distinguished. First there is the creative nonviolence pioneered by Gandhi and others, which is a natural expression of Buddhist activism.

Secondly there is a pragmatic, rationalist strain of nonviolent thinking, of which Gene Sharp has probably been the most noteworthy exponent. In his book *Social Power and Political Freedom* Sharp maintains that nonviolence is simply a more effective means of attaining a peaceful and just world than violence. Sharp acknowledges the deep personal, as well as social, roots of violence, but he is critical of heavily ideological philosophies of nonviolence not least because the moral absolutism of extreme pacifism will always, he believes, restrict its appeal to a tiny and ineffective minority. In my view, however, relying on the power of reason alone is insufficient to mobilize and sustain the impressive array of nonviolent strategies set out in his books. Whether spelled out or not, Sharp's kind of nonviolence is shared by the majority of peaceworkers and other nonviolent activists at the present time. It limits itself to rendering the authorities powerless through applying coercive "sanctions" (as Sharp calls them) and thereby effecting a transfer of power.

Thirdly, there is an ideological kind of nonviolence, which mirrors the ideology of violent resistance that believes that the practice of its form of opposition to injustice (i.e., overt violence) purifies and empowers the resistance. As with all ideology, that of nonviolence tends to have a self-confirming and righteous quality about it that distances it from disconcerting realities. It inclines to grand gestures like "the propaganda of the deed." In this respect, demonstrations of one's moral superiority, even if they amount to heroism, are as much likely to alienate others as persuade them of the truth of one's views. In *On Peace* Trappist monk Thomas Merton particularly warns of "the danger of ambiguity in protests that seek mainly to capture the attention of the press and to gain publicity for a cause, being more concerned with the impact upon the public than with the meaning of that impact." Merton associates such gestures with "the mental climate in which we live": "Our minds are filled with images which call for violent and erratic reactions.... We are swept by alternate fears and hopes which have no relation to deep moral truth. A protest which merely compounds these fears and hopes with a new store of images can hardly help us to become men of peace." Merton further remarks that "perhaps the most insidious temptation to be avoided is one which is characteristic of the power structure itself: this fetishism of immediate and visible results."

Moreover, as an ideology, pacifism tends to make absolute claims and too readily assumes the universal instrumental effectiveness of nonviolent action. Richard Gregg, in the classic *The Power of Nonviolence,* points to numerous historical successes: Hungary's resistance to Austrian rule (1867), Gandhi's campaigns in South Africa (1906–14) and India (1917–47), Denmark and Norway under the Nazi occupation (1942–45), and the struggle that Martin Luther King, Jr., led in the 1960s against racial segregation in the United States. To these might be added the experience of the Buddhist nonviolent movement in Vietnam, the Polish struggle against their Soviet client government, and the mass nonviolent movement that toppled dictator Ferdinand Marcos in the Philippines in 1986.

But we must also bear in mind that Gandhi hastened the withdrawal from India of a Britain that was already a burnt-out colonial power whose postwar Labor government was disposing of a whole empire as rapidly as possible. And Martin Luther King, Jr., campaigned in a democracy that had a public conscience that could be shaken. It is the very real achievement of these leaders that in both cases they accelerated a historical process that certainly would otherwise have been more violent. I believe that nonviolent movements should be assessed not solely in terms of instrumental success but rather as historical episodes that both won some tangible concessions and at the same time shifted the moral climate a little. Italian reformer Danilo Dolci's work to change the character of a neglected, poverty-stricken southern Italy, subject to corrupt and inefficient government and Mafia gangsterism, is a good example.

There have been many instances where conditions were such that no practicable foothold existed for a nonviolent action that could conceivably have yielded instrumental results. In the Second World War, for example, Jews and Slavs were incapable of significant nonviolent resistance because they were overtaken by unspeakably violent Nazi genocide. In the war against Nazi Germany, the timely use of violence was instrumental in terminating the escalating violence of a ruthless adversary in circumstances where nonviolent action was very unlikely to be effective. Previously I mentioned the examples of Michael Scott and Dietrich Bonhoeffer, both men of great spiritual strength and maturity, who made the decision to fight. There were others, however, who felt that nonviolent witness and service was the only course of action they could take and the only one that could be ultimately and profoundly effective.

To give another example of the ambiguity that is often present in a moral stand against violence, the left-wing regimes in Cuba (and in Nicaragua before it was destabilized by the U.S. government) were born out of a comparatively modest violence on the part of the revolutionaries, and whatever the shortcomings of its current government, Cuba is now undoubtedly less violent and more socially just and free of poverty than was the case under the crude dictatorships that preceded it. Such examples give plenty of scope for argument, of course, but my concern here is only to suggest that genuine moral dilemmas are involved.

In the great majority of *social conflict* situations there exists the possibility of remedy through nonviolent action, even when other conciliatory and noncoercive attempts have failed. More or less favorable conditions will variously obtain with respect to: (a) the nature of the protest movement; (b) its adversaries; (c) the issue in dispute; and (d) the contextual situation (the state of "external" opinion, for example). The kinds of situations I have in mind are social justice issues such as industrial disputes; community actions of various kinds (as against unwelcome "development" foisted by the authorities or private enterprise); environmental, peace, and antiglobalization movements; communal strife such as that in Northern Ireland; and movements to topple an oppressive and unrepresentative regime. Even if some violent course of action ultimately is undertaken within the limits that Jacques Ellul finds "condonable," every opportunity must surely be used to give effect to the creatively nonviolent approach outlined below.

Creative nonviolence is a natural and direct expression of Buddhadharma, which shares a common perspective with the nonviolence in other traditions of engaged spirituality. The most sophisticated and well-grounded model is undoubtedly the *satyagraha* (literally, "holding to truth") of Mahatma Gandhi, which was rooted in Hinduism, with acknowledgments also to Thoreau, Tolstoy, and Ruskin. In the discussion that follows I have drawn particularly on Joan Bondurant's valuable presentation of Gandhian creative nonviolence in her book *The Conquest of Violence: The Gandhian Philosophy of Nonviolence*.

The conventional approach to remedying a grievance (from a breach of an employment contract to the threat of global warming) is to focus all attention on confronting and defeating the adversary. Where the issue is ideological the conflict over the specific grievance is seen as no more than a step in a long and historic struggle that strengthens the protesters and weakens the adversary (as in Marxist revolutionary perspective). The creative nonviolence of engaged spirituality, however, takes place within a perspective that is not only social but human and existential. Therefore the common humanity of the adversary is recognized as a matter for compassionate concern throughout the conflict. In particular, the protesters seek to be in full awareness of the urge to violence, confrontation, and alienation that they share with their adversary.

The philosophy of creative nonviolence recognizes that both protester and adversary are caught up in the same historical web of socially supercharged bitterness and antagonism. Like other conflicts reflected in Indra's Net, the specific question at issue is no more than an expression of the whole flux of karmically freighted fear, ill will, acquisitiveness, and existential blindness. The so-called method of nonviolence by which an affliction is to be removed is therefore more important than the specific issue at hand, for it seeks to help undercut the human roots from which such afflictions arise again and again. It does this by seeking to bring into the awareness of the adversary the suffering that arises from greed and domination, and also to share with him or her something of a higher level of consciousness through the experience of mutual respect, genuine communication, and some recognition of ultimate common interest. But, as Gandhi made very clear, where necessary the minds of the powerful and wealthy are to be forcefully (but not violently) concentrated upon these realities. The struggle is directed to raising the consciousness of adversaries as well as protesters, and obliging them to explore alternatives and make choices. The afflictions at issue are not just occasions for a profound learning exercise; they are real and terrible things in themselves, and Gandhi was always adamant that there should be no compromise on fundamental, reasonable, and minimum demands.

Satyagraha is made up of two elements, *love* and *force*, which are the creative dialectic of a spiritually inspired nonviolence. Nonviolent coerciveness is present as the motive power for transforming the situation, but it is to be a *filiative* and not an *antagonistic* coerciveness, with force used minimally, without violence or hate, to set in motion the search for a "truth" in the conflict situation that both sides can recognize, a higher third on which to base a solution. Bondurant writes that the "immediate goal" for Gandhi in a nonviolent conflict

> is not the triumph of his substantial side in the struggle—but, rather, the synthesis of the two opposing claims. He does, then, all he can to persuade the opponent of the correctness of his own position but, while he carries on his own persuasive activity, he allows the opponent every opportunity and, indeed, invites him to demonstrate the correctness of his (the opponent's) position and to dissuade him of his own position.

He makes it clear that he is open to persuasion and is not seeking a one-sided triumph: "He seeks a victory not over the opponent but over the situation." As Thomas Merton observes in *On Peace,* "A test of our sincerity in our practice of nonviolence is this: are we willing to learn something from the adversary? If a new truth is made known to us by him or through him, will we accept it? Are we willing to admit that he is not totally inhumane, wrong, unreasonable, cruel, etc.?"

Writers on nonviolent campaigning and conflict resolution have variously distinguished successive stages through which it is desirable that the action should move. The following are based on those distinguished by Gandhi, Gene Sharp, and Adam Curle and presented in Curle's book *Making Peace.* To some extent the stages overlap and parallel one another, rather than following in successively exhausted sequence.

1. *Research.* In conflict situations, "truth" serves the contending parties through the same weighted polarization that is at work in most arenas of life. It is important to examine the adversary's truth carefully and respectfully, to be equally rigorous in examining one's own for tendentiousness, and to try to enlarge the view by further research that should be as independent as possible (perhaps through using intermediaries). The enlarged and more fully shared "knowledge base" can then be publicized, and attempts can be made to secure wider agreement simply regarding the facts of the situation.
2. *Negotiation and arbitration through established channels.* Every effort should be made to resolve the dispute at this stage, which should be exhausted before further steps are taken.
3. *Education, publicity, meetings, and street demonstrations.* Gandhi attached great importance to the education of protesters, adversaries, and other parties thus far uninvolved, not only about the question at issue but also about the philosophy and practicalities of creative nonviolence.

4. *Making the case to the adversary.* Gandhi counsels the need to be constructive, not to drive the adversary into a corner, not to push for more than is really needed, not to press home an advantage, and to allow the adversary to save face. By refraining from pressing the adversary to the limit throughout the conflict and from taking advantage of his every weakness, he may be jolted out of the sense of confrontation and given some emotional space in which to make a constructive proposal, free of being forced into doing so. For example, in his early days in South Africa, Gandhi deliberately refrained from pushing his advantage at a time when the authorities had to cope with a rail strike as well as with him and his followers.

5. *Preparation of the protesters for creative nonviolent action.* Gandhi emphasized that the protester should be well integrated in a self-reliant affinity group in which strong bonds of mutual trust had been built up. This preparation is the most important single precondition for the success of creative nonviolence. Protesters need to have had opportunity to work through their more obtrusive self-needs with the support of the group so that they do not use a nonviolent demonstration or other action as opportunity to vent their anger, resentment, or other unfinished emotional business upon the adversary. The practices of meditation and awareness are clearly valuable for developing a calm, unwavering, well-centered strength in the face of violence and provocation.

6. *Escalation of nonviolent action.* Escalation will begin with such constitutional action as lobbying the legislature, petitions, protest meetings, and the like and will continue through economic boycott and strikes to noncooperation with the authorities (such as a boycott of state schools or a tax strike). Beyond this lies active civil disobedience and lawbreaking (either symbolic or related to the grievance). The ability of the authorities or other target organization or institution to continue operating normally will become impaired.

Authority is normally confirmed by compliance because it is assumed to be reasonable and in the interests of those who comply with it; people also comply with authority out of habit and social conditioning, or because they feel powerless. Concerted, large-scale, and resolute refusal to comply obliges the authorities to resort to coercion and even violent coercion to intimidate and terrorize. However, if the protest movement can remain firm, even this becomes self-defeating beyond a certain point.

Before moving on to escalate the action to a higher stage, the protesters will at each stage attempt to open positive and creative negotiations with the adversary in the spirit described earlier in this chapter. If these fail, a further ultimatum may be issued and nonviolent sanctions further extended. However, even the ultimatums should offer the widest scope for agreement, should be constructive and reasonable in character, and avoid violent and confrontational language. Gandhi urged that adversaries at all levels be treated with respect and humanity and protected from physical violence and verbal abuse. The protesters' own willingness to suffer these can make a strong appeal to both adversaries and public.

It is true that in many situations nonviolence may be more difficult to sustain than open violence. And it may at times be very difficult to find a creative way forward out of confrontational and narcissistic forms of nonviolence, especially when the adversary will not open the door even a fraction of an inch to real communication. What is saddening, however, is the lack of awareness of the possibility of more creative forms of nonviolent action and of attempts to make trial of them. Unfortunately, in mass movements whose unity and morale depend very much on black-and-white picture-making and combative sloganeering, such initiatives would be likely to prove divisive and disorienting. The initiation of discussion and action around the theme of *creative* nonviolence would seem to be one of the more immediate tasks for Buddhist and other engaged spiritualities.

Peaceful Stabilization of Violent Crises

How do we establish peace in times and places that are rife with a sudden, open violence that might have been nipped in the bud? Advocates of creative nonviolence have put forward persuasive proposals as to how this might be done—and could have been done—in recent flashpoint situations in Africa, the Balkans, Iraq and elsewhere. They entail a wide range of strategies, which include addressing some of the underlying causes of violence, such as poverty and injustice, and the slow and unglamorous work of unraveling hatred through conflict resolution and reconciliation.

Creative peacework in these kinds of situations requires multiskilled teams in which a conventional military presence would play at most a small part. A start has been made, most notably through the Organization for Security and Cooperation in Europe (OSCE). Building on its experience in Yugoslavia, OSCE is establishing Rapid Expert Assistance and Cooperation Teams (REACT). These will be trained in conflict prevention, crisis management, and postconflict rehabilitation. The problem is that this work is not well known or publicized, and its funding is inadequate.

Some would question whether any form of Buddhist peacework is viable in cases where widespread and bloody violence has already broken out, antagonisms are inflamed, and opposing positions solidified. An increasing number of conflicts are fueled by ethnic hatred, and may be confusing and elusive in character, with much "mindless" violence and a general breakdown of the state and civil society (the drug-crazed adolescent soldiery of Sierra Leone is an extreme but not unique example). In his book *Another Way: Positive Response to Contemporary Violence,* Adam Curle argued that the global spread of this new chaotic violence has substantially invalidated the earlier models of negotiated and mediated conflict management. When—in the official jargon—much so-called Third World Development collapses into "non-viable national economies" and these in turn degenerate into "ungovernable chaotic entities" (such as Somalia), breeding grounds are created for the latest violent phenomenon—highly destructive international terrorist networks. The kind of conflict that arises in broken-backed countries is also impervious to economic sanctions, which would make matters worse. Economic sanctions have been an important pacifist resource, but have always been problematic. They appear to have contributed positively to the nonviolent transition from apartheid to representative government in South Africa. And the Burmese democracy movement values them as a means of putting pressure on the ruling junta. But their use in Iraq has been widely condemned as imposing terrible hardship on ordinary people while having little impact on the ruling elite. The value of economic sanctions, like so many other peacemaking strategies, is clearly situational and not absolute.

Creating Cultures of Peace

Buddhist peacework is not just about stopping wars or other armed conflicts after they have broken out; it must also emphasize the creation of cultures of peace. As Thich Nhat Hanh reminds us in "*Ahimsa:* The Path of Harmlessness":

> To prevent war, to prevent the next crisis, we must start right now. When a war or a crisis has begun, it is already too late. If we and our children practice *ahimsa* in our daily lives, if we learn how to plant seeds of peace and reconciliation in our hearts and minds, we will begin to establish real peace and, in that way, we may be able to prevent the next war.

Furthermore, to confine our definition of peacemaking to remedying open violence would be to condone the social injustice and misery that arise from the daily "violence" of our social institutions. Nonviolence must go beyond refusing to make war. It must work to create justice in the world so that war is no longer necessary. Sulak Sivaraksa spells this out in "Buddhism and a Culture of Peace":

In order to create a culture of peace, first we must make society more just, more fair, and give equal rights to all people. The imposition of so-called peace has, in fact, at times been a tool of repression. Look at the many programs for pacification undertaken throughout history and the world. In many cases the institutional definition of peace is tantamount to the suppression of righteous struggles for equal rights and justice. In other cases, the institutionalization of peace is really propaganda for maintaining the status quo of an unjust government or system.

In his book *Buddhist Peacework* David Chappell and his fellow contributors propose a variety of strategies for building a culture of peace. Giving particular attention to the need for engaged Buddhists to work concretely in areas of social reform, Chappell writes:

> The primary area of Buddhist peacework is [that of] soft power [characterized by networks of small groups]. It has three main forms: individual mindfulness, organized social development, and non-violent resistance to structural violence.... Although the Buddhist tradition has been very good in its prohibitions and very idealistic in its emphasis on universal responsibility, it has been rather weak in the intermediate steps of social responsibility—education, health, employment, welfare, and cultural development. This "middle path" needs more attention by Buddhists. Fortunately, it is in this middle area where many of the new contributions of Buddhist peacework are being made.

Beyond Buddhist Pacifism: The Ultimate Purpose of the Precepts

Kenneth Kraft, a prominent scholar of engaged Buddhism, proposes in "New Voices in Engaged Buddhism," that it might be "an opportune time to undertake a fresh critique of Buddhist pacifism.... Can it be that pacifism and just-war reasoning are *equally valid* options for present-day Buddhists? The question deserves more attention than it has yet received." There are indeed fundamentalist Buddhists who endeavour to interpret the ethical precepts literally. However, if the phenomena that are the subject of ethical decisions are ever changing, and exist only in their interconnectedness, their interbeing with other phenomena, then a Buddhist peace ethic must surely be situational. Circumstances alter cases. Certainly in situations of international and civil conflict there are many different factors to be taken into account, some of which we may be ignorant or inadequately informed about. Moreover, what would be a wise decision one week may be folly the next. Ethical principles are guidelines to be interpreted and applied contextually. Thus in *Mountain Record of Zen Talks* Zen master John Daido Loori observes: "There is no way to make a viable set of rules for what you should do, because what you should do is always determined by time, place, position, and degree—by consideration of how much action is necessary."

The foregoing recalls the writing of Jacques Ellul, which is particularly instructive in that he combines an uncompromisingly radical political stance with a scrupulous honesty about the evil of violence. For Ellul no violence can be "good, legitimate, or just," yet he believes that violence can be "understandable, acceptable, and condonable" in the following exceptional circumstances: (a) when nonviolence is impracticable or has failed; (b) when it is demonstrable that if violence were not used, greater violence would befall; (c) when violence is not "strategic," that is, an integral and fundamental part of policy; and (d) and only when means are found to mitigate the effects of violence before and afterward. For "the first law of violence is continuity. Once you start using violence you cannot get away from it," he writes in *Violence: Reflections from a Christian Perspective.* "Violence has brought so many clear and visible results; how then to go back to a way of acting that certainly looks ineffectual and seems to promise very doubtful results?"

With Ellul the argument has begun to harden into classic just-war principles. Yet Buddhists cannot afford to dismiss these. As John Kelsay argues in "The Just-War Tradition and the Ethics of Nuclear Deterrence," these criteria provide a useful set of concepts for analyzing religious traditions that must balance the claims of nonviolence against the realities of war.

Whether Christian or Buddhist, the self tends to cling to the certainties of absolute virtue; we like to know definitively where we stand.But the ultimate purpose of ethical action is to relieve suffering, not the literal enactment of the precepts. It requires the wisdom and compassion that come from an open awareness and a selfless empathy. There are many situations in which the spirit of a precept may be violated by its literal interpretation, and this is widely recognized by Buddhists. It is not difficult to appreciate, however, why the first precept, against the destructiveness of violence and killing, has almost unanimously retained a strictly literal interpretation. Nevertheless, I believe that there are now situations and possibilities evolving in the world that make it desirable to apply the first precept situationally also.

It is worth turning inward and subjecting Buddhist pacifism to Buddhist scrutiny. For pacifism is also an *ism,* another ideology. That is to say, it tends to simplify complex and uncertain situations into black-and-white choices and treats the evidence selectively in order to sustain a fixed subjective standpoint. Buddhist scholar and former monk José Cabezón describes what he calls a "top-down" peacemaking model, which "seeks to make peace descend into our midst from the heaven of ideals." This approach is "doomed to failure," he explains in "The UNESCO Declaration: A Tibetan Buddhist Perspective,"

> not only because such a model often disregards the causal process, but also because it encourages a kind of unhealthy clinging to the ideal of peace. Peace...becomes imagined (a more accurate term would be "reified") and then clung to as an absolute that is independent, not only of causes, but of time, place, cultures and the beings that inhabit these. In the end peace becomes reified/deified as a transcendent and ultimately unattainable absolute, and our proper relationship to it devolves into one of worship and awe. The deleterious side effects of such an attitude will be obvious.

If not Kosovo, then Afghanistan, and if not Afghanistan, then, sooner or later, there will be somewhere else where an irresistible case will arise for skillful international intervention that will undoubtedly save many lives and restore peaceful conditions—*but only if the use of arms is not ruled out*. As a matter of urgency we need to work for the creation of international intervention agencies that are authentically benevolent and uncompromised by the interests of the wealthiest nations or of transnational corporations. I believe this is now a realistic prospect.

A peacemaking that lets go fearlessly and unreservedly into the realities of a violent situation, dropping even pacifist conviction, is scary, liberating, and potentially creative. As elsewhere, the self assumes that, bereft of supporting beliefs, things will somehow fall apart. In fact, given some maturity of wisdom and compassion, we *do* know what to do, and our revulsion at killing and violence *does* remain undiminished—but it is no longer absolute and unconditional. However, we will have no *certainty* about our knowing what to do and will have to trust that we are making the best judgments we can. Inaction is one possibility, but we bear the same responsibility for its consequences as we do for any other course of action. It was the inaction of the young Dutch United Nations conscripts at Srebrenica that condemned thousands of innocent people to a cruel death. I can empathize with Buddhists who unconditionally refuse to condone the taking of life. But I take issue when this becomes a dogma that is never open to question. Yet none of this detracts from a belief in nonviolence as a necessary ideal and goal.

Helen Tworkov made the following statement about Buddhist pacifism in a 1999 editorial:

The first Buddhist precept is non-killing. A literal interpretation demands a crystallized commitment to pacifism. This is a position for which I have enormous respect, but it's not one that I share. I am drawn to those schools of Buddhism in which "killing" becomes part of a more complex conversation; in the Balkans the alleviation of suffering emerges as the prime motive for war, and the strategies accommodate paradox and contradiction. I cannot look at pictures of the Nazi death camps and fault the U.S. decision to enter the European theater; and as this winter went on, the massacres in Kosovo invited comparisons. Yet saving lives by bombing Milosovic into the ground doesn't make war holy.

The fact that many Buddhists had a similar response to the Kosovo crisis suggests that in the twenty-first century, pacifism will no longer be an almost universally held Buddhist belief. Will it be the last Buddhist dogma to be relinquished? And will the next book about Buddhist peacework be courageous enough to open up this question?

This chapter's exploration of peacework and social justice has ended with a discussion about the ethics of tactical, fire-fighting kinds of peacemaking—or, more properly, violence damping. Such emergency operations to save lives and win time are sensational and controversial. They should not detract, however, from the long-term, in-depth work to develop cultures of peace for which a Buddhist perspective is particularly valuable.

Chapter 13

A WORLD IN FLAMES

ONE OF THE BUDDHA'S earliest teachings was his *Fire Sermon:* "All things are on fire—with the fire of passion, with the fire of hatred, with the fire of infatuation, with birth, old age, death, lamentation, misery, grief and despair are they on fire." Evidently the Buddha had our human condition itself in mind. Yet he was addressing a world that did not yet know the conflagration that would ensue over the subsequent two and a half millennia. By the "terrible twentieth century" humankind had developed sufficient technology, wealth, and organization to inflict on itself death and every kind of suffering on an unprecedented scale.

In this new century we are faced with three interrelated conflagrations. First, there are the various and sometimes novel forms of violence, war, and terrorism spilling over from the previous century into zealous "wars against evil." Secondly, there is the structural violence of transnational free market capitalism. Thirdly, and at the deepest level, is environmental degradation and the incompatibility of the exponential growth of material consumption with a finite ecosystem.

Transnational Terror

As noted in the previous chapter, a growing number of destabilized and impoverished countries are sinking variously into civil war, ethnic conflict, and a warlordism bereft even of ideology. Such conditions breed humanitarian disasters and attract intervention by the Western powers out of humanitarian but also more questionable motives.

The terrorist attacks of September 11, 2001, on the United States can only be understood against the background of decades of American aggression against much smaller and weaker countries. Sometimes this has taken the form of conventional military action, but more usually it is officially termed *low intensity warfare*. The official definition of this "low intensity" engagement is almost identical with that of *terrorism* in the United States Code.

Scholar of linguistics and social commentator Noam Chomsky, in his book *9-11*, cites a well-documented example:

> Nicaragua in the 1980s was subjected to violent assault by the U.S. Tens of thousands of people died. The country was substantially destroyed; it may never recover. The international terrorist attack was accompanied by a devastating economic war, which a small country isolated by a vengeful and cruel superpower could scarcely sustain, as the leading historians of Nicaragua, Thomas Walker for one, have reviewed in detail. The effects on the country are much more severe than the tragedies in New York the other day. They didn't respond by setting off bombs in Washington. They went to the World Court, which ruled in their favor, ordering the U.S. to desist and pay substantial reparations. The U.S. dismissed the court judgment with contempt, responding with an immediate escalation of the attack. So Nicaragua then went to the Security Council, which considered a resolution calling on states to observe international law. The U.S. alone vetoed it.

The overall indictment of the United States, as set out in William Blum's *Rogue State,* is staggering when contrasted with the national self-image. In "Rogue Nation" Richard DuBoff elablorates further, summarizing twenty-two major instances of the American government's refusal (virtually alone) to work with other countries peacefully to resolve pressing world issues.

The foregoing is not about stoking up yet another "war against evil." But, from a Buddhist point of view, unless these unpalatable but well-documented facts are known and taken to heart, some kind of atonement cannot begin, and without that we cannot set out on the long road to global reconciliation and healing.

The attack on the United States on September 11 was dramatic, audacious, and, above all, peculiarly horrific. But its main significance is that this was the first time since the British set fire to the White House in 1812 that there has been a major attack on the United States mainland territory. This is the first time the guns have been turned round the other way. Hence the American people experienced a novel and shocking sense of vulnerability. In fact, *they* are in no danger of having their government overthrown by externally promoted insurgency, or being carpet-bombed and land-mined to destruction (as Henry Kissinger did to Cambodia).

The aim of the organization behind those terrorist attacks was to provoke a major conflict between America and the millions of Muslims angered by U.S. policy in the Middle East. The motives appear to have been primarily religious and cultural. But the Bush administration's escalation of its campaign against terrorism into an all-encompassing "war against evil" (embracing Iraq, Iran, North Korea and any other country "not with us") has alarmingly extended the scale of the conflict, broadening the questions at issue and prompting deeper inquiry.

A Historic Choice

The events of "9-11" presented the American government with a historic—and traumatic—choice. On the one hand it could, and apparently has, escalated the conflict into a kind of global war against anything that appears to threaten U.S. interests. This is the tragic but time-honored antithetical bonding response discussed in chapter 6. This will result in the death of countless innocent people and thereby ensure a plentiful supply of new terrorists.

On the other hand, the United States could—just conceivably—wake up and adopt the Buddhist remedy of seeking the higher third. This would involve stepping out of the shadow of partisan self-interest and dispassionately examining the overall global situation and the choices facing America. It would imply a radical turnabout in the foreign policies and overseas aid programs of the United States and its allies. Such changes would enhance global security rather than diminish it.

However changes in foreign policy and aid programs will not be enough. In 1999 U.S. Secretary of Defense William Cohen repeated what had been said one way or another on countless previous occasions, namely that the United States is committed to "unilateral use of military power" to defend vital interests, which include "ensuring uninhibited access to key markets, energy supplies and strategic resources." Global terrorism has complex origins, but in the final analysis they cannot be separated from the poverty and sense of powerlessness of millions of the world's peoples subject to global, free market capitalism. The whole spectrum of global problems, from the military to the ecological, require the dismantling of this system and its replacement by a much more equitable and egalitarian global economy, backed by a system of authentically democratic, global decision making. This is no mere vision splendid. A broad "antiglobalization" coalition has already proposed policies for moving in that direction. The unquestioned establishment of a world order that is leading inexorably to "the end of history" is now being questioned more widely year by year. The world is indeed at present a very dangerous place, requiring the concerted employment of a wide and flexible range of peacemaking strategies.

Profit the Measure of All Things

Free market ideology maintains that all values can be reduced to the monetary value ascribed to by the buyers of goods and services in a competitive market. Maximum value at minimum cost is thus assured. Successful livelihood depends on an acquisitive and aggressively competitive spirit (market versions of two of the "poisons" condemned by the Buddha). If individuals and groups are obliged to struggle against one another for survival, the "best" will win (popular Darwinism always comes into fashion in such periods). Giving serious weight to other values (like increasing costs by being more generous to one's employees) could make a business uncompetitive. The free market thus tends to be ethically regressive, leveling everything down to a lowest common cash denominator.

High modernity progress now lies in the evolution of an unrestricted global market. All impediments to the movement of commodities, labor, and especially capital are to be removed, so that each country exports the goods that it can produce more cheaply than any other. Capital will be attracted to where labor most needs it, and a wider and cheaper range of consumer goods will, it is assumed, become available worldwide. In fact, the transnational corporations and major states have not been content simply to use their commercial superiority to dominate the world. They have also maintained subsidies and tariffs that severely disadvantage the poorer countries. These unfair terms of trade far outweigh the value of overseas aid programs. After the last thirty years global capitalism is becoming an increasingly transparent disaster for most of the world's peoples and for the planet itself. It is the global apocalypse of the exploitative adventure that began in Western Europe some five centuries ago.

The prime movers of this system are the transnational corporations (TNCs), whose economic power typically equals or surpasses that of most of the world's sovereign states. About half of the world's biggest economic units today are states and the other half are TNCs, the biggest 500 of which now account for 70 percent of world trade. Mitsubishi is larger than Indonesia; General Motors is larger than Denmark; Wal-Mart Stores is larger than Israel. Some of their chief executives have higher incomes than the revenues of small nations. And however well-meaning the personal motivation of an individual executive may be, this is not what determines corporate policy. Corporate policy is determined by "the logic of the market," leaving senior management with relatively limited freedom of action. The traditional religious practice of applying moral precepts only to individual conduct hardly touches the great ethical problems of modernity. For this it is necessary to question the norms and imperatives that are institutionally embedded in social systems, as well as to question the ethical validity of the systems themselves.

In the first place, in order to prosper and survive, a TNC must make a competitive profit. It must keep its costs low and externalize them wherever possible, such as by operating in countries that have tough antilabor laws and minimal environmental protection legislation. Environmental and social justice policies that increase costs cannot be pursued except to the extent that a reputation for social responsibility attracts extra business. David Korten notes in *When Corporations Rule the World,* however, that some socially responsible corporations may not be able to optimize in this way and, like Levi Strauss and StrideRite, are stalked by corporate raiders.

Secondly, a TNC must *grow:* enlarge its market share, attract more investment, increase its political influence—and further degrade the ecosphere.

Thirdly, it must keep ahead of competitors by devoting considerable resources to shaping the culture of consumerism in its own interests. This means gaining as much control as possible over the mass media (90 percent of the media outlets in the United States are controlled by some two dozen TNCs).

Fourthly, TNCs must subvert the democratic process by pressuring and covertly bribing governments to deliver contracts, policies, and legislation in their interests. For the free market is a legislative and regulatory construct to ensure the unrestricted use of capital. It is typically sustained as such by government in close association with big business. Their concern is to shape a society exclusively for the good of business, with a citizenry packaged into a docile work force eager to consume and invest. At the same time, influential business lobbies ensure the legislation of state subsidies and tax breaks as incentives for private investment where mere enterprise may not be sufficient, as with privatized undertakings. Thus instead of facilitating the discussion about contending public values and their democratic translation into policy, politics is increasingly reduced to the application of a value-free "postideological" techno-rationality, with personality and presentation—politics as show business—to fill the vacuum. The latest development is to oblige previously sovereign states to throw open their education, health, and other tax-supported public services to international competition and privatization by the company that can run them most "economically." The TNCs are able to intervene thus because of their decisive influence in the regulation of the global market through the General Agreement on Tariffs and Trade (GATT) and its successor the World Trade Organization. For example, under the terms of GATT a country is at liberty to adopt whatever food standards its wishes, yet it cannot bar the import of food from other countries produced to lower standards.

Third World countries that are already heavily in debt and desperate for foreign investment (much of which may benefit corrupt local elites) are obliged to compete with one another by lowering wages, living standards, and environmental protection. To secure further loans (to pay off the existing debts) they are obliged to accept Structural Adjustment Programs, which typically include severe cuts in government spending on healthcare, education, and other social services.

The transnational corporation—perhaps the most extraordinary of the institutions of high modernity—has been summarized as follows by Peter Montague in "One Fundamental Problem":

> In sum, the publicly-traded transnational corporation is a colossus, larger than most national governments, a smiling giant [that] is unable to act upon the conscience and sense of morality its managers and directors personally have, is unable to care about place and community, is politically privileged by its size and wealth, and owns or controls all the relevant mass media, as needed.

Consumerism: The Religion of the Market

Human beings are insatiable animals. Typically they experience as *needs* all those wants that lie beyond sufficient satisfaction. It is not so much the usefulness or beauty of an object or experience that makes it desirable. What momentarily fills the sense of lack is the excitement at the possibility of acquisition, the act of possession, and what the object *stands for*. With a little self-awareness it is not too difficult to appreciate the distinction that is being made here. It is not what the acquisition *is* that attracts so much as what it *means* or *symbolizes* (and how that meaning reflects upon you). It may be an exotic holiday that "takes you out of yourself," or it may be an attractive partner, or just the logo on a garment. As a reinforcement to self-identity, for a sense of belongingness, or to set one apart, style, culture, power, prestige, *savoir-faire*, a caring "green" image, and even the promise of spiritual enlightenment can all be purchased along with the goods and experiences that signal them. Consumer culture is the water in which we swim.

We discussed in chapter 7 high modernity's personal identity crisis and its attendant inner void that insatiably *needs* to be filled. These needs—previously addressed by religion and community—have now been commodified into a whole *culture* of consumerism. If free market economics is the theology of high modernity, then consumerism is its popular religion. As David Loy puts it in *A Buddhist History of the West: Studies in Lack,* consumerism is "the most successful religion of all time, winning more converts more quickly than any previous belief system or value system in human history."

Mere production, distribution, and free-floating advertising ("Brand X is Best!") no longer ensure survival in the marketplace. The market itself has to be created and shaped to support the seductive symbolism to which the product testifies. More money may be spent on creating the image than on making the product itself: The actual manufacturing cost of a pair of Nike athletic shoes is covered by only 5 percent of the purchase price. A large percentage of a manufacturer's expenses goes toward the manufacture of seductive narcotic dreams to make high modernity's disembedded individualism tolerable and even desirable—and, of course, to make a lot of money.

In *Overworked Americans* Juliet Schor observes that "consumerism traps us as we become habituated to the good life, emulate our neighbors, or just get caught up in the social pressures created by everyone's choices. Work-and-spend has become a mutually supporting and powerful syndrome—a seamless web we somehow keep choosing without even meaning to." If everyone worked only twenty hours a week, who knows what they would get up to? Consumerism makes the beneficiaries of the culture of contentment (and those who aspire to it) stakeholders in the market system. Running on racing anxiety, it has an addictive quality about it. It creates its own disorienting virtual reality, numbing the distinction between needs and wants.

The fundamental problem with greed is more than just the maldistribution of worldly goods or its effect on the biosphere. Consumerism, as the currently fashionable form of evasion of our sense of lack, of our root sense of inadequacy, just doesn't work. After some fleeting gratification, it simply perpetuates the age-old suffering. And it readily seduces us away from the option of staring unflinchingly deep into our sense of lack itself. Here, the Buddhist perspective is in fact shared by many mainstream sociologists. Zygmunt Bauman, in his book *Legislators and Interpreters,* writes:

> Individual needs of personal autonomy, self-definition, authentic life or personal perfection are all translated into the need to possess, and consume, market-offered goods. This translation, however, pertains to the appearance of use value of such goods, rather than to the use value itself; as such it is intrinsically inadequate and self-defeating, leading to momentary assuagement of desires and lasting frustration of needs.... The market feeds on the unhappiness it generates: the fears, anxieties and sufferings of personal inadequacy it induces release the consumer behavior indispensable to its continuation.

Thirty Years of Free Market Ideology

The following figures, from the United National Development Program's *Human Development Reports,* illuminate the effects of modernity's latest great project on the quality of life of the great majority of the world's peoples.

Of the approximately six billion people in the world, half live at a bare subsistence level, and a billion of those live brief lives of cruel and abject poverty. Of the other half, two billion live on the fringes of the money economy, with an income of under $5,000 a year and no property or savings. The remaining billion make, on average, a living wage, and can at least aspire to the comfortable life achieved by a small minority within that billion. At the very top are 350 individuals whose combined estimated wealth exceeds that of the combined wealth of 45 percent of the world's population.

There has undoubtedly been an overall improvement in the living standards (measured by GNP per head) of industrializing Southeast Asia, India, and China. (This could be, however, because they are in fact the most state-regulated and least "free" markets in the world.) But in Africa there is probably not a single state that could boast a significantly higher per capita income than at independence. In Russia, the Arab states, and Latin America, income growth in the 1990s either stalled or fell backward. In 1999 almost a billion people in seventy countries consumed less than they did twenty-five years ago. Almost everywhere the gap between rich and poor has widened, often dramatically. Three of the richest men in the world now have private assets greater than the combined national product of the forty-eight poorest countries.

In the industrialized countries the steady rise in per capita GNP (that is, in incomes and consumption) conceals the fact that in the majority of these nations, the gap between rich and poor is widening and, more important, the number of people falling into poverty is increasing alarmingly. As Jeff Gates reports in *Democracy at Risk: Rescuing Main Street from Wall Street,* in the United States 95 percent of the surplus of $1,100 billion generated between 1979 and 1999 was appropriated and consumed by 5 percent of Americans. In the last decade of the century the average American family income rose by only 0.3 percent (after inflation adjustment) but its members were working the equivalent of an extra 4.5 weeks a year. And Will Hutton notes in *The State We're In* that in Britain, according to the government's own definition, a quarter of the population were living in poverty at the end of the twentieth century, caught in a vicious circle of unemployment, low pay, poor diet, dismal schools, and petty crime.

Moreover, in the United States and Western Europe there is mounting evidence, states F. E. Trainer in *Abandon Affluence!,* that rising per capita living standards no longer necessarily amount to an improved quality of life, in terms of fulfilling work and leisure, supportive social relations, a clean and healthy environment, adequate healthcare and housing, opportunity for self-development, and freedom from theft and violence. One source of evidence is in the studies of people's perceptions of quality of life at different periods, showing a progressive decline through the increasingly prosperous 1960s, 1970s, and 1980s. Also, a variety of statistical indicators alternative to GNP have been developed, aimed at measuring the variables that contribute to quality of life. This is clearly a debatable subject, but there are nonetheless pronounced similarities in the changes charted by different indicators over recent decades. One of the earliest is the Index of Sustainable Economic Welfare, which is a personal consumption-based measure adjusted for factors relating to social welfare and environmental quality, outlined by Herman Daly and John Cobb in *For the Common Good.* In both the United States and Britain the graphs of GNP and ISEW rise together until the mid 1970s. At that point the GNP continues to rise but the ISEW commences a downward trend. Clifford Cobb subsequently extended the scope of ISEW in a Genuine Progress Index (GPI), which takes in additional social factors, such as crime and the diminution of leisure time. The latest figures suggest that the average American currently has an almost one-third poorer quality of life than in 1950.

Of the three economic building blocks of millennial modernity, the culture of contentment (or, rather, of gratification and anxiety) is pushed by the second, the free market system, and pulled by the third, consumerism. For visionary liberals and socialists, the emancipatory project of modernity was about the satisfaction of all of the needs for a civilized life, and the leisure and opportunity to develop creativity and humanity to the fullest. For the last quarter of a century, however, the momentum of this progress has for the most part been reversed. The quantitative, or certainly the qualitative, well-being of the vast majority has gone into decline. For many, freedom has become no more than the freedom to escape into a commercialized fantasy world, to which an ever increasing number of the world's poor aspire. The predicament of the growing number of the impoverished, disempowered, and uprooted is becoming increasingly desperate, as reflected in violent crime, addiction, and mental depression. Buddhists need to renew their understanding of *dukkha* (suffering) by looking deeply into our wounded contemporary global society and the roots of its misery, reflecting on how it might be healed—and then putting their insight to good use.

The Ecological Question Mark

The prime mover of modernity is an urgent striving to find some fulfillment *within* by liberation *without*—liberation from all that discomfits the fragile sense of self, from all that deepens the sense of lack. By the end of the second millennium of the Christian era this ultimately futile striving has invested itself with so much technological power as to have literally knocked planet Earth itself out of alignment. According to Norman Myers's "Problems of the Next Century," the axis of rotation has been pushed some 60 centimeters away from the North Pole toward western Canada. Scientists ascribe this to the huge quantity of water impounded by the high dams that have been a feature of so many twentieth-century development projects. This has reduced mass around the equator and shifted it into the northern hemisphere.

Tom Athanasiou reports in *Slow Reckoning: Ecology of a Divided Planet* that in 1990 the global economy produced in seventeen days as much in goods and services as took a year in 1900. The economy is now four times as large as in 1950, and on present projections, by 2050 will be five times as large *again*. It was this escalation of growth that first brought ecological sustainability into question in the 1970s. The official discovery of the ozone hole in 1985 was the first apocalyptic warning. Less disputably than the other problems discussed in this chapter, the ecological crisis has a more terminal imperative about it, for the ecosystem is indeed "the bottom line" of our survival. More certainly than anything else it may force a transition to a qualitatively different kind of society—a true *post*-modernity. However, although the writing is now quite clearly on the wall, year after year passes without any sufficient corrective action being taken. What is remarkable is the momentum with which global society is so helplessly driven, recalling the fate that the Easter Islanders heedlessly brought upon themselves.

To be ecologically sustainable, society would need to be able to operate indefinitely within the *carrying capacity* of the planet. And since the ecosystem knows no national frontiers, such a society needs to be conceived in global terms.

The carrying capacity of the planet sets limits on the environmental impact that the economy can make over time. Each key environmental resource, such as energy, land, water, and wood, has an "environmental space" that defines the global limits to the rate at which it can be used. For example, if it takes fifty years for a tree to grow to maturity, then we can fell no more than a fiftieth of the trees in our forests each year, assuming that we are able to replant at the same rate.

The overall outlook regarding ecosystems' carrying capacity, that is, the sustainable supply of *renewable* resources such as soil, water, and forests, is alarming. In 1997 the United Nations Environmental Program "Global Biodiversity Outlook 1" concluded that these resources have now passed their natural renewable capacity. Deforestation is a global problem affecting biodiversity, topsoil (lost through run-off), and climate (forests absorb carbon dioxide, which accounts for half of global warming). Less sensational is creeping worldwide desertification. Between 1970 and 1990 global topsoil losses were equivalent to the whole of India's cropland.

Environmental impact is a function of total population multiplied by consumption per head. Population increases are expected mainly in parts of the world where consumption is relatively low, whereas consumption per head is expected to continue to grow relatively fast in the industrialized countries. *Increases in per capita consumption are likely to have a more significant amount of environmental impact than population increases.*

In the last thirty years world population has risen from two to six billion. The United Nations expects it to peak at nine billion or less by 2040 and then to fall back. It can be stabilized by 2050 if the poor have the security they require before having smaller families and if women have improved education, status, and rights. Therefore, as part of any global strategy to address the ecocrisis, a rise in Third World living standards will be necessary over the next fifty years. It has been estimated that ten billion people could be fed by 2050 if food could be more fairly distributed and if land hunger could be satisfied by breaking up the big estates. According to the United Nations' World Food Program, one and a half times the amount of food needed to provide everyone in the world with a nutritious and adequate diet is already being produced.

Turning our attention next to global resources, the first point to note is that the availability of raw materials (fossil fuels, minerals, and metals) is a less pressing question than the capability of nature to absorb the pollution and wastes arising from their extraction and use. For example, the problem with fossil fuels is less the extent of resources and much more the atmospheric and climatic effects of emissions from power stations and motor vehicles. Global warming is the most dramatic of those effects, with a speed, scale, and consequences that are difficult to forecast. Even the important international Kyoto agreement for reducing greenhouse gas emissions (in which the United States has refused to participate) can do only a little to slow down the process, which will lead to the flooding of low-lying centers of population, increased desertification, and an unprecedented refugee problem.

Nature (including our human body) can only break down and recycle so much, and we are now up against those limits. Pollution not only includes vehicle and industrial emissions and nuclear wastes but also some 70,000 synthetics—artificial fibers, paints, industrial chemicals, pesticides, fertilizers, and so on—with 1,000 more added each year. Nature has little or no capacity to absorb many of these, and they are rapidly accumulating in the air we breathe, the water we drink, and the soil that produces our food. No one really knows what the consequences of this continuing build-up will be, but there is growing evidence linking it to a wide range of health issues, affecting reproduction, causing cancers, and harming immune systems. For example, in July 1999 a report commissioned by the Worldwide Fund for Nature, in the United Kingdom, found that two-month-old infants were taking in forty-two times the safe level of dioxin in their mothers' breast milk.

There is no doubt that the ecological closure of modernity's industrial frontier is the most significant event in human history. However, the catastrophic metaphor of an industrial locomotive on a collision course toward a fixed ecological barrier is misleading. A better analogy is a car plowing into thickening mud, with a skillful driver weaving and skidding and trying to continue on. On present trends high modernity will maintain its steepening economic trajectory well into the twenty-first century, with piecemeal adaptations to the need for ecological sustainability. Sooner or later these will hopefully tip over into more radical shifts, as the situation becomes increasingly dysfunctional. The slower and later the transition—if there is one—the more difficult it will be to achieve sustainability, and the more extreme and intractable will the global economic and political situation become.

Global sustainability is technically feasible and provides a breathtaking agenda for the human family at last to come of age on planet Earth. A sustainable society would evidently have to be so fundamentally different from modernity that I have called it *postmodernity* (at the risk of confusion with postmodernism—the characteristic intellectual movement of high modernity). Indeed, it will need to be radically different from any previous society in history, entailing a social and cultural revolution surpassing the neolithic five thousand years ago. To shape it and maintain it will require no less than a different kind of person from what we typically are now. Our previous history has made it clear that nothing less will do than some kind of psychospiritual revolution.

Dharma Gaia

Ecology and Buddhism are both about the interdependence of all forms of existence, the former from a scientific viewpoint, the latter in the existential and experiential sense. *Interbeing,* a term coined by Thich Nhat Hanh, is a more suggestive term in the case of Buddhism, as expressed in the metaphor of Indra's net. As the self becomes more transparent through meditative practice, so does it become more intimate and eventually at one with its environment. In the words of the Chan sage Yuansou, from Thomas Cleary's *Zen Essence:*

> The mountains, rivers, earth, grasses, trees and forests are always emanating a subtle precious light, day and night, always emanating a subtle precious sound, demonstrating and expounding to all people the unsurpassed ultimate truth. It is just because you avoid it even as you face it that you are unable to obtain the actual use of it. This is why Buddhism came into being, with its many expedients and clever explanations…these are all simply means of stopping children from whining.

As discussed in chapter 8, ecologically speaking, humankind is a paradox. Neither an anthropocentric view is appropriate (for, as to ecological collapse, we are as vulnerable as the rest of the planetary community) nor an ecocentric one (because we stand out on account of our immense power and responsibility). In this respect Buddhism is *acentric*.

In recent decades a succession of anthologies have been concerned with establishing and documenting Buddhism's "green" credentials. (Two recent and outstanding titles are *Dharma Rain: Sources of Buddhist Environmentalism,* edited by Stephanie Kaza and Kenneth Kraft, and *Buddhism and Ecology: The Interconnection of Dharma and Deeds,* edited by Mary E. Tucker and Duncan R. Williams.) Much of this literature is replete with "Buddhist values" but short on how we can employ those values at a level and on a scale that will catalyze real change. Its emphasis is for the most part environmentalist. In this context, by *environmentalism* I mean a green consumerism that nevertheless goes on consuming at an exponential rate. It is about global climate change conferences aimed at reducing the emissions of the existing industrial economy rather than changing the nature of that economy. It is about grand visions like the Earth Charter, which have no social edge or political will behind them. It is about cycling to work, using biodegradable dishwashing liquid, and planting a few trees—all necessary and worthwhile, so long as we appreciate that on their own such lifestyle changes cannot make a significant difference to the massive global industrial *system* that is wrecking the planet.

What is generally absent is a truly radical agenda based on an effective Buddhist social theory—in short, a Buddhist political ecology. Buddhism is an urgent and practical remedy for the suffering arising from our human condition. Any worthy Buddhist social theory must offer a no less urgent and practical remedy for the suffering arising from the social evolution of humanity (which is inseparable from the existential predicament of each individual). The acquisitiveness and aggressiveness characteristically rooted in that condition have over the centuries developed a power that is now degrading the ecosystem itself and its many life forms, killing off whole species. This degradation puts the future of humankind in doubt and has already greatly added to the burden of its suffering.

How can we shift to an ecologically sustainable, steady-state economy that is no longer dependent on continuous material growth? This would require a steady-state society that is free of the gnawing greed to have more tomorrow if not today, and the competitiveness that goes with it. If we relinquish the promise of jam tomorrow, we can establish an egalitarian society of *qualitative* growth, ensuring a satisfying livelihood and lifestyle for all citizens, in a climate of social justice. This implies restraint, sufficiency, and mutuality in place of the culture of expansive individualism.

Many will not take easily to the end of their unlimited airline tourism, for example, or to a more vegetarian diet because so much grain produced in poor countries can no longer be fed to raise food animals for rich countries. If restraint cannot be internalized so that it is no longer even experienced as such, the only alternative will be some kind of ecological authoritarianism (which is inherently unstable anyway). Clearly the steady-state economy without which ecological sustainability will be impossible will in turn need to be sustained by a new breed of "steady-state citizens."

When the futile outlets of modernity are no longer available to us to fill our sense of lack, might this not be an incentive to turn inward to authentic contemplation and the transcendence of the pain of being human? Might not the greatest benefit of ecological sustainability be the joy and contentment—as well as the necessity—of living lightly and harmoniously as planetary creatures?

Chapter 14

SOCIALLY ENGAGED BUDDHISM:

WHAT IS IT?

The Anatomy of Engaged Buddhism

AT ITS BROADEST DEFINITION socially engaged Buddhism extends across public engagement in caring and service, social and environmental protest and analysis, nonviolence as a creative way of overcoming conflict, and "right livelihood" and similar initiatives toward a socially just and ecologically sustainable society. It also brings a liberal Buddhist perspective to a variety of contemporary issues, from gender equality to euthanasia. It aims to combine the cultivation of inner peace with active social compassion in a practice and lifestyle that support and enrich both. In the first edition of this book, "engaged Buddhism" required some special pleading within the Western Buddhist community. It has now come of age.

The following diagram distinguishes the different kinds of social activism within the context of Buddhist practice.

In the West, so-called inner Buddhism is usually practiced in a group or at a teaching center within some specific Buddhist tradition, such as Theravada, Zen, or Tibetan. However there are many advantages in having an "umbrella" Buddhist group in each region that can bring together people who are practicing in the different traditions, others who are unaffiliated, and also inquirers and beginners. Such a group can provide talks, discussions, meditation sessions and instruction in basic meditation, and general fellowship and support. It can present basic Dharma, introduce the range of traditions represented in its membership, and periodically host sangha and other outside speakers. Unlike a closely focused practice group in a specific Buddhist tradition, the area umbrella group can provide a natural forum for discussion on the relevance of Buddhism to everyday situations at work, in the family and other relationships, in the local community, as well as wider social issues. The group can provide a channel of representation for the Buddhist community in the town or district in terms of interfaith events, religious teaching in schools, local environmental protection, and social problems such as homelessness, hospital and prison chaplaincy, displays and stalls at community events and in the public libraries, local press and radio, and other demands made on a recognized local religious group that has come of age.

BUDDHISM

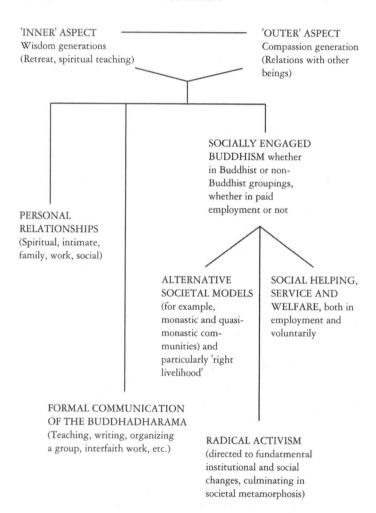

'INNER' ASPECT
Wisdom generations
(Retreat, spiritual teaching)

'OUTER' ASPECT
Compassion generation
(Relations with other beings)

SOCIALLY ENGAGED
BUDDHISM whether
in Buddhist or non-
Buddhist groupings,
whether in paid
employment or not

PERSONAL
RELATIONSHIPS
(Spiritual, intimate,
family, work, social)

ALTERNATIVE
SOCIETAL MODELS
(for example,
monastic and quasi-
monastic com-
munities) and
particularly 'right
livelihood'

SOCIAL HELPING,
SERVICE AND
WELFARE, both in
employment and
voluntarily

FORMAL COMMUNICATION
OF THE BUDDHADHARAMA
(Teaching, writing, organizing
a group, interfaith work, etc.)

RADICAL ACTIVISM
(directed to fundatmental
institutional and social
changes, culminating in
societal metamorphosis)

Socially engaged Buddhism is best practiced if possible in some degree of association with fellow Buddhists who are working toward the same ends,

Peace Fellowship in the United States or the Network of Engaged Buddhists in Britain. Such networks can provide support and increased organizational effectiveness (pooling of experience and knowledge, division of labor and specialization in publicity, research, coordination, education, lobbying). And as specifically Buddhist networks they can, through retreats, affinity groups, workshops, and co-counseling, help individuals to remain centered amid the pressures and distractions attendant on campaigning, lobbying, and other social action.

Such social action networks and affinity groups are also, incidentally, valuable in dissolving any "holier (or more enlightened!) than thou" inclinations among Buddhists who had previously confined themselves to their own particular Dharma traditions. They may also include some of the many people of Buddhist persuasion who nevertheless do not regard themselves as formal, "card-carrying" Buddhists. The presence of such "Buddhist humanists," "Buddhist Christians," and "Buddhist Greens" makes for valuable fellowship and mutual learning as well as providing links with other social action networks.

The different kinds of engagement can be arranged along a continuum. At one end of this spectrum there is *personal* engagement, as with friends, family, and fellow-workers. This is about mindfully changing diapers, working through a disagreement with a spouse, caring for a sick parent, dealing with collegial problems at work, and so on. The definitional boundary is blurred (and doesn't really matter), but we might say that *social* engagement begins with the cultivation of a lifestyle that is conscious and well informed—ecologically, politically, economically, and culturally. This is about, for example, "right livelihood" (one of the steps on the ancient eightfold path of Buddhist practice), ethical consumption, how we relate to others in terms of gender and ethnicity, and the whole shaping of our lives. It is no longer sufficient just to sip one's coffee mindfully: Was it produced under conditions of social justice and ecological sustainability, and marketed through a "fair trade" scheme?

Extending out from "lifestyle politics" is social engagement in public and organized forms of service and caring—therapy, healing and healthcare, prison work, education, social welfare, and environmental projects. In Buddhist Asia and in Western countries where Buddhism is well established there is a growing mosaic of projects, organizations, and networks in all these fields.

At the other end of the spectrum of engaged Buddhism is what I shall term social *activism*. This refers to action for social and environmental change, particularly radical, long-term social changes. This is a much more problematic and controversial level of engagement, and it is this level of engagement that we will examine within the rest of this book. Buddhist radical social activism includes many forms of mass protest, whether demonstrating, lobbying, or just bearing witness to suffering and calamity.

Radical activism is concerned with fundamental changes in social policies, practices, and institutions in areas such as disarmament and defense policy, Third World poverty, environmental protection, women's rights, prisoners of conscience, the persecution of ethnic minorities, and so on. In particular, nonviolent protest and the advocacy of nonviolent solutions to social and international conflict have been prominent in both East and West. Indeed, engaged Buddhism in the West had its origins in the movements against nuclear weapons and the war in Vietnam. There has also been a common concern to halt environmental degradation.

It is noteworthy that issues such as mass unemployment, cuts in social services, poverty, and attacks on civil rights have received less attention, at least from Western Buddhists. They might well ask themselves, for example, why it is that there have been so many publications on Buddhism and the environment and so few on Buddhism and global, free market capitalism? Social activism must inevitably be involved in questions of power and conflict, confrontation and partisanship. Buddhists have to find ways of coming to terms with these without being taken over by them.

Ultimately, Buddhist social goals surely need to be no less radical than is the "inconceivable liberation" of the individual. That is to say, the work needs to be directed toward the creation of a global society free of war, poverty, curable disease, and the many forms of oppression and exploitation, through the evolution of a compassionate and cooperative commonwealth. Above all, such a Good Society will aim to provide conditions of freedom and responsibility favorable to the evolution of consciousness.

Compassion in Action

The great majority of socially engaged Buddhists are not "activists" in the sense used above. They are concerned predominantly with various kinds of caring and service. Many would doubtless share the view expressed by Bo Lozoff, who is renowned for his dedication to offering spiritual care to prison inmates, in *We're all Doing Time:*

> I see very little hope for really turning things round and entering an age of compassionate government, so I don't really get frustrated by the lack of success. But there are people who are really suffering and struggling to whom we can extend friendship. And right away that's the kingdom of heaven. Right away there's success. Because when we're involved with each other in a compassionate way, with friendship and good-will it instantly "works." We have success constantly.

Compassion has been called the *daily face* of wisdom. And helping others is compassion in action, whereby we seek to transcend the sense of a separate, self-absorbed ego. Helping and serving others raises questions in every sphere of our lives, questions that we cannot evade if we believe that we are truly brothers and sisters of one another. These questions extend from how we relate to other individuals, as parents, lovers, workmates, and so on, across into the areas of social engagement and planetary responsibility. Although truly effective helping everywhere has the same quality, it does pose different challenges in different areas of life. For example, trying to be helpful in a close relationship can put us on the spot more than "saving the world," where we can more readily preserve consoling delusions. Getting into wholesale helping may even mask evasions in other areas of our lives. From time to time it is worth quietly reflecting on how we are getting on in the helping (or not helping!) business in different arenas of life.

So, what is it that lies at the heart of spiritual care? Perhaps the most valuable feature of inner-path spiritualities like Buddhism is the way in which they relentlessly direct our attention back to the self.

We begin with that gap between self and other. The needy person—or the needy world—is somehow other than me, and I am able to make myself significant and my life meaningful, and aggrandize myself, if I can do some "good" out there. As Buddhist activist David Brandon observed, "The only way I can let you know that I need your help is to insist on helping you." Indeed, in severe cases of do-gooding or frenzied activism it is a good idea just to stop for a while and to contemplate one's own sense of helplessness. Activists do need to get some feeling for the supreme paradox that *nothing matters; everything matters.*

The most delusive kind of helping arises from the conviction that one is the possessor of some great liberating truth that needs to be impressed upon others. On the contrary, any truly liberating truth must be discovered by the people who might benefit from it, and not delivered as solidified ideology by others. Thus the Dalai Lama asked of Bo Lozoff, "You're not trying to make more Buddhists in prisons, are you? Because the world doesn't need more Buddhists. We don't need to convert more people to any particular religion. We need kindness and compassionate friendship."

Spiritual care requires a self-withdrawal so that the other has space. This space is liberating for the other and helps to build mutual trust. It also enables us truly to see the other in his or her own light and not in ours. From this arises empathy, which is the power to see into another's personality, imaginatively experiencing their experiences. In these conditions grow friendship, warmth, and trust—even fun—and even joy. Often there is a journeying with people, as they reflect on their life and on the way in which their sense of meaning and worth has been challenged by misfortune. It involves discussing hopes and fears, which often manifest themselves in the great *Why* questions: Why me? How should I and can I respond to my misfortune? From there the exploration may lead naturally to the practice of meditation, and then, maybe, to questions about this thing called "Buddhism."

There is no inclusive prescription; each situation has to be played by ear. If the helper is truly open, what needs to be said will be said. And this may especially be so when the helper feels they have no more "help" they can give. "Helper" and "helped" disappear as each opens to a liberative acceptance of just how it is. Buddha speaks with Buddha. Buddha laughs with Buddha at the black comedy of being. Then, in the words of Christian theologian Paul Tillich, "We experience the grace of being able to look frankly into the eyes of another, the miraculous grace of union of life with life." I used to think that the bodhisattvas of old "saved all beings" mainly by preaching Dharma to them. Now I believe that this helping situation is closer to the truth. It gives a fresh resonance to the ancient resolves:

> In my heart I turn to the Three Jewels [of Buddha, Dharma, Sangha]
> May I save suffering beings and place them in bliss,
> May the compassionate spirit of love grow within me
> So that I may complete the enlightening path.

Is Engaged Buddhism a Distinct and Coherent Phenomenon?

The *Journal of Buddhist Ethics,* inviting papers for an online conference, defined socially engaged Buddhism as

> a reorientation of Buddhist soteriology and ethics to identify and address sources of human suffering outside the cravings and ignorance of the sufferer—such as social, political and economic injustice, warfare and violence, and environmental degradation…a new form of Buddhist activism that seeks to transform the self and the world through awareness and compassionate service. The walking-bodhisattva-as-activist is venerated alongside the sitting-Buddha-as-awakener as traditional disciplines and virtues of Buddhist practice are directed to the challenges of the modern world.

However, many Buddhists, including some of the socially engaged, believe that a needless distinction is being made here. Even Thich Nhat Hanh, who is credited with inventing the term *engaged Buddhism,* believes that, "in a sense" it is redundant. "Buddhism means to be awake—mindful of what is happening in one's body, feelings, mind and in the world," he writes in a 1983 Buddhist Peace Fellowship Newsletter. "If you are awake you cannot do otherwise than act compassionately to help relieve suffering you see around you. So Buddhism must be engaged in the world. If it is not engaged it is not Buddhism."

At the level of mere definition such arguments are pointless, since we do need to be able to put a name to what is now a widely recognized phenomenon. However, when viewed from an Asian standpoint the question becomes more significant. Traditionally, it can be argued that, first, Buddhism has always been socially engaged. And, secondly, it has been and is engaged in such a variety of ways as not to warrant identification as a single distinctive and coherent movement or even as a worldwide trend in Buddhism. In "Socially Engaged Buddhism and Modernity," Santikaro Bhikkhu, an American Buddhist activist in Southeast Asia, writes:

> The way most of my Asian Buddhist friends explain their being "Buddhist" is not the same as the Western thing with meditation. The former don't venture definitions or textual arguments; they take it for granted. The same with engagement: "we are acting socially; isn't that socially engaged Buddhism?" There are connections and overlaps, of course, but not enough for a coherent or unified movement.... It seems to me we have disparate local and national movements, but are far from one socially engaged Buddhist movement. In Siam, we don't have a *national* movement, despite our famous engaged Buddhist heroes. Furthermore, the International Network of Engaged Buddhists is weak as far as international organization is concerned. If engaged Buddhism is more unified and coherent than I think it is, it needs to be shown rather than merely assumed.

In contrast to this model of a historically continuous yet fragmented engaged Buddhism is the model of a *new* and *coherent* worldwide movement of modernity. This seems to be the view of most Westerners and has been strongly argued by Christopher Queen and others in two substantial anthologies on engaged Buddhism in Asia and the West (Christopher Queen and Sallie King, eds. *Engaged Buddhism: Buddhist Liberation Movements in Asia,* and Christopher Queen, ed. *Engaged Buddhism in the West*). In the Introduction to his survey of engaged Buddhism in the West, Queen argues that the "voices and actions" of his contributors display a world view which is arguably fresh and unprecedented in the history of Buddhism. This Buddhism is endowed with many, if not all, of the themes and techniques of the past: interdependence, mindfulness, compassion, skillful means, chanting and walking meditation, community practice, right livelihood, and many, many more. But it is also endowed with a sensitivity to social justice, institutional evil, and political oppression as sources of human suffering, that has not been central to Buddhist analysis in the past.

In the same book Queen goes so far as to claim that engaged Buddhism is the fourth *yana,* or vehicle, of Buddhist belief and practice, following Theravada, Mahayana, and Vajrayana (Tibetan) Buddhism: "The general pattern of belief and practice that has come to be called 'engaged Buddhism' is unprecedented, and thus tantamount to a new chapter in the history of the tradition. As a style of ethical practice, engaged Buddhism may be seen as a new paradigm of Buddhist liberation…a *fourth yana* in the evolution of the Dharma."

Those who support the idea of establishing a "new Buddhism" locate its origins in the impact of modernity, geographically and culturally. In the first place, the Buddhist homelands were invaded by a modernizing, missionary Christianity, which carried all the prestige of a triumphant and therefore culturally superior colonialism. Social engagement was the Buddhist response to the Western liberal and socialist emancipatory project, as well as to its rationalism and science. In the second place, engaged Buddhism in the West grew out of the endeavor of Western converts to remain true to their culture of active social responsibility and social justice. This view can be convincing when combined with the persistent Western emphasis on the otherworldly character of Asian Buddhism, which tends to ignore its considerable history of social involvement.

However, while some Western Buddhists who are engaged in various forms of charity or activism may define themselves as "socially engaged Buddhists," they are unlikely to lump themselves together in the same boat with Burmese Buddhists who are struggling to establish a democratic government. What about the small group of rural Thai monks who do not protest overtly and know little about what is going on in other countries, yet are doing remarkable grassroots work to improve social conditions in their own villages? How do the small, fragmented Japanese Buddhist groups supporting various projects in developing countries fit in with the wealthy, powerful, international Japanese Soka Gakkai movement? Is it "one animal or many?" asks veteran activist Santikaro Bhikkhu.

Distinguishing Characteristics
of Engaged Buddhism

For a start toward answering Santikaro Bhikkhu's question, its practitioners and literature implicitly define socially engaged Buddhism as not just social engagement but *ethical* engagement. Hence it excludes Japanese Imperial Way Zen and the hawkish monks of Sinhala Heritage who support the ongoing, bloody territory battle in Sri Lanka. But how about the mindfulness training offered to Japanese and American executives of transnational corporations to improve their business efficiency?

While there are enormous differences in the various approaches to engaged Buddhism worldwide (which I will outline in detail in the next chapters), there are also a number of distinctive and defining characteristics, in terms of shared values and common ways of working.

First, engaged Buddhism is firmly based on the core tenets of the Dharma—compassion, interdependence, selflessness, and the practice of morality and mindfulness. The inner work of radical personal change is generally seen as essential for creating social conditions for both reducing material affliction and fostering the personal growth of all.

Secondly, there is a humanism that lies at the heart of engaged Buddhism. It joins hands with the secular humanism of Western modernity, whether in the face of religious fundamentalism or the cruelties of free market ideology. Buddhist humanism refers to that buddha nature that both validates every human being yet at the same time exists only in the mutuality of all humankind. Each person, and indeed each creature (and even the insentient) exists just as it is, in its own suchness, beyond the relativity of either denial or affirmation. The absolutely "given" quality of that reality has been superbly expressed by Zen master Dogen in his *Shobogenzo* in the chapter "Genjokoan" (frequently translated as "the way of everyday life"):

> No creature ever comes short of its own completeness;
> Wherever it stands, it does not fail to cover the ground.

Thirdly, the interbeing of Indra's net is limitless, and implies a concern for a harmonious and sustainable planetary system. Since natural resources (and their synthetic derivatives) are ultimately limited, this implies a lifestyle of frugality and simplicity for affluent Westerners (supported by a very different kind of society than the present one), and a decent sufficiency for the poor of the world.

Fourthly, as we discussed in detail in chapter 12, engaged Buddhism is characterized by its use of positive nonviolent strategies, which recognize the common humanity of the adversary and his or her dignity and autonomy. Change can only come through creative interaction.

Fifthly, equal rights and partnership between men and women are aspirations consistently found in engaged Buddhist movements, as is respect for ethnic minorities.

Sixthly, engaged Buddhists share an active internationalist perspective, particularly with regard to positive relations between the peoples of the affluent industrial world and the great majority of the world's economically deprived peoples.

Seventhly, engaged Buddhism (at least the mainstream forms) is characterized by pluralism and inclusiveness, and an open-minded, nonsectarian spirit.

In short, it is remarkable that in terms of key values, there is substantially a single, global engaged Buddhism. For although the movement has developed on the ground in different ways in the East and West, engaged Buddhists do appear to share much the same values, goals, and perspectives, as is testified by the writings of leading thinkers in the different countries.

Overcoming Fragmentation

Nevertheless, it is also true that *fragmentation* is another characteristic of engaged Buddhist organizations and initiatives, and in this sense it is very far from being a coherent phenomenon, even at national level.

In two of the biggest international Buddhist movements, the Soka Gakkai and Thich Nhat Hanh's Community of Interbeing, individual members and local groups are for the most part encouraged to pursue their own separate agendas. In work for the terminally ill and prison inmates even in a small country like Britain, there are several separate initiatives with apparently little or no cooperation to improve the effectiveness of their care giving. Sarvodaya, the Sri Lankan village self-help movement, is the remarkable exception of a unified movement that at the same time appears to have remained open and flexible notwithstanding the pressures to which it has been subjected.

The International Network of Engaged Buddhists (INEB) and the national networks (where they even exist) in effect function only to provide background support for a multiplicity of separate and generally uncoordinated projects. Alan Senauke, until recently director of the (American) Buddhist Peace Fellowship, testifies that, in the various manifestations of engaged Buddhism worldwide,

> what seems common is maybe nothing more than a loose agreement that our practice includes engagement with pressing social issues. Beyond that, I don't think we have much agreement. Even within BPF there is a wide

range of thought, action, and practice.... As to engaged Buddhism worldwide, the failure (so far) of INEB, and the tensions I have encountered among [Bernie Glassman's] Peacemaker Communities, suggest that we are not ready for globalization.... Would that our differences were on the basis of ideology! For me the difficulties and divergences are based on local, national, or group interests and needs, personalities, and the lack of any real ideology or common process beyond buddhadharma and dharma practice. So it becomes a fuzzy but well-intentioned mess.... Socially engaged Buddhism [has become] anything that you think is interesting/important to do [if] you happen to be a Buddhist. But that will not lead to social change. In fact, if we assert that our personal social leanings are engaged Buddhism then that will prove to be a barrier to inner change as well.

The radical activists do have their visions of the ideal society of the future, and these visions doubtless have much in common. Nevertheless they appear to be unwilling to cooperate together on a coherent, graduated, and multifaceted national and international enterprise designed ultimately to achieve their common goal. They have not even shown any interest in talking together about it. Santikaro Bhikkhu proposes training as a way forward:

We already have individuals and groups consistently practicing socially engaged Dhamma. However, for socially engaged Buddhism to make its mark on samsara...will require the collective practice of diverse aggregations of individual engaged Buddhist practitioners. To matter, they must do so coherently and consistently. This points to a central role for training. Just as individual practice requires suitable training, so does group-engaged Buddhist practice. Thus, we need organizations capable of providing such training and others to facilitate the application of the fruits of such training.

The fragmentation of organizations and goals is accompanied by a symptomatic paucity of critical and creative open dialogue among engaged Buddhists, with some rare exceptions such as the international Buddhist think-tank ThinkSangha or publications from within the groves of academia, such as the *Journal of Buddhist Ethics*. Most of the literature to date has consisted of interminable anthologies of reportage by overexposed Dharma celebrities, and is beginning to assume a formulaic character. The Russians have two useful words for truth. *Pravda* is official or public truth. *Istina* is the truth that lies beneath it—awkward and potentially dangerous realities; the way things really are, beloved of investigative journalists, whistle blowers, and rockers of boats—the truth that always sooner or later comes out. How grateful we are at such times for its bitter, salty, liberating taste! I have the impression that many Buddhists are apprehensive about honest dialogue, though in fact it can be a very valuable practice, personally as well as instrumentally.

I believe that as engaged Buddhism continues to come into its own, it will be increasingly important for Buddhist activists to develop constructive dialogue around two vital but neglected issues. First we need to work toward developing an intellectually adequate Buddhist social theory. Secondly, we need an ongoing and overarching strategy for radical social change that will enable us to work *together* to real effect.

Chapter 15

ENGAGED BUDDHISM IN ASIA

S IGNIFICANT ENGAGED Buddhist movements, which share many features in common, have developed in most of the Buddhist countries of Southeast Asia. In many cases these movements have arisen as a heroic response to extreme conditions of invasion, civil war, and tyrannical government. Over several decades they have been inspired and led by several personalities outstanding for their integrity, steadfastness, and shared values. They include: A. T. Ariyaratne of Sri Lanka, Thich Nhat Hanh of Vietnam, Ajahn Buddhadasa and Sulak Sivaraksa of Thailand, Daw Aung San Suu Kyi of Burma, and Samdech Preah Maha Ghosananda of Cambodia. In addition, sharing and contributing to their joint vision, is His Holiness the Dalai Lama and the Tibetan liberation movement. When one gets to know these movements better, one encounters a host of fine men and women of the same mettle.

Sri Lanka: Sarvodaya

Sarvodaya, which means "the awakening and welfare of all," is a Buddhist-inspired village self-help movement outside the official rural development program. It is arguably the largest and most comprehensive example of socially engaged Buddhism in the world today, although the mass Buddhist movements of Japan have a comparable claim. Today 12,000 of the 30,000 Sri Lankan villages are involved in the movement, involving some 4 million people.

Sarvodaya aims at an economy of modest sufficiency, employing appropriate low and middle technology, with equitable distribution of wealth and concern for the quality of the environment. Local and national cultural identities and diversity are respected and nurtured, and the movement seems to make its strongest impact in the more traditional kinds of community. Sarvodaya's Village Awakening Councils enjoy program and budget autonomy, but receive much specialist support from area and regional centers, which are backed by extensive training programs and international aid. Projects include roads, irrigation works, preschool facilities, community kitchens, retail cooperatives, and the promotion of village handicrafts (though impact on agriculture appears to have been disappointing).

Joanna Macy, in *Dharma and Development: Religion As a Resource in the Sarvodaya Self-Help Movement,* describes the typical *shramadana,* or voluntary cooperative work project, as being "like a combination of road gang, town meeting, vaudeville show and revival service—and these many facets build people's trust and enjoyment of each other."

A. T. Ariyaratne, the movement's founder and leader over four decades, emphasizes that "the chief objective of Sarvodaya is personality awakening." This is a kind of consciousness raising that represents a start on the gradual path toward "the ultimate goal of Buddhism." "Every human being has the potential to attain supreme enlightenment," for which such personality development is an essential precondition. The root problem of poverty is seen as being a sense of personal and collective powerlessness. Personal awakening is interdependent with the awakening of one's local community, and both play a part in the awakening of one's nation and of the whole world. "We make the road and the road makes us" is an oft-quoted Sarvodaya slogan.

The necessary spiritual foundation for all-around social development is kept in the forefront through Sarvodaya's creative interpretation of traditional Buddhist teachings in forms that can be understood and experienced in social terms. Thus, the shared suffering of a community, the poverty, disease, exploitation, conflict, and stagnation, is explored together by the members as is also the individual suffering experienced by each one of them. But, crucially, this suffering is shown to have its origins in individual egocentricity, distrust, greed, and competitiveness, which demoralizes and divides the community and wastes its potential. In place of the corrupted traditional meaning of karma as *fate,* Dr. Ariyaratne emphasizes the original Buddhist teaching. "It is one's own doing that reacts on one's own self, so it is possible to divert the course of our lives," he explains, as reported by Macy in *Dharma and Development.* "[Once we understand that,] inactivity or lethargy suddenly transforms into activity leading to social and economic development."

Similarly, each of the practices includes the traditional Buddhist eightfold path amplified socially. A Sarvodaya trainer is quoted as follows: "Right Mindfulness—that means stay open and alert to the needs of the village.... Look to see what is needed—latrines, water, road.... Try to enter the minds of the people, to listen behind their words. Practice mindfulness in the shramadana camp: is the food enough? are people getting wet? are the tools in order? is anyone being exploited?"

The traditional Buddhist virtues and precepts provide guidelines for joint endeavor and a significant shared vocabulary for the open discussions that are the lifeblood of the movement. Thus dana, which had come to be identified specifically with giving alms to the monks and nuns, has been restored by Sarvodaya to its original, wider meaning of sharing time, skills, goods, and energy with one's community. Sarvodaya's practice of dana demonstrates the liberating power of sincere and spontaneous generosity to dissolve barriers between individuals and groups.

These inspirational guidelines are presented in symbols, slogans, posters, murals, songs, and stories, not as catechisms and commandments but as pointers and as tools of analysis. Above all, they are made fully meaningful through the practice of meditation, which is incorporated into Sarvodaya meetings and training sessions. The local knowledge and influence of the sangha and the respect in which it is held at all levels of society enable the monks to make an extensive and significant contribution to Sarvodaya. And, in turn, the movement's ideology and expectations help to revitalize the monastic order and its sense of vocation.

Since the late 1970s Sarvodaya, in part as a result of its success, has been subjected to new pressures. In particular, the increasing scale of its activities and the growth of its influence have made it more difficult for it to confine itself to relatively uncontroversial areas, raising questions about the future direction of the movement.

Detlef Kantowsky reports in *Sarvodaya: The Other Development* Dr. Ariyaratne's statement that "when some aspects of the established order conform with the righteous principles of the Movement, the Movement co-operates with those aspects. When they become unrighteous, in those areas the Movement does not co-operate and may even extend non-violent non-co-operation [though so far it has never done so]. In between these two extremes there is a vast area…in which establishments like the government and the Sarvodaya Movement can cooperate." Since there has been virtually a national consensus about the desirability of rural self-help schemes, Sarvodaya has been able to operate on politically neutral ground, cooperating with government policies and accommodating to the national and local power structure.

However, since the 1980s international investors have been getting involved with successive Sri Lankan governments and the moneyed elite in the creation of a competitive consumer society promoting a materialist and Westernized culture. This is characterized by urbanization and bureaucratization; the erosion of local economic, social, and political self-reliance; the progressive impoverishment of the rural population; and reliance on huge infrastructure projects (such as the Mahaveli hydro program) that emphasize centralized, top-down development and mainly benefit those already in control of land and marketing. These developments conflict dramatically with Sarvodaya values, and with a movement that has become a powerful national entity, rivaling the government in terms of its popularity, integrity, and the success of its programs. Between 1989 and 1993 Sarvodaya was subjected to an intensive government campaign of defamation and destabilization, ending only with the death of President Ranasinghe Premadasa. In his essay "Waking Everybody Up," Dr. Ariyaratne forthrightly declares that

> my dream is to get 16,000 villages in Sri Lanka to build a truly alternative system (without calling it alternative), and then one day declare our freedom. Instead of confronting a government, we confront the whole system. If the spiritual, moral and cultural value systems of the people are destroyed, then everything is lost, and more and more coercive instruments of the State—the police, the armed forces—are needed to bring about order.

The bitter, long-running civil war between Tamil separatists and a government representing the Sinhalese majority is one of several factors to postpone the realization of Aryatratne's "dream." In Joanna Macy's book, *Dharma and Development: Religion As a Resource in the Sarvodaya Self-Help Movement,* Ariyaratne places the movement in line with Buddhism's long history of religious pluralism. He states, "the Sarvodaya Movement, while originally inspired by the Buddhist tradition, is active throughout our multi-ethnic society, working with Hindu, Muslim and Christian communities and involving scores of thousands of Hindu, Muslim, and Christian co-workers. Our message of awakening transcends any effort to categorize it as the teaching of a particular creed." In his "Declaration on National Peace and Harmony," he blamed the conflict on the destruction of the Sri Lankan value system "founded on the ancient Hindu-Buddhist Code of Ethics," and he outspokenly maintained that the Sinhalese community had the "onus of responsibility" for redeeming the situation. Sarvodaya has established refugee camps for Tamil refugees, made strenuous attempts to mediate some solution to the conflict, and organized huge peace marches and rallies, attracting as many as 200,000 people at a time. Facing up to the terrorists, Ariyaratne declared in a speech at a 1986 peace walk ceremony: "Let it be known to those who bear arms that there are about two million members in Sarvodaya who are prepared to brave death anywhere at any time." Among Sarvodaya's opponents on this issue is Sinhala Heritage, an organization of Buddhist monks urging a tougher policy against the Tamils.

In 1999 Dr. Ariyaratne's son, Vinya, assmed the position of Executive Director of Sarvodaya. Future plans include a target of 10,000 fully developed Sarvodaya villages, together with a policy of decentralization down to grass-roots level. The training of village people is to be prioritized, to make rural communities less dependent on Sarvodaya workers. These changes had in part been prompted by a major financial crisis in 1995 due to a massive cut in donor funds. As Vinya Ariyaratne explained: "What had originally begun as a partnership based on dialogue had by the mid nineties become a sub-contractorship based on commands and sanctions." Essentially these plans amount to a continuation of Sarvodaya's previous mission—but more and better. There is no sign yet of a move toward a qualitatively different type of engagement at the urban level, with the self-help welfare perspective extended to the creation of alternative national institutions. The new programs for "Social, Economic, and Technological Empowerment" may, however, be a step in that direction. Nevertheless the fact that Sarvodaya has been able to retain its integrity and orientation, and continue its expansion, over five decades in the face of major difficulties is itself a remarkable achievement.

There are also new plans to promote a global network, establishing links with international organizations and agencies. In fact Sarvodaya movements have existed for some years in several Western countries, and Sarvodaya Shramadana International was founded in 1981. Together with the "right livelihood" initiatives to be examined later, the Sarvodaya movement offers a valuable contribution to a strategy for building in the West a radical culture of awakening.

Thailand

In Thailand there are a number of projects and networks of Buddhist-inspired organizations that have much the same outlook and methods as Sarvodaya. They are, however, more fragmented and limited in scale of achievement. In particular, there are a number of rural cooperative self-help projects, such as rice banks and buffalo banks, initiated by members of the *sangha*.

A wide and diverse range of projects owes much to the energies and talents of Sulak Sivaraksa, the country's best-known Buddhist intellectual and social critic. A tireless organizer, publicist, orator, and thinker, he has over a hundred books to his credit, and has founded a whole raft of national and international organizations. These address issues of peace, social justice, and civil and human rights, and often work with marginal peoples—the rural poor, slum dwellers, disadvantaged women, and the war ravaged. Others support Dharmicly inspired cultural, educational, and artistic interests. The Asian Cultural Forum on Development (ACFOD), an international and interreligious network of organizations that work for the empowerment of the rural and urban poor, illustrates Sulak's concern to build networks of people within Thailand, between Thailand and other countries, and among different religious traditions and organizations. The long-established Thai Inter-Religious Commission on Development and the International Network of Engaged Buddhists, together with two of Sulak's more recent initiatives—the Alternatives to Consumerism Network and the Spirit in Education Movement—are promoted and publicized by the Bangkok magazine *Seeds of Peace.*

Sulak's Buddhism, which owes much to his mentor, Ajahn Buddhadasa (below), is what Sulak has called "Buddhism with a small *b.*" It is a core Buddhism stripped of the acculturations of the civil religion that he associates with Thai chauvinism. And it is a personally transformative Buddhism that Sulak believes has much in common with the essentials of the other great world religions. At the same time, Sulak is well embedded in Siamese culture and traditions, which he believes to be an indispensable resource and support in the work for radical change. In this he exemplifies the *radical conservatism* found in many forms of socially engaged Buddhism, which seeks to foster all that is best in traditional culture, particularly the sense of community and ethnic identity. Change has to be authentic and organic in character—from the roots—rather than imposed, mechanistic, and manipulative. The old way of doing things, or some adaptation or evolution of it, may still be the best way.

Sulak and his associates work for a Buddhist-inspired economic and social development that is opposed to the dominant Western model of Third World development. He associates the latter with a widening gap between rich and poor, landlessness, environmental degradation, the growing power of transnational corporations, the militarization of society, and an insidious Western intellectual and cultural imperialism. He argues for locally based democracy, appropriate Asian social institutions and national self-reliance, and refers approvingly to Gandhi's network of "village republics" and philosopher and economist E. F. Schumacher's "Buddhist economics."

Another influential—and radical conservative—figure in Thai engaged Buddhism was Ajahn Buddhadasa (1906–1993). He was concerned at the crisis in traditional Thai Buddhism, which is being eroded and devitalized by Western secularism, leaving an increasingly empty shell of public and national ceremony combined with quasi-magical ritual designed to bring personal good fortune. In contrast to traditional doctrinal and prescriptive teaching, Buddhadasa's Dharma teaching is experientially and meditatively based. It draws freely upon Mahayana Buddhism as well as upon Theravada and holds that all religions are ultimately and fundamentally the same.

Buddhadasa offered a vision of *Dharmic socialism*, which contrasts both with "vengeful" and "angry" dogmatic Marxist socialism, on the one hand, and, on the other, with what he saw as the selfishness and irresponsibility of individualism and liberal democracy (and the downright immorality of capitalism). Socialism here simply means "living for the benefit of society, not for the individual benefit of each person"; politics is not about power but about morality.

We encountered in chapter 5 Buddhadasa's belief in the need for "enlightened dictators" in order to buttress a Dharmic socialist society against the root selfishness of the individual. How to negotiate this root selfishness has been a pervasive question also in Western political theory. It seems apparent that men and women have felt insufficiently at peace and secure within themselves as to be able to sustain an equitable commonwealth. So, how can we do this without resorting to dogmatic ideology, mass movements, and authoritarian saviors, on the one hand, or the discipline (and gratification) of market capitalism and a questionable species of democracy on the other? Buddhadasa evidently felt that the Dharma in Dharmic Socialism might not provide sufficient stabilization for a sufficient number of citizens—hence the need for "Dictatorial Dharmic Socialism." Although we may not accept Buddhadasa's solution, it is important that he has raised this perennial problem within the context of engaged Buddhism. Unfortunately it has gone virtually unrecognized—apart from some special pleading on Buddhadasa's behalf that his argument for benevolent despotism be included in the radical interpretation of engaged Buddhism.

Burma

In 1988 the people of Burma rose in spontaneous revolt against twenty-six years of political repression and economic decline. Aung San Suu Kyi, the daughter of General Aung San, who had liberated Burma from colonialism, joined in and helped form the National League for Democracy. Suu Kyi quickly emerged as an articulate and effective leader, and the League won a colossal election victory in 1990. However, the military junta refused to acknowledge defeat, instituted one of the most brutally repressive regimes in the world, and confined Suu Kyi to house arrest for six years.

In the face of state terrorism Suu Kyi and her associates have been extraordinarily steadfast and successful in sustaining the opposition. They have maintained a nonviolent stance, refusing to admit to any hatred and anger toward their oppressors, and have been open to the possibility of any negotiated settlement that did not compromise their principles. Suu Kyi herself has faced down rifles on more than one occasion. And the remarkable Deputy Chairman of the League, U Tin U, is a former soldier who had been imprisoned for seven years for his part in earlier democracy struggles and who subsequently spent two years as a monk. He later spent another nine years in solitary confinement, where he shared with his jailers the small amounts of food brought in by his wife. Again and again Suu Kyi and her comrades have testified to the crucial importance of their Dharma practice in sustaining them in the face of repeated discouragements.

Cambodia

Torn apart in the killing fields of civil war and devastated by extensive U.S. air attacks and by the genocide that followed the Khmer Rouge takeover, Cambodia is now undergoing a slow recovery, amid material hardship, political faction fighting—and nearly 3 million land mines. Maha Ghosanada, Supreme Patriarch of Cambodian Buddhism and cofounder of the Inter-Religious Mission for Peace in Cambodia, has done much to introduce and inspire several initiatives for Buddhist social engagement. The Dhammayietra peace marches are the most inspiring and visible manifestation of this endeavor. Beginning in 1992, these walks, usually lasting several weeks, through dangerous, heavily mined countryside, have been maintained and developed by the newly emergent people's movements. Led by Maha Ghosananda and the sangha, they provide a compassionate space that is free of violence and partisan politics.

Vietnam and Thich Nhat Hanh

In the 1960s South Vietnam endured a long and bloody struggle between the communist National Liberation Front and the American-backed Saigon government. The Unified Buddhist Church and the Buddhist Struggle Movement inspired a historic campaign of mass nonviolence for a third way that could bring an end to the war and establish a neutral Vietnam. The Buddhists sought allies in people of other faiths and beliefs who were willing to work for peace and independence, and, in particular, large numbers of Catholics made common cause. The movement for peace was linked with action for social justice and social revolution. Young people went into the country to work alongside the peasants on rural development projects, and a number of unions and other organizations were formed that also embraced urban workers, women, youth, and students. An extensive antiwar literature flourished, of poetry, satire, song, and prayer.

This movement would have succeeded perhaps, had it not been for an American-inspired coup. It remains as a truly historic example of activist spirituality, ranking with Gandhi's satyagraha movement and Martin Luther King's civil rights movement, but the more remarkable in that it was not led by a single charismatic leader. Increasingly prominent, however, was a monk named Thich Nhat Hanh, who in 1966 embarked on an influential speaking tour of nineteen countries to put forward the Buddhist case for peace in Vietnam.

After the tour, Thich Nhat Hanh was unable to return home for fear of his life and had to go into exile in France with a few associates. In 1982 he established the Plum Village retreat center and went on to develop a worldwide peace movement. Next to the Dalai Lama he is now the most influential figure in engaged Buddhism, with over sixty books to his credit. By 1998 some seventy-five *dharmacharyas* (monastic and lay Dharma teachers) had been ordained into the Tiep Hien Order (the Order of Interbeing), committing themselves to practicing the Order's fourteen precepts of engaged Buddhism and mindfulness training (see chapter 11), and at least sixty "mindfulness days" a year. There are now some three hundred sanghas worldwide, and the Maple Forest Monastery and Green Mountain Dharma Center have been established in Vermont for monastic and lay practitioners.

Central to Thich Nhat Hanh's teaching is mindfulness—bare awareness—in everyday life. Engaged Buddhism is ultimately about the way we each live our lives. Through mindfulness practice we cultivate insight into interbeing (the nonseparate self).

Thich Nhat Hanh's Community of Interbeing is enjoined to work to end war and to achieve social justice, but "without taking sides." Thus, Nhat Hanh responded to the 1991 Persian Gulf War as follows, from *Love in Action: Writings on Non-Violent Social Change*:

> The night I heard President Bush give the order to attack Iraq, I could not sleep. I was angry and overwhelmed.... But after breathing consciously and looking deeply, I saw myself as President Bush.... In our collective consciousness there are some seeds of non-violence, and President Bush did begin with sanctions. But we did not support and encourage him enough, so he switched to a more violent way. We cannot blame only him. The president acted the way he did because we acted the way we did.

While the activities of the members of the Community of Interbeing cover the whole spectrum of engaged Buddhism, such engagement appears, however, to be isolated to individuals and local *sanghas*, with a relatively small number involved specifically in social action. David Brazier, leader of the Amida Community for engaged Buddhism, in the United Kingdom, and formerly a member of the Order of Interbeing, charges in *The New Buddhism* that "few white supporters—a few areas of the USA excepted—have any real enthusiasm for engaged Buddhism. Rather, what many want is a form of religion that teaches mindfulness and gentleness in daily life and offers them freedom from stress and anxiety." Patricia Hunt-Perry and Lyn Fine report in "All Buddhism Is Engaged: Thich Nhat Hanh and the Order of Interbeing" the results of a survey in which some critics complain that Thich Nhat Hanh

> is not engaged enough with Buddhist collective action in the public arena; or that he does not address fundamental issues of class and power, institutional and structural violence. Several people we heard from and interviewed suggested (and lamented) what they see as a shift in emphasis in Thich Nhat Hanh's teachings in the later 1990s from the more politically engaged and collective Buddhist activism of the 1960s in Vietnam to a more individual- and sangha-based practice in the West. The assumption that individual transformation and even small sanghas functioning as base communities can effect real social transformation is naive and idealistic, according to some critics.

The survey revealed that there are many former activists who now "focused less on social activism, as traditionally defined, and more on 'practicing mindfulness in daily life.'"

Thich Nhat Hanh has also been criticized for his lack of emphasis on traditional, intensive practice for lay supporters and his lack of concern with deep insight. On the other hand, it can be argued that these limitations are also strengths if seen as a contribution to broadening the overall field of engaged Buddhism. In place of a heavy and rather exclusive focus on sitting meditation, Thich Nhat Hanh offers a training that is accessible and family orientated and weaves a variety of individual and group practices into daily life—not only mindfulness per se but also walking meditation, *gathas* (short verses for sustaining everyday mindfulness), bowing, reconciliation and atonement practices, guided and "loving-kindness meditations, mantra chanting—and "hugging meditation." Moreover the emphasis on individual and collective mindfulness and nonpartisanship can offer a valuable counter to the seductive pull of conventional activism, where it is all too easy to lose one's balance.

Tibet and the Dalai Lama

The Dalai Lama has become not only the world's best-known—and much loved—Buddhist, but also the most prominent exemplar of a Buddhism that is socially engaged. Out of the Tibetan response to the Chinese occupation of their homeland there have evolved universal social principles, all of which originate from Mahayana philosophy.

The overarching principle is that of compassionate and universal *responsibility* as a duty laid on all of us by the fact of being human. However, as the Dalai Lama wrote in the foreword to the first edition of this book: "The fundamental aim of Buddhist practice, to avoid harming others, and if possible to help them, will not be fully achieved simply by thinking about it."

Secondly, there is the principle of nonviolence and love of one's enemies. This does not, however, imply passivity. "For example, if you are genuinely a humble and honest person and *act* that way, some people may take advantage of you," explains the Dalai Lama in an interview with Buddhist scholar José Cabezón. "So in such a situation it may be necessary to react. But we should react without bad feelings. Deep down, tolerance, compassion and patience must still be present."

Thirdly, all human beings are fundamentally equal, since all have buddha nature. All have the potential to be fully human. Therein lies the Buddhist basis for human rights.

Fourthly, contemporary society is increasingly characterized by interdependence at every level. Hence there is a need for worldwide cooperation. But at the same time it is important to celebrate and appreciate the value of diversity. As the Dalai Lama explains in *Ocean of Wisdom*:

Deep down we must have real affection for each other; a clear realization or recognition of our shared human status. At the same time we must openly accept all ideologies and systems as means of solving humanity's problems. One country, one ideology, one system is not sufficient. It is helpful to have a variety of different approaches on the basis of a deep feeling of the basic sameness of humanity.

Fifthly, like Ajahn Buddhdasa, Thich Nhat Hanh, and many other engaged Buddhists, the Dalai Lama believes in the fundamental unity of all religions and the need for pluralism. "In the past centuries there have been many learned teachers who have laid down various paths to show the Truth," he writes in a 1967 newsletter. "Among these Buddhism is one, and according to it my opinion is that, except for the differences in the names and forms of the various religions, the ultimate truth is the same."

Sixthly, there is a recognition of the potential of science, technology, and other material achievements of modernity to relieve much suffering. However, the Dalai Lama notes in *Universal Responsibility and the Good Heart* that "without inner peace material things alone are not sufficient…. There is something lacking. Therefore, the only way is to combine the two."

Finally, the Dalai Lama maintains that the truth will always eventually prevail over all obstacles. Nevertheless, he clearly believes that effort is required to effectively manifest it. Here is his prescription for the ultimate achievement of the engaged Buddhist agenda, from the 1982 book *Collected Statements, Interviews and Articles:*

> We need human qualities, such as moral scruples, compassion and humility. In recognition of human frailty and weakness, these qualities are only accessible through forceful individual development in a conducive social milieu, so that a more human world will come into being as an ultimate goal. A dynamic revolution is deemed crucial for instigating a political culture founded on moral ethics.

Japan and the Soka Gakkai

For Japan, defeat in the Second World War brought despair and disillusionment and a search for new values and orientations. Japanese Buddhism was deeply involved in this process, which has some similarities with the postcolonial modernizing developments in Theravada Buddhism in Southeast Asia. In chapter 10, I referred to the humanist and pacifist Zen of intellectuals and activists such as Hisamatsu Shin'ichi and Ichikawa Hakugen. The latter wrote of a *Buddhist socialism* rooted in self-emptiness and hence imbued with a humble and open spirit cleansed of the will to power and working toward a cooperative commonwealth. Today something of this tenuous tradition is to be found in the small but lively INEB-Japan (the Japanese branch of the International Network of Engaged Buddhists).

The above developments are overshadowed, however, by the postwar development of the "new religions." These are Buddhist lay organizations that, with some 15 percent of the population in membership, are among the most striking manifestations of Buddhist activism in the world today.

Although noteworthy variations exist among the new Buddhist movements, most of them share certain characteristics, which are especially marked in the case of the largest, the Soka Gakkai (with about 9 million members in Japan and some 3 million more in 162 other countries). All offer strong, simple doctrines and practices of ready appeal. Soka Gakkai, socially and psychologically, has much in common with Christian evangelical fundamentalism, even linking religious faith with entrepreneurial success. They tend to be mass, ideologically driven movements with strong charismatic leaders at all levels of their hierarchies. They generally require an exclusive commitment from their loyal and dedicated adherents. One scholar has likened them to "a nation within a nation," with their own collective self-identity. They are characterized by a paternalistic, "one big family" type of Asian organization, and their members feel they belong to a caring and compassionate movement. Co-counseling in small groups *(hoza)* is a feature of many (including Soka Gakkai). The following is from a brochure published by Rissho Kosei-kai, the second largest new Buddhist movement, with 6.5 million members in Japan and worldwide:

> In a *hoza* session, a group sits in a circle with a leader who plays the role of advisor, creating a warm, intimate atmosphere for open discussion. The spectrum of problems and questions raised at *hoza* ranges from personal worries at home or work, through matters of human relationships, to issues of religion and ethics. One member describes his or her problem and the others listen with compassion, seeking to understand the speaker's situation and emotional state. When the member with the problem feels that it has been thoroughly understood and that the sufferings described have been shared by all, the speaker's heart is opened to the others and he or she becomes awakened to mistaken thoughts or deeds. Such honest speaking helps to purify the speaker in a healing process, thus manifesting the speaker's spirituality.

All the new Buddhist movements are involved in a wide range of activities, particularly extensive in the case of the Soka Gakkai, which include education, peace activism, environmental concerns, and cultural development. Thus Soka Gakkai sponsors a major political party, a large university, two art museums, and several publishing houses and mass circulation newspapers. Typically, concern is not with radical social change but rather with morally "toning up" society, with a leaning to social democratic welfarism. Certainly, however, Soka Gakkai's long-term perspective is ambitious, if vague. Its leader, Ikeda Daisaku, is quoted in Edward Norbeck's *Religion and Society in Modern Japan,* declaring: "The purpose of the Soka Gakkai lies in the attainment of *kosen rufu,* the propagation of True Buddhism throughout the country, and further to the entire world.... Religion should be the basis of all cultural activities. In a sense the Soka Gakkai aims at an unprecedented flowering of culture, a Third Civilization." (*Third Civilization* refers here to a fusion of the best in capitalism and socialism.)

Most of these movements proclaim the superiority of their own beliefs over all others, but do acknowledge the value to be found in other religions. Rissho Kosei-kai, for example, cooperates directly with other religious bodies in a variety of areas. Not so Soka Gakkai, which is uncompromisingly dogmatic in its righteousness. It has, however, mellowed since the zenith of its proselytizing zeal in the 1970s, and now works together with a wide range of nonreligious bodies, including the United Nations, in strictly secular and social programs.

Soka Gakkai is an extreme example of the peculiarly Japanese Nichiren Buddhist tradition that has inspired most of these movements. Nichiren, a poor fisherman's son, founded this messianic sect in 1253, proclaiming that self-transcendence could be brought about only by the devotional chanting of a prescribed mantra. From the beginning the Nichiren sect was marked by an intolerant and missionary dogmatism, and is differentiated from other Buddhist schools by what the eminent scholar Edward Conze described as "its nationalistic, pugnacious, and intolerant attitude." He concluded that "it is somewhat doubtful whether it belongs to the history of Buddhism at all." Similarly, in his Introduction to the anthology *Engaged Buddhism: Buddhist Liberation Movements in Asia,* editor Christopher Queen noted that the inclusion of a chapter on the Nichiren offshoot Soka Gakkai "has raised objections." These included "its intolerance of other Buddhist sects," "its aggressive missionary outreach," its personality cult of its leader Daisaku Ikeda, and its grandiose, publicity-grabbing projects.

Soka Gakkai is certainly one of the world's most controversial Buddhist organizations, and this applies, with less intensity, to some of its international affiliates. It continues to be dogged by accusations of power seeking, corruption, and cultic exploitation. The Soka Gakkai sponsors the only explicitly Buddhist political party in the world, and many observers feel that this may be more a liability than an advantage for engaged Buddhist movements worldwide. Komeito, the political party established by the Soka Gakkai in 1964, dissolved in 1994 as part of the reorganization among Japanese opposition parties but was reformed in 1998 as the New Komeito. After winning a record 7.8 million votes in a general election, it became in 1999 a junior partner in the Liberal Democratic government and pledged to work for a new anticorruption law, equal rights for women, and stronger welfare and environmental legislation.

Daniel Metraux, a longtime Western authority on the Soka Gakkai, has offered the following harsh conclusion:

> The Gakkai's strong adherence to its own doctrines and worldview is both a source of its strength and a weakness. Its anchor is its big following and strong leadership, but its exclusivism makes it a suspect organization to most Japanese, who distrust its motives. This distrust dooms most Soka Gakkai attempts to influence Japanese society and minimizes its influence on the national scene.

Notwithstanding their peculiarly Japanese character many of the new Buddhist movements have attracted considerable numbers of adherents in North

America and Europe. For these are missionary movements that offer a reassuring belongingness identity and a belief system beyond question, in contrast to the awareness identity and the "living in doubt and uncertainty" of more open Buddhist formations.

Chapter 16

ENGAGED BUDDHISM IN THE WEST

The United States

A STRONG, DIVERSE, and articulate socially engaged Buddhism exits in the West only in the United States. This reflects the sense of a nationwide Buddhist community (or at least a European American one) that is broader than the different traditions and centers, and that finds a voice in several influential magazines and in various occasional gatherings that transcend sectarian differences. In many parts of this community, but particularly in the Zen and Vipassana centers, there is a groundswell, a predisposition, in favor of social and environmental engagement.

The activist stance is invariably a radical, left-wing one, manifested in peacework, environmental protest, and work for social justice and human rights. The organizational picture is generally one of local and statewide initiatives, open and nondogmatic, sometimes linked through networks, and with a striking absence of the kind charismatic leaders found in Asia. With respect to terminal illness, HIV/AIDS, and support for the 2 million inmates of America's prison gulag, there is a particularly wide range of Buddhist caregiving services and networks, whether autonomous or supported by centers in the different traditions.

The Buddhist Peace Fellowship

Many individual activists from different traditions network through the Buddhist Peace Fellowship (BPF), an organization that facilitates individual and group social engagement in the United States and Asia and often works together with the International Network of Engaged Buddhists (INEB). The BPF is the largest and most effective of the engaged Buddhist networks. Founded in 1978, it is a loose association of some 7,000 members organized mainly in autonomous local chapters. With its outstanding quarterly journal, *Turning Wheel,* it has been indispensable in establishing socially engaged Buddhism as a legitimate and well articulated presence, not only in the American Buddhist community but world-wide. However, one of its limitations appears to be its failure to develop an adequate, in-depth social analysis to underpin its work. Another is the absence of a unifying strategy for social change and the leadership to implement it. Both problems are evident in the wider field of engaged Buddhism, reflected in a fragmentation of concerns and activities, short-term perspectives, and a tendency to see Buddhist practice as little more than an adjunct to conventional secular activism.

A noteworthy support network is the BPF's "Buddhist Alliance for Social Engagement" (BASE). Initiated in 1995, this alliance operates in various locations and forms, usually through successive programs. The Buddhist activists each work on a specific project (ranging from caring for the dying to promoting community gardens) but form a closely knit learning and support group. Each has an experienced mentor, and all come together at frequent intervals for sharing experience and for mentor guidance in balancing the inner and outer work.

The Buddhist Peace Fellowship's commitment to social activism is evident in the following goals articulated in its mission statement:

1. To make clear public witness to Buddhist practice and interdependence as a way of peace and protection of all beings;
2. To raise peace, environmental, feminist, and social justice concerns among North American Buddhists;
3. To bring a Buddhist perspective of nonduality to contemporary social action and environmental movements;
4. To encourage the practice of nonviolence based upon the rich resources of traditional Buddhist and Western spiritual teachings;
5. To offer avenues for dialogue and exchange among the diverse North American and world *sangha*s.

Bernie Glassman and the Peacemaker Order

Beyond the Buddhist Peace Fellowship, but with the same perspectives, are the many projects for social engagement founded by Bernard Tetsugen Glassman. A tireless, challenging, and controversial innovator, Glassman received Dharma transmission from Taizan Maezumi and is lineage-holder of the White Plum (Soto) Zen sangha.

A former physicist with strong business acumen, Glassman's first project was the Greyston bakery in Yonkers, an economically deprived district in New York State. The aim was to enable unemployed people to learn livelihood skills— and also to provide compassion and awareness practice for his Zen students. Housing for the homeless followed, together with numerous other social service projects.

Glassman also began doing "Street Retreats" in which he took his students with him to live for a week "on retreat" on the streets with the inner-city homeless. Subsequently he organized a meditation pilgrimage and vigil at Auschwitz, and it was out of this that his most ambitious project has emerged—the Peacemaker Order.

The Peacemaker Order was founded on three basic tenets. The first is not knowing, letting go of fixed ideas. The second is bearing witness, totally immersing oneself in the situation one is involved in. And the third is healing oneself and others out of the ingredients that arise from bearing witness. One of the tools of the Order is the "plunge"—plunging into a situation that is completely unfamiliar and commonly evokes fear. The initial members of the Zen Peacemaker Order, together with those forming the wider Interfaith Peacemaker Assembly (who are not Zen practitioners) exemplify different ways of "taking the plunge": working with terminally ill people, in prisons, with ethnic minorities in the inner city, with Native Americans, and on peace and environmental issues.

It is intended that the Order and the wider Assembly will evolve as a network of villages, both physical and "virtual." This wider peacemaker community will be based on the four principles that the last World Congress of Religions could agree upon: commitment to a culture of nonviolence; a just economic order; tolerance and a life based on truthfulness; and equal rights and partnership between men and women.

Glassman has a long-term vision of a global spiritual network that goes beyond institutional religion. He explains in *Shambhala Sun*'s feature "Zen on the Street": "Groups in many different traditions are coming from the same basic place of the oneness of life, the interconnectedness of life, and the place of not knowing. I can see this happening all over the place, and I see us spinning together a web of support. That's what I envision."

Identity Politics

Another important development in engaged Buddhism is the pioneering work that has occurred over the past few decades in the area of *identity politics*—how we perceive ourselves and others in terms of gender, ethnicity, and sexual preference. This certainly lies at the radical end of our spectrum of engagement, but differs from other kinds in that it lies mainly within the Buddhist community itself. The subject of identity politics has inspired a penetrating inquiry not only about Dharmic lifestyle, but also about issues of sexism, racism, and homophobia, in the first place within Buddhism itself. And, more positively, this movement is exploring the emancipatory potential of Buddhism to relieve the suffering arising from these experiences.

Probably the single most significant achievement of the Buddhism of modernity has been, in Asia, to challenge the patriarchal tradition, and, in the West, to have already achieved so much toward sweeping it away completely. There are now a number of women teachers and writers of distinction. And in some sanghas women are beginning to make practice and organization less "top-down" and more relational. Although very much an established part of engaged Buddhism, Buddhist feminism has evolved as a substantial field in its own right, with a considerable literature. Regretfully, to afford it the treatment that it deserves would have enlarged this book beyond what is practicable.

An important area of identity politics involves people who identify themselves as gay, and who wish to practice Buddhism in the conscious acceptance of this, both in themselves and by others. Here *gayness* refers to a distinguishing self-identity, as compared to homosexuality as no more than same-sex genital activity. A sense of gay community has resulted in a deepening awareness of a personal and group woundedness, amounting in extreme cases to guilt and even self-hatred. Here, then, is a specific form of suffering previously barely acknowledged. How is the Dharma to be understood, practiced, and internalized as a liberation from this suffering? A variety of gay Buddhist groups have come into being to work through these questions together.

Other areas in which identity politics needs to be further addressed in the United States are race and economic class. American Buddhism is split into two sectors. On the one hand are the Zen, Vipassana, and Tibetan groups whose membership (if not leadership) consists almost entirely of educated, middle-class European Americans. On the other hand—and with very little intercommunication—are the groups founded by Asian immigrants, providing cultural as much as religious support. In between, and largely left out, are the many million African Americans and Latin Americans. Racial discrimination (usually unconscious) is compounded by the less widely recognized discrimination by social class. In the strongly meditation-based European American sector, not only do you have to have the money and leisure to sustain an optimum practice, you also need to have the assertiveness and confidence to handle a highly individualistic social culture that is comparatively lacking in inclusive community support.

Soka Gakkai International

Here the American affiliate of Soka Gakkai International (SGI-USA) plays a uniquely important role. Not only is it by far the largest Buddhist group in the United States, claiming 330,000 members, it has also attracted a greater diversity of races and classes than any other Buddhist organization, and has made a strong, explicit commitment to promote diversity. (The Jodo-Shinshu Buddhist Churches of America, or "Pure Land Buddhism," is the second largest, incidentally.)

The various international satellites of the Soka Gakkai are formally autonomous bodies, although Ikeda Daisaku remains the global movement's spiritual leader, teacher, and spokesman. These organizations do not differ in any major respect from the Japanese parent body, other than in their more modest scale of operations.

Sandy McIntosh, a former SGI-USA member, offers the following explanation for the Soka Gakkai's success in the United States in "An Insider's View of Nichiren Shoshu":

> To an observer, the practices of Soka Gakkai seem tailor-made for the American fast-food, instant wish-fulfillment culture. You can chant for money, for a better job, for love, for any of the 108 human desires represented by the prayer beads which members hold as they chant. An observer would note that Soka Gakkai practitioners spend far more time in discussion meetings and other group activities than they do in disciplined contemplation or consultation with Buddhist teachers. Because its emphasis falls on action rather than view, Soka Gakkai appeals to a broad range of Americans with varying educational backgrounds, even as it may alienate those who enjoy meditative Buddhist traditions.... The appeal [of materialism] attracts many Americans living in the inner cities who are desperate for a way to improve their lives. For these people who know little material prosperity, the more conventional Buddhist view—that enlightenment is encouraged by abandoning all attachment to material things—is virtually senseless.

David Chappell, a scholar specializing in engaged Buddhism, offers a contrasting assessment in "Racial Diversity in the Soka Gakkai":

> [SGI-USA's] primary mediums of work are twofold: personal transformation through religious practice and educational programs. The political fight for equal rights and economic justice, or practical relief for the

dying, homeless, or sick, is encouraged among its members but is not institutionalized within SGI-USA. It is fair to say in 1998 however that…Soka Gakkai in America has committed more resources, has impacted more lives, and has created more substantial institutions to implement programs for social and cultural improvement than any other American Buddhist organization.

Soka Gakkai International currently sponsors two major transnational projects: "Abolition 2000" (which collected 13 million signatures to a petition for the abolition of nuclear weapons), and the Earth Charter (concerned with the eradication of poverty, social justice and a culture of peace, as well as ecological sustainability).

Britain—and Right Livelihood

Prominent in British Buddhism are three relatively large movements—the Friends of the Western Buddhist Order (FWBO), with some 2,500 members; SGI-UK, with an estimated 5,000; and the New Kadampa Tradition, with approximately 4,000. The first two are variously engaged socially. The pattern of SGI-UK activity is similar to that of the Soka Gakkai elsewhere. The main contribution of the FWBO is to offer a British-grown model of right livelihood enterprise whose wider relevance merits closer attention.

The engaged Buddhist scene in Britain has all the features with which readers will by now have become familiar. The radical activism wing is represented by the U.K. Network of Engaged Buddhists, which was founded in 1983, and inspired by the American Buddhist Peace Fellowship. Its membership is currently less than two hundred, and its main activity is to publish a quarterly magazine, *Indra's Net*. Larger, and growing, is the Amida Community, led by David Brazier and his wife, Caroline. Amida has for some years offered psychotherapy training programs, but in 1999 became involved in humanitarian outreach to the Balkans and Africa. More recently Amida has moved into direct action initiatives, and was involved in street demonstrations against the war in Afghanistan. In 2002 Amida began offering a part-time, distance-learning, field-based course in "Fully Engaged Buddhism."

There are a variety of social and environmental projects within the United Kingdom, most notabley those sponsored by Samye Ling, the Tibetan center in Scotland. The Tibetan Buddhist Rigpa organization and the Buddhist Hospice Trust offer care to the terminally ill, and Angulimala and the Phoenix Trust have well-developed support services for prison inmates. Educationally there is the Dharma School in Brighton and the Sharpham College for Buddhist Studies in

Devon. There are also several Buddhist psychotherapy initiatives. In short, engaged Buddhism in Britain is diverse, well-rooted—and fragmented.

One of the most important developments in engaged Buddhism in the West lies in its exploration of right livelihood. Right livelihood, of course, has been emphasized from the very beginning in the scriptures, though limited to listing occupations considered "unwholesome" (like arms trading and drug dealing). Claude Whitmyer, editor of *Mindfulness and Meaningful Work: Explorations in Right Livelihood,* the only substantial contemporary work on the subject, has questioned the very possibility of right livelihood, given "the complexities of life in the modern world," especially with regard to "the long term consequences of our work."

One response is to establish independent businesses run according to Buddhist ethical principles. Several such enterprises have been started as adjuncts to Buddhist centers, not least to provide them with a steady source of income. A more ambitious response lies in enterprises designed, among other things, to prefigure an entire and radically different future society (as with Glassman's network of Greyston Mandala businesses, and Sarvodaya—the biggest right livelihood enterprise of all). In the West, however, it is the Friends of the Western Buddhist Order's cooperative movement that has been particularly well conceived and enduring.

The Western Buddhist Order was founded in Britain in 1967 by a talented Buddhist innovator known as Sangharakshita (born Dennis Lingwood). In practice and belief it is a skilful blend of traditional ingredients plus some idiosyncratic additions supplied by the founder. Order members are men and women, single, married, or living in celibacy, some with full-time jobs and others working wholly for the FWBO. Many live in residential communities, usually near an FWBO urban center. The movement is now a worldwide organization of centers, communities, and right livelihood businesses. Outside Britain the FWBO is strongest in India, where it is known as Trailokya Bauddha Mahasangha Sahayak Gana (TBMSG), and where, funded by the U.K.-based Karuna Trust, it works to enable some of India's poorest people to achieve educational and economic self-reliance.

Right livelihood criteria for the FWBO are that a job be ethical, meaningful, useful, and beneficial—both for society and for the individual's spiritual growth. If at all possible the work should be carried out with like-minded co-workers who can inspire and support one another. There are now many successful FWBO enterprises not only in Britain but also in the United States, India, Germany, and elsewhere. One of the biggest businesses is Windhorse Trading in Cambridge (England), which runs a wholesale and retail gift business. It has been listed as one of the hundred fastest-growing companies in Britain, with 1996 sales worth

US$60 million. The FWBO businesses are worker cooperatives in which members have an equal stake and equal voting rights, and receive a basic living wage with the option of requesting a raise to meet any special needs. Martin Baumann, in "The Application of Buddhist Right Livelihood in the Friends of the Western Buddhist Order," describes the FWBO's businesses, together with its outreach centers and residential communities, as major contributors to achieving its goal of creating a "new society" radically different from the present one, which it views as detrimental to human growth.

Buddhist Humanism

In a valuable paper entitled "Political Values for an Age of Scarcity: Buddhist Politics," political scientist William Ophuls points out that the principle of equality that recognizes the autonomy, uniqueness, and potential of each person should not be confused with the mass egalitarianism that often substitutes for it. False egalitarianism "tends to reduce the social diversity that fosters genuine individuality and at the same time throws people into conflict as everyone tries to climb to the top of the same pole." Therefore, a Buddhist humanism seeks to support a social climate that encourages individuals to have confidence enough to enjoy just being who they are, doing what needs to be done, and ripening their awareness of the richness of life—instead of feeling driven to prove they are the equals of others either through aggressive and competitive behavior or through sinking into the consoling security of a mass mediocrity.

Humanistic engaged Buddhism supports a whole raft of interrelated social values, as is evident in the survey of engaged Buddhism worldwide presented in this and the preceding chapter. There is an emphasis on individual responsibility and personal development as the means of sustaining local and community empowerment and self-reliance, in contrast to both the top-down bureaucratic functionalism of modernity and the hierarchical paternalism of tradition.

In engaged Buddhism, grass-roots democracy has the character of the "radical conservatism" mentioned previously, in that while it seeks radical change, it at the same time works to strengthen the sense of community and the values and ethnic identity of traditional cultures. Rather than forcing or imposing change, a humanistic engaged Buddhism knows that change must emerge and establish itself in an authentic and organic manner. Traditional methods are often employed or adapted as the best approach. There is a particular concern to pioneer a third way of social and cultural development alternative to either Western capitalist-style "development" or the traditional paternalism.

These social values have roots in the West, in the long and complex tradition of libertarian socialism, syndicalism, and anarchism. This has now crystallized into a whole "green" political theory, first popularized by E. F. Schumacher, with his "small is beautiful" theory of "Buddhist economics." Sallie King, in her Conclusion to *Engaged Buddhism: Buddhist Liberation Movements in Asia* notes that a similar "green" social and political theory—an "environmentally friendly, people-friendly politics and economics"—is emerging in Asian Buddhism.

These "green" and "radical conservative" perspectives together amount to a set of coherent and common political values found in the engaged Buddhist mainstream worldwide.

Chapter 17

THE GROUNDING
OF SOCIALLY ENGAGED BUDDHISM

Validation

AS IS EVIDENT from the four noble truths and its other fundamental
scriptures, Buddhism is primarily a religion of personal transcendence of the ordinary human condition—a religion of salvation. It has been and
still is commonly regarded as "other worldly." Some explanation is therefore
called for as to how a religious philosophy with this soteriological preoccupation
translates into social engagement, and in what forms. It also begs the question
of the relationship between enlightenment and engagement. This is a necessary
undertaking even if we were to argue that traditional Buddhism *was* substantially
engaged.

The rationale for the Buddhist social theory adopted in this book will already
be evident. I have taken the essentials of the Buddhist diagnosis of the existential predicament of the person, and most particularly the sense of lack, or the root
anxiety, and its consequences. I have then drawn upon phenomenological social
theory to explain how the three fires of acquisitiveness, aggressiveness, and existential ignorance (and their many variants) have driven human history, have
shaped social structures and institutions, and have been expressed in cultural
norms. And just as the Buddhist diagnosis of the root human condition carries
within it the remedy, so does the societal extension of this diagnosis carry the liberative goal of a radical social culture of awakening. This in turn I believe to be
the necessary foundation for a commonwealth of mutuality that has so far eluded
humankind. There is thus a rationale and agenda here for Buddhist social
engagement as well as for Buddhist social theory. Their validation lies in how far

they contribute to understanding the world in which we live and to providing a well-founded guide to action.

A socially engaged Buddhism needs no other rationale than that of being an amplification of traditional Buddhist morality, a social ethic brought forth by the needs and potentialities of present-day society.

The great bodhisattva vow to "liberate all beings" now also implies a concern for changing the social conditions that in every sense discomfit us, whether through gross affliction or through supercharging the existential folly through which we make what William Blake called our "mind-forged manacles." These are surely among the conditions that the Buddha declared

> lead to passion, not release therefrom; to bondage, not release there-from; and to the piling up of rebirths; these to wanting much, not want-ing little; to discontent, not to contentment; these to sociability, not to solitude; these to indolence, not to exertion; these to luxury, not to fru-gality; of these things know with certainty, this is not the Dhamma, this is not the Discipline, this is not the word of the Teacher. (Anguttara Nikaya IV, 280)

The argument for Buddhist social activism may be outlined as follows:

1. We cannot work selflessly and fully effectively to change society so long as we are driven by divisive and delusive self-need.
2. Delusive self-need is the ordinary root response of the individual to the predicament of being human.
3. This individual response is compounded in sociohistorical conditions that *institutionalize* alienation, ill will, aggressiveness, defensiveness, and acquisitiveness.
4. In turn those social conditions are karmically inherited by each new generation, whose delusive personal struggle for identity and meaning is socialized and supercharged by the aforementioned norms and insti-tutions.
5. Therefore out of *wisdom* we need to create different social conditions of a kind that nurture positive personality change; and out of *compas-sion* we need to create those conditions because the present ones give rise to so much gross physical and mental affliction.
6. If our work to effect these social changes is at the same time undertaken as a meditative training that ripens inner awareness, then we shall at the same time contribute to our own eventual "inconceivable liberation" from self-need—or at least become a little more human!

7. Thus we shall be more free to see clearly and act effectively so as to meet the material and spiritual needs of others, facilitating both personal and social change.

The above rationale I shall term *socioexistential,* in contrast to the various *scriptural* rationales. David Loy has independently adopted a similar approach. And in the same spirit Joanna Macy has related the doctrine of dependent co-origination to general systems theory.

It will be evident by now that the discussion and arguments in this book rely directly on the social implications of fundamental Buddhist teaching, or Dharma, which I have taken to mean the four noble truths, the eightfold path of training and practice, and the root insights of Mahayana Buddhism arising from these. In this I share the view expressed by Edward Conze in *Thirty Years of Buddhist Studies:*

> The cornerstone of my interpretation of Buddhism is the conviction, shared by nearly everyone, that it is essentially a doctrine of salvation, and that all its philosophical statements are subordinate to its soteriological purpose [its goal of salvation]. This implies…that each and every proposition must be considered with reference to its spiritual intention, and as a formulation of meditational experiences acquired in the process of winning salvation.

The classic depiction of ancient Buddhism as "otherworldy," "antipolitical," and "salvation seeking" is found in Max Weber's *Religions of India: The Sociology of Hinduism and Buddhism,* published in 1958. Revisionist scholars of postmodern bent are inclined to dismiss Weber's interpretation as a superimposed Western "orientalism." And to the extent that it ignores the not inconsiderable evidence of social concern in ancient Buddhism noted elsewhere in this book, such a revisionist critique is justified. Nevertheless, Christopher Queen claims in *Engaged Buddhism: Buddhist Liberation Movements in Asia* that "today, after eighty years of new research, many specialists are inclined to agree with Weber that, in its essence, primitive Buddhism was not based on service to others, but on the quest for individual enlightenment." Queen quotes the following measured conclusion by Asian studies scholar Bardwell Smith, from "Sinhalese Buddhism and the Dilemmas of Reinterpretation":

> The primary goal of Buddhism is not a stable order or a just society but the discovery of genuine freedom (or awakening) for each person. It has never been asserted that the conditions of society are unimportant or

unrelated to this more important goal, but it is critical to stress the distinction between what is primary and what is not. For Buddhists to lose this distinction is to transform their tradition into something discontinuous from its original and historic essence. Even the vocation of the bodhisattva is not as social reformer, but as the catalyst to personal transformation within society.

The inner work has primacy over the outer work; existential liberation has primacy over social emancipation. *Primacy* here means that social conditions have their ultimate origin in the human condition. And, more profoundly, how we experience social conditions—and create them—is dependent ultimately on the extent of our liberation from self-need. However, *primacy* is here a preliminary formulation. For the mature spiritual practitioner neither is primary: There is only a single, seamless practice experience, and activism. Wisdom and compassion are one. Note also that reference to the primacy of existential awakening still leaves open the questions about the *extent* of Buddhist social engagement, its *nature,* and its historical *continuity or discontinuity.*

My method of validation can be characterized by terms such as existential, perennial, epistemological. It contrasts with the other method of validating Buddhist social analysis and justifying social activism, which is exegetical, culture-bound, and contingent in character, relying on specific scriptural evidence and historic Buddhist practice to give prescriptive guidance. These primary and secondary methods of validation exemplify the distinction emphasized by Ajahn Buddhadhasa between *patipatti-dhamma* (the teaching of the Way, the practice) and *pariyatta-dhamma* (scriptural teaching). The two methods are not exclusive, of course, but complementary. However, I believe that the main weight must be put upon the first, with the second only supplementary, suggestive, and confirmatory. There are two reasons for this.

First, even where scriptural and historical evidence apparently does carry some spiritual authority, it is, notwithstanding, more or less the application of Buddhadharma within the specific conditions of a bygone culture. Meaning must therefore be scrupulously teased out of that context and translated back into a transcultural core Dharma before it can be related to present-day conditions.

Secondly, Buddhism is not a "religion of the book," and its relationship to its scriptural record is highly ambiguous. Scripture is intended only to signpost the way to direct experience of reality and not to be a sufficient substitute for that realization. In a nontextual religion the only ultimate value of the texts is as vehicles for the insights of sages. As emphasized in the celebrated Kalama scripture (see chapter 6), Buddhism enjoins seekers to rely first and foremost upon their own experience, while working all the while to deepen this and so make it a more reliable guide. Rather than bringing to bear the weight of scriptural authority I would prefer to call upon readers' own personal and social experience as validation. In "Justify Your Love: Finding Authority for Socially Engaged Buddhism," a useful taxonomy of the means of validating an engaged Buddhism, Diana Winston writes:

> Put simply, what goes on in one mind is mirrored in the world; *looking inward is a hallmark of a socially engaged Buddhist critique.* We can discover "where am I implicated?" For example, where are the same structures of greed, hatred and delusion present in my own mind? How do my inner *kilesas* (defilements) create or mirror external reality/institutions? This "turning inward" invokes compassion for others who perpetuate structures of violence as well as providing insight into understanding just how and why these structures work, and what could be done about them. (Italics added.)

Winston quotes the example of the driven speediness of American culture whose ultimate origins we can experience in the flurry we find in our own minds when first we sit in meditation and whose remedy may be suggested also when we become experienced in calming the mind.

The Literal Textual Rationale

The texts offers us three kinds of evidence for a Buddhist social concern and for the nature of that concern. First, there is social theory and analysis. Secondly there are injunctions and prescriptions for social engagement. (And it is desirable to distinguish between engagement in service and engagement for radical social change.) Thirdly there is the record of the practice of engagement.

Diana Winston identifies two textual approaches. The first, which I shall call the *literalist,* involves drawing directly from the texts. The other, *socializing textualism,* I shall examine later in this chapter.

As to the literalist approach, my first reservation (though Winston does not refer to it) is the danger of reading modern meanings into the scriptures of very different cultures. At worst this can secularize both scriptural meaning and engaged spirituality by annexing both to contemporary social categories and perspectives. This tends to be a reductive modernist interpretation that reduces the Dharma solely to a humanism. Thus in the past, Western Buddhist intellectuals were concerned to present it as a national, democratic, and even socialist ideology for today. Buddhism was claimed to be no less rational, scientific, and "modern" (and therefore relevant) than either the technological capitalism or the Marxian scientific socialism that challenged it.

Of Western secularizers of Buddhism perhaps the most distinguished has been professor of religious studies Trevor Ling, for whom the historic role of Buddhism "to end the disease of individualism" is perceived essentially in cultural and social terms. His achievement may be likened to taking the wheels off a splendid Rolls Royce automobile, putting it in a farmyard, and then extolling its virtues as a very superior chicken coop. For Ling, Buddhism is a sociocultural phenomenon based on a "psychosocial philosophy" rather than a system of personal transcendence.

He does maintain in his book *The Buddha* that "the reordering of human consciousness and the reordering of human society were the two complementary aspects of the Buddha's teaching.… These two complementary concerns constitute the Buddhist prescription for curing the ills of the human condition." But note that social transformation is not seen here as a supportive condition for "reordering human consciousness" or as an outcome of that more fundamental transformation but as the other major limb of the Buddhist project. Moreover, as to this "reordering of consciousness," the Buddha's enlightenment itself is, for Ling, "a process of analytical reasoning," which is "discovered by strenuous effort of the mind" that is "almost superhuman." There is no sense here of an arduous path of meditative humility and self-surrender, leading to a numinous turning about at the very root of self, with a revelation "given" by the falling away of delusion. It is, of course, possible to write about this phenomenon in terms that illuminate rather than reduce, as scholars as varied as D. T. Suzuki, Hubert Benoit, and T. P. Kasulis have demonstrated.

The above absolute misunderstanding of Buddhism as being no more than a historic culture or a sublime humanism or a brilliantly insightful metaphysics is furthered by the assumption that there are, on the one hand, only theistic religions and, on the other, only humanisms (or religions without God). Buddhism is nontheistic, so it is a humanism, free of "the supernatural and the superhuman," as Ling puts it, though he does not explain what he means by those words.

There is no way that Mahayana Buddhism can be crammed into this superficial schema, so it has to be pictured as some kind of degeneration into superstition and arcane mysticism. After Ashoka the history of Buddhism is downhill all the way—"a long process of misinterpretation, perversion, and distortion," according to professor of Indian philosophy N. V. Banerjee. In Ling's words, "It ceased to be a civilization" and "suffered also a transformation of its original humanistic character: it became a theistic religion."

All that having been said, since much of scripture is the expression of a high level of spiritual consciousness, it must carry considerable weight in validations of social theory and action. What is really at issue here is not the legitimate guidance of scripture as understood within its spiritual context and in terms of its soteriological purpose. What is being contested is the modern tendency to displace the scriptures from this original context and purpose and to interpret them instead in terms of contemporary social values and norms, which secularizes and reduces both scriptural meaning and engaged spirituality. And, of course, the fundamental Dharma on which I have tried to base this book does itself necessarily go back to scriptural record, though only at the most generalizable level.

There are other reservations about a literalist approach to the texts, to which Winston does refer: "Which texts? Who is the authority here? The Buddha? The Pali Canon? The commentaries? The Mahayana sutras?... Contemporary teachers? What texts and traditions have the so-called final word? And what if they conflict?"

When we have accounted for reservations of these kinds, what can we learn from the texts in terms of theory, injunction, and practice? In Chapter 5 I noted the rudimentary character of Indian Buddhist social analysis, notwithstanding some astute perceptions. In chapter 2, in the discussion of the Bodhisattva ideal, I presented evidence of an impressively large concern with compassionate social engagement in the Mahayana scriptures in particular. As to practice in India, and East Asia also, the following conclusions by Stephen Jenkins in "Do Bodhisattvas Relieve Poverty?" are noteworthy:

> Because of the paucity of resources for study, particularly in comparison to East Asia, it is very difficult to say in regard to India how, or to what degree, Indian Buddhism in practice was "socially engaged." However, we do know that in the more historically clear environments of China and Japan, Buddhist activities included road and bridge building and public works projects; social revolution; military defense; orphanages; travel hostels; medical education; hospital building; free medical care; the stockpiling of medicines; conflict intervention; moderation of penal codes; programs to assist the elderly and poor including "inexhaustible treasures" to stockpile resources for periods of hunger and hardship; famine and epidemic relief; and bathing houses. Perhaps this was purely the unique response of East Asian culture to Indian Buddhism, but we can at least make the weak initial observation that it is reasonable to speculate that East Asians were following the Indian models of Buddhist activity.

However, the above welfare picture needs to be qualified by the following important reservation from Buddhist scholar Gregory Ornatowski, from "Continuity and Change in the Economic Ethics of Buddhism":

In terms of issues of economic equality and distributive justice...Buddhist teachings were generally less interested in changing the current distribution of wealth than in cultivating the proper attitudes toward wealth, which were defined as those of giving and nonattachment. This position relied upon a karmic interpretation of social and economic inequalities which served to justify them (and therefore view them as a type of economic justice). Such a position also served as a rationale for a cooperative attitude toward the ruling authorities and for upholding the social, political and economic status quo. Of course, this was the dominant tradition in the form of the teachings of the majority of Buddhist schools. A minority tradition also existed (in particular in China) of movements which called for political upheaval based upon an interpretation of teachings concerning Maitreya, the future buddha.... However, in China and Japan in particular, the political situation which Buddhism faced for most of its history there made a strong and independent role both economically and politically difficult.

Continuity or Discontinuity? Ancient or Modern?

A discussion of the textual evidence for Buddhist social engagement in the past raises the continuity/discontinuity issue to which I referred earlier. In his examination of this question in "Engaged Buddhism: New and Improved!" religious studies scholar Thomas Yarnall takes the "traditionalist" continuity view:

> The Buddhadharma has *always* had a more or less fully articulated sociopolitical dimension in addition to its (supposedly "other-worldly") spiritual/soteriological dimension. Modern forms of Buddhism ("engaged" or otherwise) are essentially contiguous with traditional forms in spite of any superficially apparent differences.

Yarnall contrasts this with the view of discontinuity writers:

> While this group admits that there have been doctrines and practices with socio-political relevance *latent* in Buddhism since its inception, it insists that these "latencies" have always remained relatively "untapped," that they have not been (or often *could* not have been) until Buddhism encountered various Western elements unique to the modern era.

I believe the polarization and schematization in Yarnall's essay is unhelpful. As one of his "modernist" targets I certainly do not believe that the sociopolitical dimension was no more than "latent" in traditional Buddhism, but I do believe that it was shaped by a social culture very different from that of modernity. The element of discontinuity is imposed by the radical disjunction between pre-modern and modern cultures. (And hence in contemporary Asian societies where the influence of modernity has not been so all-encompassing, traditional forms of engagement would have greater continuity.)

Yarnall contends that the discontinuity thinkers' assertion "that the modern (and future) context is something historically unique and unprecedented" is a thoroughly mistaken "modernist strategy." His position is perhaps more readily understandable in light of the fact that he argues from a postmodern ideological standpoint. This perspective questions any claims for authentic social and cultural evolution with the above kinds of radical disjunction as mere "metanarratives." Similarly, any value judgment of a phenomenon in one culture from the viewpoint of another (typically Western modernity) brings a charge of political incorrectness. For example, my claim that early Indian Buddhist social theory was "rudimentary"—a view with which no sociologist could disagree—exposes me to being identified as an "Orientalist."

At all events, emphasis on continuity can do nothing but provide support and encouragement for a contemporary Buddhist social engagement, so in this respect it is certainly beneficial.

A Socializing Textualism

Diana Winston distinguishes a second, more sophisticated use of scripture for validating engaged Buddhism:

> Unlike (the first), we are not asking "What did the Buddha say?" but instead questioning, "What *would* the Buddha have said?"... We can take the classic Dharma teachings and consider them as basic principles underlying socially engaged Buddhism [and] deliberately "socialize" them (abstract them out to social and political situations) within particular contemporary contexts. For example, what would be a "social reading" of the first precept of non-harming, and how could it be used to critique militarization and nuclear weapons? [Finally] we can systematize this research...to create a body of dharma-based social teachings that help us better understand and critique structures of injustice.

Another example of a social reading of the texts would be Thich Nhat Hanh's expansion of the ethical precepts into the social sphere, noted earlier. And A. T. Ariyaratne extensively reinterpreted the basic teachings in a social context in order to underpin his Sarvodaya grassroots movement in Sri Lanka.

Several members of the engaged Buddhist think-tank ThinkSangha have also used this approach. For example, Santikaro Bhikkhu has offered a contemporary analysis of each of the eight *kilesa,* or "defilements," to illustrate how, in the final analysis, social cultures and structures originate in the personal defilements of our humanity—the greed, lust, anger, hatred, conceit, and so on. But at the same time, these social conditions impact back upon individuals, making it even easier to be greedy, lustful, angry, and so on. For example, the third *kilesa,* hatred, Santikaro extends to "three forms of structural hatred—racism, classism and exclusivism." And he expands upon the fifth *kilesa,* ignorance or delusion, to offer a critique of contemporary education and the media.

Socializing textualism differs from my approach to engaged Buddhism only by degree. My doctrinal basis is limited to the existential essentials, centering upon *dukkha,* root anxiety, or, as David Loy prefers, our sense of lack. To this it adds the all-important dimension of contemporary social theory. If this is not done then the direct application of "Buddhist principles and themes" to "contemporary problems, institutions, and social structures" tends to produce simplistic analyses. An example would be the direct equation of personal aggressiveness with war and militarism, whereas even a slight acquaintance with the literature of the subject suggests a much more complex situation. If social scientists are to take socially engaged Buddhism as seriously as most professional psychotherapists take Buddhist psychology, then we shall have to do better than this.

Chapter 18

ROOT PROBLEMS
OF BUDDHIST SOCIAL ACTIVISM

IN THIS CHAPTER I address some of the most basic challenges and questions faced by the socially engaged Buddhist community. Essentially, I believe the three issues I discuss here—the "balancing" of inner and outer work (and ultimately coming to see them as nonseparate); the challenge to not become disempowered or burned out in the face of seemingly insurmountable obstacles; and the embracing of the essential emptiness of nonetheless committed social action—are interrelated. The only transformative way to loosen the knot that our struggles continually tighten is through the work that has to be done within.

Liberation—Inner and Outer

Once upon a time there was an enlightened king who wished to relieve all his subjects of suffering. Everywhere, there were thorns and sharp stones underfoot. His chief minister suggested carpeting the kingdom in leather, wall to wall. But the finance minister objected that it would be impracticable. Then the king had the bright idea that each of his subjects should tie their own piece of leather to their feet. With sandals they could each "be a refuge" unto themselves.

This was in a premodern time when there was not the accumulated wealth, science, technology, and social organization that would enable changing the world *out there* to be an imaginable possibility. However, it was a spiritually saturated culture familiar with the possibility of shifts in consciousness itself, so that the world out there could be *experienced* differently. The alternative—or, rather, the *complementary*—liberation project proposed by the chief minister had to be put on the back burner for another millennium and a half.

Yet in both Theravada and Mahayana scripture the practical relief of suffering is commonly given first priority. The Buddha declined to preach to a hungry man until he had been fed. The bodhisattvas in the *Vimalakirtinirdesha Sutra* and other Mahayana scriptures are always at hand to give some direct, practical assistance, but their ultimate motive of inspiring enlightenment is never in doubt, and they are "skilled in means" to that great end. All of the foregoing refers to social cultures in which there could be virtually no expectation of change in the harsh conditions of life (even for the rich). To help people to release themselves into an absolutely different way of experiencing those conditions was—*and still is*—a truly revolutionary gift.

The great thirteenth-century Zen master Dogen warned in his *"Gyoji"* (Ceaseless Practice) teaching in the *Shobogenzo* that "if we wish to build a temple [that is, to engage in any intentional activity] we must remember that the main purpose is not form, fame or fortune. But it is rather the ceaseless practice of the Buddha Dharma that is important." In other words, we undertake bare awareness and other spiritual practices not primarily in order to lubricate the wheels of social change. On the contrary, the challenge of social activism is a valuable opportunity to further our practice of the Dharma, as mindful *action,* mindful *service.* This is so because it is our root existential condition that is primary. It is from this that our social condition originates, and the radical remedy for the ills of that social condition depends on a no less radical change in the kind of people we typically are. It is essential to get this right. Then with practice we may mature sufficiently to be able to combine this inner and outer work in a single seamless lifestyle, where activism *is* practice, and practice *is* activism. (The higher third referred to earlier in this book). It is then that we come to understand the better-known claim by Dogen in his "Bendowa" (Wholehearted Practice) essay in the *Shobogenzo:* "He who regards worldly affairs as an obstacle to his training only knows there is no Way in worldly affairs, not knowing that there is nothing such as worldly affairs to be distinguished from the Way." Thus Mahatma Gandhi, when questioned about his motives for doing good in the world, said that he was grateful to the poor for the opportunity of perfecting his spiritual practice, but it was because of that practice that he could do no less than his best to relieve poverty.

In the light of the above, the culture of modernity is one of secular inversion. For the young American radicals of the 1960s, 1970s, and 1980s who became interested in Buddhism, emancipatory modernity—the wall-to-wall carpeting project—was simply the absolute, taken-for-granted truth, to which the Dharma had to be accommodated. Thus one of the first concerns of the American Buddhist Peace Fellowship was to secure some historical validation by assiduously seeking out "exemplars of engaged Buddhism" from the past, ranging from the bodhisattva who offered himself as a meal to a starving tigress to the emperor Ashoka's Buddhist welfare state.

Eventually it began to dawn in some quarters that such readings were decontextualized exceptions to the cultural norms of premodern Buddhism, where inner transformation was necessarily the paramount goal. In his confessional essay "How Shall We Save the World?" commemorating twenty years of the American Buddhist Peace Fellowship, one of its founders, Nelson Foster, wrote:

> Naïveté...played a part in BPF's creation, I now see, at least on my part, naïveté about Buddhism itself and the bodhisattva way of saving beings. While innocence may have served BPF well in other respects, I think in this respect it did not. As I reflect on the developments of the past twenty years, it seems to me that BPF and other Buddhist projects of a similar nature have suffered from a failure to resolve crucial differences between the world view implicit in Buddhism and the world view that we absorb unintentionally as children of this culture.

To work for social change in modernity, and yet appreciate received Buddhism for what it authentically is, it is therefore necessary to be acutely aware of the magnetizing effect of secular inversion (such as attachment to results, and the disempowerment and burnout that can follow). This requires a kind of distancing from the outer emancipatory pull of modernity (which is difficult if one is strongly identifying with it) while at the same time not losing one's commitment to that noble project. I believe that this magnetic attraction is an ever present challenge, certainly for engaged Buddhists in the West, and that it is insufficiently appreciated. But, contrariwise, unengaged Buddhists have to come to terms with modernity's vastly expanded potential for active and effective compassion.

On the opposite side of the middle way set out above is what has been cleverly called *manyana Buddhism*—the Buddhism of *mañana,* the Spanish word for "tomorrow." This approach is one of being caught up in quietism, instead of in activism. It is the belief that a Buddhist should postpone all overt social action until such time as he or she may have fully opened to that wisdom and compassion without which truly selfless and effective intervention is impossible. Otherwise they will be caught up in the delusiveness of the social process and will themselves become part of the problem they set out to resolve. Thus, Milarepa, the eleventh-century Tibetan sage, warned, as quoted in W. Y. Evans-Wentz's *Tibet's Great Yogi, Milarepa:*

> Even without seeking to benefit others, it is with difficulty that works done even in one's own interest are successful. It is as if a man helplessly

drowning were to try to save another man in the same predicament. One should not be over-anxious and hasty in setting out to serve others before one has oneself realized Truth in its fullness; to be so, would be like the blind leading the blind. As long as the sky endureth, so long will there be no end of sentient beings for one to serve; and to every one cometh the opportunity for such service. Till the opportunity come, I exhort each of you to have but the one resolve, namely to attain Buddhahood for the good of all living beings.

Therefore, according to this view, effort should be directed to, as articulated by Masao Abe in "Zen Comes West," "dissolving the root of social evil within each individual" instead of cutting back its branches by social action. This is to be effected by the quiet, radiant example and spiritual teaching of all sincere followers of the Way.

I do not dissent from such statements as they stand; they can be valuable warnings. What I disagree with is the interpretation that they have received in some quarters in the context of contemporary social activism.

It may be added that, at the extreme end of this position, there are some very unengaged Buddhists lost in emptiness, such as a certain Kelsang Rabtan, who expressed an unmitigated quietistic view in the Winter 1996 correspondence column of *Full Moon,* the magazine of the New Kadampa Trust. Dismissing concern for the environment he declares that "the environment and the mind are like the body and its shadow. Likewise to the same degree that I purify my mind, my environment will be purified."

I believe that most Buddhist activists do acknowledge the danger in strong social engagement of being pulled off-center by headstrong partisanship and ideology. (It is ironic, however, that there are fewer warnings from the traditionalists about the no less dangerous spiritual hazards of business enterprise, professional ambition, and, of course, falling in love!) Even the hazards of everyday morality in the mainstream of traditional Buddhist practice are common enough: helping other people can be very self-deceiving.

Zen master Robert Aitken offers a trenchant rebuttal of the "perfectionist" position in *The Mind of Clover: Essays in Zen Buddhist Ethics.*

[It is not the case that] before one can work for the protection of animals, forests, and small family farms—or for world peace—one must be completely realized, compassionate, and peaceful. There is no end to the process of perfection, and so the perfectionist cannot begin Bodhisattva work. Compassion and peace are a practice, on cushions in the meditation hall, within the family, on the job, and at political forums. Do your best with what you have, and you will mature in the process.

"If Nothing You Can Do Is of Any Avail..."

In the aftermath of the events of September 11, in my mad scramble to understand what was going on and then to act appropriately, I have been most struck by a disturbing, though predictable phenomenon: my own and others' sense of disempowerment. It doesn't matter that I have been an activist for twenty years. It doesn't matter that I work at a social justice non-profit. It doesn't matter that in the past months I've been to rallies, painted signs, organized response groups, and called my congresspeople. At the bottom of it all is this terrible feeling that it's all kind of hopeless.

Disempowerment is one of the most unpleasant conditions of the human heart and mind, and in some ways it has been the norm for the last decade and certainly before. It just got really clear and ugly in this past month. Those of us opposing the war are disempowered. There's really nothing we can do. We just have to sit and take it.

This correspondence, from Diana Winston, associate director of the Buddhist Peace Fellowship, is an example of the powerlessness commonly experienced by social activists. Winston notes many objective reasons for this: "a tangled web of causes and conditions that might take years of studying," together with the lack of "good information" and the disinformation from the American media. I believe, however, that we tend to magnify such objective problems. Research into organizational decision making suggests that we commonly feel the need for more information than is strictly necessary for us to be able to decide and to act, and that much of the information we do obtain we do not use. There appears to be some unconscious evasion or procrastination at work here. Moreover there is in my experience a more than adequate range of publications and Web sites on most topics, global or local, to enable most would-be activists to get started.

Relevant also is the sense of powerlessness induced by our tendency to reify and solidify social forces, discussed earlier, in chapter 6, under the heading "The Emperor Has No Clothes." And certainly what has been called "the fetishism of results," a dependence on achievement, can disempower us. But note that non-attachment to results does not imply an absence of goals. What it implies is the absence of any emotional preoccupation with one's goal, during or after an activity, and whether the goal has been achieved or not. Christopher Titmuss, who is both a British Green Party parliamentary candidate and an international meditation teacher, reflects on this issue in "A Passion for the Dharma":

> Focusing too much on results brings nightmares—literally and metaphorically. There is a perversion of perception, and this is something which each of us must watch with the same kind of vigilance as if we had a cobra in a small room with us. The ego comes up in the form of "I" or " we" and says, "We are too small. I am too small." We can't confront the huge circumstances and crises of life. It deadens the spirit. And this wretched system we live under, day in and day out, is putting out that message.

We discussed previously how the inner work of practicing mindful bare awareness can open us to a wholehearted acceptance of the powerlessness within and the terrible power without. This acceptance unblocks the space where self-less love and fearlessness are revealed. And this releases confidence, clarity, and energy. This is an "empowerment" very different from the self-empowerment that is the usual meaning of the word. It is the empowerment simply to do our best, to make mistakes, and perhaps not to be able to do anything at all. Sadly, sometimes that's just how it is; but there's no need to take it personally.

The activist may, however, choose to make use of an ancient Far Eastern device for releasing spiritual insight called the *koan*. This is a seemingly paradoxical statement that conceals a profound truth (like, for example, the "emptiness" of phenomena). This truth may reveal itself when the koan is dropped into a still, meditative mind. Or it may come from wearing out the urgent, questing self by battering away at questions like that which the Japanese Zen activist Hisamatsu Shin'ichi gave to his students: "Right now, if nothing you can do is of any avail, what do you do?" Jack Douglass, a veteran war resister, explains the classic paradox of radical activism as follows, from *Resistance and Contemplation: The Way of Liberation:*

> The very intensity of my recognition of evil, necessary to my resistance and humanity, heightens the consciousness of my self that is the source of my powerlessness. I resist, therefore I am; powerless to *be* a liberating force, [and so] my resistance will become an egotistic duel with external powers because I have not come to terms with the fundamental absence of power within myself.

Struggling unavailingly with Hisamatsu's koan, ego eventually may surrender, exhausted, and, getting out of its own way, allow this truth to emerge, and with it a great sense of liberation.

For Douglass, an extraordinary self-honesty is required:

> The truth which comes in solitude is that the struggle for [social] libera-
> tion must begin by recognizing the terrifying emptiness of that self of
> mine which is prepared to pose on the outside as a redeemer of others....
> For the prophet goes to the depth of the double poverty in the world and
> himself, in the terrible suffering of the innocent and in the radical empti-
> ness of himself. The prophet who is able to endure this double struggle
> defines all over again the beauty and tragedy of man: the dignity of man's
> commitment to his limitations.

How to be a practical idealist is a seemingly baffling paradox to those who are
hanging on to their mysticism or their militancy. Practical idealists are accepting of their fear (and there is plenty to be afraid of) without being possessed by
it. Living beyond hope and hopelessness, optimism and pessimism, they are
patient and clear-sighted *possiblists*. Just released from one of his periodic impris-
onments, Jack Douglass was asked whether he really felt there was any hope.
"Not hope, but there are possibilities" was his reply.

There are many ordinary folk who can testify. Cathy McCormack, a tenant
in Easterhouse, a huge, squalid housing project on the outskirts of Glasgow,
Scotland, speaks of her despair after seven years of unemployment and crushing
adversity:

> I was so broken by it that I felt there was no point in living. I wanted to
> go to sleep and never wake up again. Then one day something happened.
> It was a kind of awakening; almost a spiritual experience.... I understood
> that my life is here in this place, and no fantasy of escape would help.
> This is where the wains [children] must grow up and make their lives;
> here we must survive or perish together.

Cathy McCormack was enabled to empower her fellow tenants and to initiate
housing regeneration projects to reverse the cycle of despair and deprivation.

Moreover there are larger economic and political situations where this kind
of clarity provides the fortitude and resolution for a long-haul strategy instead
of a knee-jerk activism that may only create further problems—like the armed
uprising that creates an even more intractable situation, or the war that is "won"
at the cost of an enduring peace.

Finally, here is the Buddha's response to the problem of disempowerment,
from the Sutta Nipata (I, 1032–36): "What is it," said Ajita to the Buddha, "that
smothers the world? What makes the world so hard to see? What would you say

pollutes the world, and what threatens it most?" "It is ignorance which smothers," said the Master, "and it is carelessness and greed which make the world invisible. The hunger of desire pollutes the world, and the great source of fear is the pain of suffering." "In every direction," said Ajita, "the rivers of desire are running. How can we dam them and what will hold them back? What can we use to close the flood-gates?" "Any river can be stopped with the dam of mindful awareness," said the Buddha, "I call it the flood-stopper. And with wisdom you can close the flood-gates."

Engagement and Emptiness

When situations are *emptied* of self-need they can be seen as the unfolding, transient, insubstantial flux of phenomena—*and yet, at the same time, they are no less real.* The human experiment of global civilization may, for example, prove to be ecologically unsustainable, or a community campaign to halt a destructive development may fail—yet we may know that we have done our best, and can accept that's just how it has turned out to be. This can enable us to return once again, clearing our minds for appropriate response. We can, for example, treat our adversaries with the respect and humanity due to fellow human beings, instead of needing to demonize them and perpetuate the problem we have with them. Dwelling in *emptiness* can clarify *form,* nevertheless, for the activist trapped in the two-dimensional struggle between *this* and *that,* the third way that emerges from the dialectics of mysticism may be difficult to access.

So what is that elusive smile playing about the Buddha's face? Is it his compassionate acknowledgment to us of the cosmic joke? If we really care, we shall not take ourselves so seriously that we cannot be freed into enough space to see the black humor, the cosmic irony. Given that space, we can begin to sense the dance of possibilities. Dogen offers this poem, pointing to a way to step out of the dualistic trap of self versus the world:

Like tangled hair
The circular delusion
Of beginning and end,
When straightened out
A dream no longer

I recall a contentious and wide-ranging correspondence in *Tricycle* magazine some years ago, provoked by John McClellan of Boulder, Colorado. Critics felt that McClellan was insufficiently committed to our planetary future. His response, in the Spring 1994 edition, was the rarely heard voice of the necessary emptiness of Buddhist activism. He asserted that he saw

> no reason for a simplistic "either/or" attitude in this area. Yes, everything is perfect, and yes, there is still much to do. The dishes need to be washed up, and deep contemplatives are expected to do their share....

We care passionately about the world, almost too much at times; this is understandable, as our very lives are at stake. But a deep and constantly refreshed detachment must lie at the core of any really passionate relationship. When this is forgotten, lost in the heat of caring, the relationship becomes greedy, possessive and materialistic; it becomes deluded, self-centered, and blind, and ultimately unhelpful.

Traditionally Buddhist practice has emphasized the need to balance *virya* (energy, forcefulness) with *kshanti* (humility, contemplation, acceptance of thusness). Overemphasis on *kshanti* makes for social quietism. But too much *virya* dims awareness of the underlying ego-impulsions that draw us into a driven, self-affirming activism. We then tend to become righteous. Since ours is the only true Buddhism, authentic dialogue becomes impossible. A muscular "Buddhism with attitude" develops. Dogmatism solidifies into ideology. Ideology generates a telltale predictability in the literature of "the movement." Righteousness leads to the antithetical bonding of "our movement," providing its members with a reassuring belongingness identity, relieved of the ambivalence, uncertainty, and other disturbing challenges encountered on more exposed spiritual paths. Yet movements get things done, often very worthwhile things, too, and this attracts further support (though history suggests that in the long term the price can be high). Dependency inflates the authority of a charismatic leader, and this can generate further dependency. An underlying conformism is socialized into the membership and requires no overt imposition by the hierarchy.

The above dangers, inherent in an activist Dharma, will become more evident as engaged Buddhism becomes more successful, influential, and—whether it likes it or not—more powerful. Soka Gakkai and the Friends of the Western Buddhist Order are Buddhist movements that have already been the subject of much criticism in this regard.

A recent book by David Brazier, leader of the U.K. Amida Community, entitled *The New Buddhism* is an invigorating call to get all those Buddhist boats "rotting in the harbor" out to social action. Brazier's "ship" is perhaps the more superficially attractive in that he has jettisoned as "unnecessary mystification and hindrance" emptiness, buddha nature, and nonduality! However, with this "ballast" thrown out, can it really be seaworthy and deep keeled enough for the ambitious voyage to the global "Dhammic Republic of Sukhavati" that the author has in mind?

Here we risk abandoning what is grave and essential in perennial Buddhism, and what engaged Buddhism has particular need of. The introduction of *both* of Buddhism's "Two Truths"—of Emptiness and Form—into engaged Buddhist dialogue can be a source of confusion and conflict, which is perhaps why it rarely happens. Yet modernity's gravitational pull to social liberation does need to be balanced by profound insight into *existential* liberation."

In this context it is a dangerous mistake to characterize engaged Buddhism as "the fourth *yana*," that is, a new and distinct Buddhist tradition. Indeed, I would rather not call it engaged *Buddhism* at all, but prefer to speak simply of engaged *Buddhists*. Engaged Buddhism must be free of the secularizing weight of modernity so that it can be truly a Buddhism of modernity.

In "Practicing Peace: Social Engagement in Western Buddhism," Kenneth Kraft, one of engaged Buddhism's most astute observers, is very frank:

> At this stage it may be difficult to identify the signs of realization in the actions or the ethics of engaged Western Buddhists. Yet one should not conclude hastily that such a dimension is entirely missing. It remains to be seen whether Buddhism's indigenization in the West will yield an ersatz (essentially Western) Buddhist ethics, *an attenuated Buddhist ethics (lacking enlightened awareness)* or a robust Buddhist ethics that brings the essentials of the tradition to bear upon contemporary conditions. (Italics added.)

Santikaro Bhikkhu, sobered by many years of activism in Southeast Asia, distills the only real solution to the various challenges of Buddhist activism addressed in this chapter:

> These days, I am thinking that socially engaged Buddhism is to be found in those with a solid Dhamma practice—not just fuzzy, nice intentions— who can bring it to bear on social issues in real live situations. What Dhamma practice can give is enough mindfulness to be present in the moment, enough non-bias to see the situation from various angles (including one's own inner dynamics), enough compassion to want to end suffering, enough wisdom to understand the major causal relationships at play (including intra- and interpersonal) and enough effort actually to do something effective on the ground.

Chapter 19

BUILDING A RADICAL CULTURE OF AWAKENING

THROUGHOUT THIS BOOK I have maintained that war, poverty, and social injustice have existential origins and are endemic in the human condition. They can only be fundamentally remedied by a profound personal transformation such as that found in Buddhist and other traditions of spiritual training. However, if such a psychosocial transformation is to take place on a significant scale, it will require the creation of social conditions that are supportive and conducive, in contrast to those that at present tend to deepen existential ignorance and push the global society into deeper crisis.

The Dalai Lama, in *Collected Statements, Interviews, and Articles,* expressed a similar sentiment:

> In recognition of human frailty and weakness, the qualities of [moral scruples, compassion, and humility] are only accessible through forceful individual development in a conducive social milieu, so that a more human world will come into being as an ultimate goal.... A dynamic revolution is deemed crucial for instigating a political culture founded on moral ethics.

Many different themes introduced earlier in this book converge upon this final chapter, which sets out various principles and characteristics of a Buddhist Good Society—or a socially radical culture of awakening.

Liberation Is Indivisible

The task that Buddhism proposes is a lifelong training directed to the transcendence of the self. This is a training in interbeing, a compassionate at-oneness with others and with society at large. When fully embraced, the fate of global society becomes our fate. Its historic greed, rage, and delusion require a no less radical remedy than the complete transcendence or transformation of our own destructive appetites.

In the contemporary society of high modernity there is an urgent need for radical change at all levels, ranging from planetary sustainability to the elusive predicament of the self. At the same time, our civilization has developed all the wealth, organization, and knowledge that are required to solve its problems. But it is unable, and indeed unwilling, to put them to effective use, squandering them instead on war and mindless acquisitiveness and frivolity.

There is, of course, a long tradition of social emancipation aiming to liberate humanity from want and oppression. But whether it is social democratic reformism or revolutionary socialism, its achievements have at best been limited, flawed, and problematic—and at worst disastrous failures.

Elsewhere in this book I have argued that a radically different society needs to be underpinned by a culture of existential awareness sustained by the inner work agenda of each of its citizens. History suggests that, without some such change in the human condition itself, even if we achieved an equitable commonwealth of social justice, global pluralism, and environmental sustainability, it could not for long be maintained. Always the old appetites have reasserted themselves. The revolutionaries become self-serving, paternalistic elites. The reformers are co-opted by those whom they had sought to reform. "Free men and women" turn with relief to charismatic authoritarian populists and, latterly, to addictive consumerism.

Socially engaged Buddhists, with their inner-path allies in other faiths and in the transpersonal therapies, therefore have to make a convincing case for the importance of inner work to support and transform the outer work of all who are striving for radical social change.

In particular it is necessary to counter classic liberationist assumptions originating with Rousseau and the romantic enlightenment of the eighteenth century. This view asserts that we are born with an innate goodness that is warped by morally corrupting social conditions; we grow up violent in a violent society. (A socially aware Buddhist would agree with this while adding that social conditioning is, however, nowhere near an adequate explanation.) Radical social change, it is claimed, is therefore necessary to create the conditions that will bring out our previously inhibited capacity for mutual care and cooperative endeavor, enabling us "to become fully human."

The problem, however, is how such a positive conditioning process is to be effectively initiated if we are not yet in fact "fully human." Here arises the temptation for an "advanced" elite to seize power and embark on a course of socially engineering the New Man. Hence socialism has come to be seen as either dangerously authoritarian or impracticably utopian. And beyond the "hard" ideology of socialism we have the "soft" ideologies of neo-romantic visionaries, for whom modernity itself is a tragic aberration. There is a broad spectrum here, from the nostalgic Arcadian autarchy of Wendell Berry to the libertarianism of Murray Bookchin.

In the above context—as in many other senses—engaged Buddhism is a radical conservatism. On the one hand it has a revolutionary vision originating in its insight into human potential. On the other, it remains grounded in the stubborn realities of our ecological and social predicament, and rooted in the deep, tangled texture of history.

A Just and Sustainable Commonwealth

No social system can by itself create a revolution in human consciousness, though it can provide more favorable conditions for such personal endeavor. The social changes set out below coincide with quite widely held democratic and egalitarian ideals, while at the same time being ultimately at variance with both capitalist free enterprise and collectivist social systems. It is not so much that the values themselves are Buddhist; the Buddhism lies rather in the manner of their cultivation and how they are to be sustained. Like the Buddhist moral precepts, they are to be taken as guidelines for personal and public learning. They are to be understood as social expressions of the more highly evolved consciousness to which we must aspire. Just as the traditional precepts exemplify how the compassionate and selfless person behaves, so are these social changes intended to suggest something of how a whole society would organize and function if it were composed of such people. The psychosocial transformation suggested here is a continuously sustained metamorphosis, in which a significant number of people change the whole social climate by actualizing these social values in their own experience.

Most fundamentally we must bring social activity back into harmony with the ecosphere. This entails a society in which development is no longer equated with endless material growth—always more jam tomorrow. We can no longer rely on economic growth as a rising tide painlessly lifting all boats; everyone can no longer aspire to become rich or even richer. A much more egalitarian order will be necessary, both within society and between different global societies. This goes deeply against the root assumptions of our acquisitive and competitive culture. Faced with the need for a lifestyle of restrained simplicity and a culture of sufficiency, how will erstwhile consumers and big money-makers fill their sense of lack?

Society must be reshaped so that basic human needs are adequately met, even though, with finite planetary resources, this must be at the expense of limiting the satisfaction of some people's wants. One condition for establishing such a society is a much more direct, localized, and egalitarian kind of democracy than the present facades of patronage and populist manipulation that pass under that name.

Populist authoritarianism will lose its power to seduce as citizens experience their own sense of empowerment in a civil society of small groups and networks, and in self-governing local and regional communities. To this end, following the principle of subsidiarity, power should be exercised locally except where it is functionally desirable for it to be exercised at regional, national, continental, or global levels. This implies confederal tiers of governance and a political—and economic—culture of balance, negotiation, and mediation, instead of coercion by political elites or by the "laws" of the market.

The economic democracy I propose necessitates a shift from transnational free market capitalism and neoliberal ideology to a well-regulated stakeholder capitalism, plus a large "social" sector of cooperatives and other not-for-profit kinds of ownership. It implies geographically more self-reliant markets that function within a culture of mutual responsibility. This has been called a "mindful market economy."

This must be more than a visionary dream of the future. It needs to be lived here and now. However, the weakness of this nascent radical alternative is that it may be limited to lobbying and publicity, and to gradually changing the climate of opinion in which policy is made. However, changes in public awareness are beginning to be reinforced by the power of consumers who are developing a will of their own, as in the dramatic rejection of genetically modified foodstuffs (particularly in the United Kingdom). Public opinion is a powerful instrument but also a very blunt one in tilting the state toward the kind of society outlined above.

Just as in an earlier period the labor and socialist movement was in the forefront of modernity's emancipatory thrust, so in postmodernity the main push must, it seems, come from a civil society of local, national, and international voluntary, nongovernmental organizations—a third sector between corporate capitalism and the state. This civil society is much the same the world over, and includes a spectrum of specific-issue social movements. But reinventing civil society also means retrieving intermediate institutions like hospitals, universities, and even the professions, which have seen their social purposes distorted by state control and enforced dependence on the market economic model. Moreover, the development of civil society itself depends in part on the state and local government adopting a more enabling role—supporting the widening range of community economic enterprises, and funding voluntary organizations in new partnerships to provide a range of local services.

By the turn of the century a radical change in the social climate was discernible in many countries. Environmental studies scholar Michael Mason has noted the emergence of

> a broad social and civil democracy movement. Its targets now range across global institutions, corporations, inner cities, transport, food, pollution and all the traditional targets of environmental groups. The movement is animated by social concerns. It is seeking broadly to stop the juggernaut of globalization. There is a sense of people losing control of what is going on and reacting.

As noted earlier, engaged Buddhists share with this broad coalition for radical change much the same social vision and values.

The Making of a New Citizenry

In Buddhist terms the Good Society would be one in which all citizens would be enabled to fill their material *and existential* needs to their common benefit and the stability of society. It would need to develop a culture in which it was both antisocial and unjustifiable to try to fill one's own, or one's group's, sense of lack at others' expense. It would also be essential to provide favorable conditions for addressing the personal sense of lack in the only ultimately conclusive way, that is, through awakening to the futility and needlessness of trying to satisfy our deepest needs in the way we commonly do. On such a culture of awakening the social stability of an authentic postmodernity would depend.

Because individualism and the world it has created are now increasingly unsustainable, an authentic postmodernity will need to be, rather than individualism-obsessed, truly person-centered. By *person-centered* I mean that our attention shifts to the attributes of personhood needed to sustain society, *instead of vice versa*. Note that this is no mere reassertion of collectivism over individualism, of responsibilities over rights (or of willed "character" over narcissism). The argument spirals up beyond such a self/society conflict. A higher third is possible beyond these dichotomies. And because the genie of reflexive individuality cannot be put back into any premodern bottle, we have either to transcend this dualism or eventually be forced to choose between an increasingly destructive individualism or a desperate resort to authoritarian collectivism.

The self can only become unreservedly socially responsible by penetrating the mystery of the self. To penetrate that mystery is to experience the paradox of simultaneous separateness and interdependence, like the jewels in Indra's net, and to experience rights and responsibilities as one. Thus Gandhi once responded to a question about his motivation by saying that "in serving these people I serve myself; in serving myself I serve these people."

The higher third to which I have repeatedly pointed manifests the personality attributes needed to *transcend* our sense of lack, beyond just trying to *fill* it in tolerably restrained and benign ways. It frees us into a spontaneous and situational morality beyond the traditional character-building that is dependent upon willpower and conditioning.

The first cluster of such attributes arises from an awareness-identity. This is a self-awareness that recognizes a feeling as it comes up, so that, with practice, we are not possessed by it and unaware that it is moving us. Self no longer requires any external validation. Antithetical bonding loses its historic attraction. Deep convictions are freed of ideology and fanaticism. Discipline is possible without rigidity; intimacy without addiction; assertiveness without aggression (or submissiveness).

Secondly, inner awareness unblocks outer responsiveness, freeing us to respond wholeheartedly, without fearing failure or loss of self-control. Instead of identifying with our response we can allow the response to reflect the situation. As occasion requires, we can be temperate extremists or passionate moderates, radical conservatives or reasonable revolutionaries. Karmic patterns of guilt, resentment, and the like begin to lose their power. We no longer need to identify with getting results, and hence we are no longer disabled from getting started, nor do we end up burned out. We still heed guiding principles and are inspired by visions splendid—but the means are the ends and the ends are the means. Nothing matters; everything matters. It was said of the bodhisattvas, the liberative saints of Buddhism, that they could wander around hell as if it were a fairground. This is not because of their indifference to suffering, but because their great compassion frees them to give of their best even in places where affliction would otherwise be unbearable.

Thirdly, the postmodern commonwealth envisioned in this chapter would require an unprecedented public-spiritedness, depending in turn upon the above attributes. This requires awareness of, and hence some freedom from, those ego agendas of power and dependency that have capsized all such previous projects.

Finally, true citizenship implies a practice of mutuality that is spiritually enhancing—or, in other words, nurtures humanity's deepest potential.

The culture of postmodernity envisaged here will rate interpersonal ability and empathy as greatly as high modernity rates acquisitiveness and aggressiveness.

Yale psychologist Peter Salovey identified five "key abilities" as marking the *emotional intelligence* subsequently popularized by author Daniel Goleman. The fourth key ability of emotional intelligence, being sensitive to others' emotions, leads to the fifth, that of handling all kinds of relationships skillfully and positively. In *Emotional Intelligence* Goleman writes of these abilities as follows:

> Being able to put aside one's self-centered focus and impulses has social benefits: it opens the way to empathy, to real listening, to taking another person's perspective. Empathy, as we have seen, leads to caring, altruism and compassion. Seeing things from another's perspective breaks down biased stereotypes and so breeds tolerance and acceptance of differences. These capacities are ever more called upon in our increasingly pluralistic society, allowing people to live together in mutual respect and creating the possibility of productive public discourse. These are basic arts of democracy.

These capabilities are not as unrealistic as might at first appear. From the way they talk and act, what kind of reality has this or that person or group made for themselves? How well are they able to take care of the rancor, edginess, competitiveness, and sense of inadequacy we all keep about our persons? When faced with a contentious problem, do they usually stir their own personality into it? Or are they able to free their talents into full attention to the problem itself?

In 1986 Christine McNulty of Taylor Nelson Applied Futures identified seven "social value groups," based on research into values and attitudes in the United Kingdom. A replication of the study ten years later showed an increase in the proportion of "self-explorers," with similar trends in other Western industrial countries. These "self-explorers" are "inner directed" individuals concerned primarily with personal growth and the search for meaning in life—ethical, creative, expressive, and with high self-esteem. They are relaxed and tolerant of others, and open to change.

However, the research suggests that, apart from strong and active environmental concerns, these "self-explorers" are typically preoccupied with personal development rather than radical social change. The study suggests that the group labeled "interactivists" (who fit the description of the "new citizenry" characterized in this chapter) would probably number less than 10 percent of the United Kingdom population. That is, however, quite an encouraging potential catalyst. It suggests that the kind of sociopersonal development proposed here is already under way. And it can be facilitated by a wide range of psychotherapeutic and spiritual practices.

Mainstreaming the Dharma

So far I have sketched out the kind of future society, embodying many Buddhist values, envisaged by a broad coalition for radical change. I have also argued that the agenda for social change needs to be supported by, and integrated with, an inner work of individual, personal change. This would amount to a veritable "culture of existential awakening," of the kind proposed by Stephen Batchelor (chapter 10). To this we shall now turn.

Something of this culture does, of course, already exist in a very small way in the various groups already practicing contemplative, inner-path, nondualistic spirituality. However, in North America much wider anticipations of a culture of awakening are beginning to make their appearance. We can now envision valuing spiritual development on a par with social, cultural, and technical work—a value it lost with the ascendancy of materialist modernity. The meditative "workout" could become as much a part of the daily routine as the physical workout. We could maintain mindfulness just as we maintain bodily hygiene. Reflective solitude could be as normal as the social round.

There are now a growing number of meditation and mindfulness programs that are available not only in medical and therapeutic settings and in the caring professions but also in education, the media, business, and the professions. These initiatives are coming together in bodies such as the Center for Contemplative Mind in Society, founded in 1997. The Center "has worked primarily in mainstream institutional and organizational channels, bridging the inner life with the outer world of social engagement." It has organized "contemplative retreats and meetings" for members of the legal profession and the mainstream media, and executives of major corporations. It also "coordinates a program of Academic Fellowships for professors to teach the study of Contemplative Practices in colleges and universities."

Jon Kabat-Zinn is a pioneer and leading advocate of the movement to integrate meditation and mindfulness practice into both healthcare and society as a whole. His Center for Mindfulness in Medicine, Health Care, and Society at the University of Massachusetts Medical Center operates Stress Reduction Clinics out of some three hundred centers worldwide. These have been remarkably successful in their contribution to conventional clinical treatment. The clinics "serve as a kind of safety net," Kabat-Zinn explains in "Indra's Net at Work," that is "capable of catching people falling through the cracks of the health care system and challenging them in a meaningful way to see if there was not something they could do for themselves as a complement to what medicine would be trying to do for them."

The title of the clinics is significant. Kabat-Zinn is undoubtedly a seasoned Buddhist practitioner, and his "treatment" is based on traditional and well-tried meditation methods. He has made it clear that he wishes to offer these healing practices "in ways that are authentic and true to the heart of the Dharma" but also to make them widely available. This is impossible if they are "locked in or wedded to tradition and vocabulary" that can deter both prospective patients and professional colleagues.

Developments of this kind raise three questions. First, is this not dumbing down the Dharma to just another therapy? In fact the Kabat-Zinn clinics make quite rigorous demands on those who enroll in the eight-week course, who commit themselves to at least an hour a day of meditation and hatha yoga (with a silent, one-day retreat in the sixth week). This supports what is the heart of the treatment—round-the-clock practice of bare awareness (mindfulness). And the dropout rates are very low.

More generally, a culture of awakening does need to be as broad and inclusive as possible, and this in no way diminishes the value of more demanding practices and higher levels of consciousness change.

My second concern is the apparent narrowing of Dharma to meditation practice. This question has already been examined more broadly in chapter 9, "Beyond Meditation." As we have seen in chapter 10, particularly the discussion of Japanese Imperial Way Zen, disregard of ethical guidelines and moral resolves in a religious culture and in personal practice can have disastrous social consequences. This may not be relevant to the functional use of meditation in the ethical context of the caring professions. But what, for example, of meditation programs to enhance the effectiveness of the chief executives of rapacious corporations? If mindful robbery *by* usurious banks is acceptable, then why not the mindful robbery *of* banks?

Thirdly, are these programs no more than a therapeutic and specific application of Dharma rather than a veritable awakening to fuller human potential—and the remedying of society's ills? (Though of course, even if they were not, this would still be a valuable and compassionate use of Dharma.) In fact, meditation practice does inevitably affect the whole person in an existential sense beyond clinical treatment, and Kabat-Zinn is very happy to acknowledge this. Radical social implications are another matter, however. Yet Kabat-Zinn believes that the widespread adoption of contemplative values and practices would have profound economic and political benefits. In a paper presented to the Contemplative Mind Working Group in Society, he refers to a "radical scenario...a real opportunity for seeding a second Renaissance." He underlines, however, the problems with ambition and power and "the potential resistance to any efforts to further a contemplative orientation in our society and its institutions." Moreover, "our efforts must transcend religion as we know it with its historically parochial and sometimes evangelical and messianic interests."

Kabat-Zinn makes ambitious proposals for establishing national training and research centers

> for the in-depth training of a new breed of inventive and creative meditation teachers: for the most part people who are already professionals in a particular area, hold other jobs and who wish to introduce the meditative/contemplative dimension into their work and into their places of work.... Of course, the deeper their grounding and commitment to mindfulness practice before they undergo such specialized training the better.

He envisages "second-generation foci" being established by "this new breed," from which a meditative culture would be propagated in virtually every kind of institution and cultural milieu.

Toward a Socially Radical Culture of Awakening

Whatever reservations one might have about this broad mainstream of awareness practice, there can be no doubt about its value in at least supporting a *socially radical* culture of awakening. I call it *socially radical* because it would be dedicated to sustaining the inner work of the diverse movements for radical social change described earlier in this chapter. It would draw its strength from Buddhist and allied inner-path faith traditions but, to be sufficiently inclusive, would for the most part embrace the broad meditation practice described above.

This socially radical culture of awakening would be distinguished from the broader culture of awakening in three respects.

First, it would be distinguished by its dedication to a strong, well-informed activist ethic—a true "opening of the fourth eye" of social awareness and responsibility. Some groups might even offer formal vows or resolutions of commitment to engagement and activism.

Secondly, activists and other change agents would support one another in the inner work through small affinity groups, linked into wider networks. The American Buddhist Peace Fellowship's BASE project, referred to in chapter 16, is a well-proven working example.

Thirdly, there would also need to be training and practice in the inner/outer work that is more specific to the needs of radical change agents, such as mediation and small group process. The widespread NVDA (Non-Violent Direct Action) workshops, which are already well-established, provide another excellent working model.

There will also be a wide variety of other kinds of organizations and activities shaping the radical culture of awakening. Inspiring examples already exist, from Sarvodaya to the right livelihood projects described in an earlier chapter.

In short, I believe that it is only through the Buddhadharma and allied spiritual traditions (explicit and implicit)—together with the transpersonal therapies—that the promise of emancipatory modernity can finally be fulfilled. And this, in turn, creates the most favorable conditions for the existential liberation of humankind. Here, at the start of a new century, the bodhisattva way becomes clearer by the year. This is the new social face of Buddhism.

Life passes like a flash of lightning
Whose blaze lasts barely long enough to see,
While earth and sky stand still forever.
How swiftly changing time flies across our face.
You who sit over your full cup and do not drink,
For what are you waiting?

Li Po

REFERENCES

Abe, Masao. "Zen Comes West." *Blind Donkey* (Diamond Sangha, Honolulu) 8, no. 1: 19.

Aitken, Robert. *The Mind of Clover: Essays in Zen Buddhist Ethics,* pp. 21–22. San Francisco: North Point Press, 1984.

———. "Two *Teishos*: The First Precept." *Blind Donkey* (Diamond Sangha, Honolulu) 5, no. 4 (August 1979) 1.

Ariyaratne, A. T. *Collected Works,* vol. 1, p.133. Moratuwa, Sri Lanka: Sarvodaya Research Institute, 1978.

———. "Declaration on National Peace and Harmony." In *Dharma and Development: Religion As a Resource in the Sarvodaya Self-Help Movement,* by Joanna Macy, revised edition, p. 102. West Hartford, Conn.: Kumarian Press, 1985.

———. Quoted in *Dharma and Development: Religion As a Resource in the Sarvodaya Self-Help Movement,* by Joanna Macy, revised edition, p. 76. West Hartford Conn.: Kumarian Press, 1985.

———. "Speech Delivered on 9/26/86 at the Peace Walk Ceremony in Vavuniya on Behalf of Mr. K. Kadiramalai." *Dana* 2, nos. 10–11: 16.

———. "Waking Everybody Up." In *Engaged Buddhist Reader,* edited by Arnold Kotler, p. 96. Berkeley: Parallax Press, 1996.

Armstrong, Karen. *Islam: A Short History.* New York: Modern Library, 2000.

Astor, David. Obituary for the Reverend Michael Scott. In *The Oberver* (London), 18 September 1983.

Athanasiou, Tom. *Slow Reckoning: Ecology of a Divided Planet,* p. 62. London: Secker & Warburg, 1997.

Banerjee, Nikunja V. *Buddhism and Marxism: A Study in Humanism,* p. 30. New Delhi: Orient Longman, 1978.

Basham, A. L. "Asoka and Buddhism: A Reexamination." *Journal of the International Association of Buddhist Studies* 5, no. 1 (1982): 131–43.

Batchelor, Stephen. *The Awakening of the West,* p. 275. London: Aquarian, 1994.

———. *Buddhism without Beliefs: A Contemporary Guide,* pp. 38, 111, 114, 115. London: Bloomsbury, 1997.

———. "Monks, Laity, and Sangha." In *The Middle Way* 58, no. 1 (May 1983): 27–33.

Bauman, Zygmunt. *Legislators and Interpreters,* p. 189. Cambridge: Polity Press, 1989.

Baumann, Martin. "The Application of Buddhist Right Livelihood in the Friends of the Western Buddhist Order." *Journal of Buddhist Ethics* 5 (1998).

Bellah, Robert N. *Beyond Belief: Essays on Religion in a Post-Traditional World,* pp. 65, 227. New York: Harper Row, 1970.

———. *Tokugawa Religion: The Cultural Roots of Modern Japan,* p. 188. New York: Free Press, 1957.

Benoit, Hubert. *The Supreme Doctrine,* p. 239. New York: Viking, 1959.

Berger, Peter L., Brigitte Berger, and Hansfried. Kellner. *The Homeless Mind: Modernization and Consciousness,* pp.74–75, 166. New York: Random House, 1973.

Berman, Morris. "Metapolitick." *Resurgence* 115 (March/April 1986): 17–19.

Blum, William. *Rogue State: A Guide to the World's Only Superpower.* 2nd ed. London: Zed Books, 2001.

Blythe, R. H. *Zen and the Zen Classics.* Tokyo: Hokuseido Press, 1960.

Bondurant, Joan V. *The Conquest of Violence: The Gandhian Philosophy of Nonviolence,* revised edition, p. 193. Berkeley: University of California Press, 1971.

Brandon, David. *Zen and the Art of Helping,* p. 59. London: Routledge & Kegan Paul, 1976.

Brazier, David. *The New Buddhism.* London: Robinson, 2001.

Buddhadasa, Ajahn. *Dhammic Socialism,* edited by Donald K. Swearer. Bangkok: Thai Inter-Religious Commission for Development, 1986.

———. Quoted in *Engaged Buddhism: Buddhist Liberation Movements in Asia.* Edited by Christopher S. Queen and Sallie B. King, p. 166. Albany: State University of New York Press, 1996.

———. *Toward the Truth,* translated by Donald K. Swearer, p. 26. Philadelphia: Westminster Press, 1971.

Burke, Edmund. *"Reform of Representation in the House of Commons."* [1784], in *Thoughts on the Present Discontents and Speeches,* London: Cassell, 1904.

Cabezón, José Ignacio. "The UNESCO Declaration: A Tibetan Buddhist Perspective." In *Buddhist Peacework: Creating Cultures of Peace,* edited by David W. Chappell, pp. 183–88. Somerville, Mass.: Wisdom Publications, 1999.

Chah, Ajahn. *A Taste of Freedom,* p. 64. Thailand: Bung Wai Forest Monastery, 1980.

Chakravarti, Uma. *The Social Dimensions of Early Buddhism,* pp. 180–81. Delhi: Oxford University Press, 1987.

Chang, Iris. *The Rape of Nanking.* New York: Basic Books, 1997.

Chappell, David W., ed. *Buddhist Peacework: Creating Cultures of Peace,* pp. 212, 214. Somerville, Mass.: Wisdom Publications, 1999.

———. "Racial Diversity in the Soka Gakkai." In *Engaged Buddhism: Buddhist Liberation Movements in Asia,* edited by Christopher S. Queen and Sallie B. King, pp. 184–217. Albany: State University of New York Press, 1996.

Chomsky, Noam. *9-ll,* pp. 24–25. New York: Seven Stories Press, 2001.

Cleary, Thomas. *Entry into the Inconceivable: An Introduction to Hua-yen Buddhism,* p. 2. Honolulu: University of Hawaii Press, 1983.

———. *Zen Essence,* pp. 155–56. Boston: Shambhala, 1995.

Cobb, Clifford, et al. *The Genuine Progress Index.* San Francisco: Redefining Progress, 1995.

Conze, Edward. *A Short History of Buddhism*, pp. 113–14. London: Allen & Unwin, 1980.

———. *Thirty Years of Buddhist Studies,* p. 217. Oxford: Casirer, 1968.

Cook, Francis. *Hua-yen Buddhism,* p. 109. Pittsburgh: Pennsylvania State University Press, 1977.

Curle, Adam, *Another Way: Positive Response to Contemporary Violence.* Oxford: Jon Carpenter, 1995.

———. *Making Peace.* London: Tavistock Press, 1971.

———. *Mystics and Militants: A Study of Awareness Identity and Social Action,* p. 41. London: Tavistock, 1976.

Dahui Zonggao. Translated and edited by Thomas Cleary. In *Zen Essence,* p. 113. Boston: Shambhala, 1995.

Daly, Herman E., and John B. Cobb. *For the Common Good,* pp. 401–55. Boston: Beacon Press, 1989.

Davies, Norman. *Heart of Europe: A Short History of Poland,* pp. 66–67. Oxford: Clarendon Press, 1984.

Dogen Zenji. "Gyoji." In *Shobogenzo*, vol. 3, translated by Kosen Nishiyama, p. 33. Tokyo: Nakayama Shobo, 1983.

————.Quoted in *The Zen Poetry of Dogen,* edited by Steven Heine, p. 110. Boston: Tuttle, 1997.

Douglass, James W. *Resistance and Contemplation: The Way of Liberation,* pp. 141, 142, 144. New York: Doubleday, 1972.

Dowman, Keith, comp. and trans. "Song Thirteen." In *The Flight of the Garuda,* p. 110. London: Wisdom, 1994.

DuBoff, Richard. "Rogue Nation." <http://zmag.org/sustainers/content/2001–12/2duboff.cfm>.

Ellul, Jacques. *Violence: Reflections from a Christian Perspective,* pp. 118, 135. Oxford: Mowbrays, 1978.

Emmerick, R. E., trans. *Sutra of Golden Light [Suvaranaprabhasa Sutra],* p. 15. London: Luzac, 1970.

Foster, Nelson. "How Shall We Save the World?" *Turning Wheel* (Summer 1998): 13–17.

Fayen Ching-yuan. Translated and edited by Thomas Cleary. In *Zen Essence,* p. 82. Boston: Shambhala, 1995.

Fromm, Erich. "Psychoanalysis and Zen Buddhism." In *Lectures on Zen Buddhism and Psychoanalysis,* edited by D. T. Suzuki, E. Fromm, and R. De Martino, p. 108. London: Souvenir Press, 1974.

————. *The Revolution of Hope.* New York: Haper & Row, 1970.

Gendun Rinpoche. Extract from a *doha.* In *The Profound Path of Peace* (journal of the International Kagyu Sangha). Nova Scotia.

Ghosananda, Samdech Preah Maha. *Step by Step: Meditations on Wisdom and Compassion,* Berkeley: Parallax Press, 1992.

Giddens, Anthony. *Modernity and Self-Identity: Self and Society in the Late Modern Age,* pp. 177, 185, 208, 211–13. Palo Alto, Cal.: Stanford University Press, 1991.

Glassman, Bernard Tetsugen. Quoted in "Zen on the Street." *Shambhala Sun* (November 1997).

Goldstein, Joseph, trans. *Kalama Sutta* in "Tasting the Strawberry: Theravada Buddhism—Path of Awareness." *Naropa* magazine 2 (1985): 22.

Goleman, Daniel. *Emotional Intelligence,* p. 285. New York: Bantam Doubleday.

Gregg, Richard B. *The Power of Non-Violence.* 2nd edition. London: James Clarke, 1960.

Gross, Rita M. *Soaring and Settling: Buddhist Perspectives on Contemporary Social and Religious Issues,* p. 105. New York: Continuum, 1998.

Gyatso, Tenzin (H. H. the XIV Dalai Lama). *Collected Statements, Interviews, and Articles,* pp. 83-84. Dharamsala: Information Office of H. H. the Dalai Lama, 1982.

———. In *H. H. The Dalai Lama: The Bodhgaya Interviews,* edited by José I. Cabezón, p. 32. Ithaca. N.Y.: Snow Lion, 1988.

———. "Love, Altruism, Vegetarianism, Anger, and the Responsibilities of Teachers: Questions Answered by H. H. the Dalai Lama." *The Middle Way* 60, no. 2 (August 1985): 69.

———. *Newsletter,* Dharamsala. (January 1967).

———. *Ocean of Wisdom,* p. 13. San Francisco: Harper & Row, 1990.

———. *Universal Responsibility and the Good Heart,* p. 16. Dharamsala: Library of Tibetan Works & Archives, 1976.

Harrington, Alan. *The Immortalist,* pp. 138–89. New York: Random House, 1969.

Heelas, Paul. "The New Age in Cultural Context." *Religion* 23, no. 2 (April 1993):104–105.

Hisamatsu, Shin'ichi. "Vow of Mankind." Translated by Christopher A. Ives. In *Zen Awakening and Society,* p. 82. Honolulu: University of Hawaii Press, 1982.

———. Quoted in *Zen Awakening and Society,* by Christopher A. Ives, p. 70. Honolulu: University of Hawaii Press, 1982.

Hughes, James J. *A Green Buddhist Declaration,* para. 2.7. Moratuwa (Sri Lanka): Sarvodaya Press, 1984.

Humphreys, Christmas. *Both Sides of the Circle,* pp. 259–62. London: Allen & Unwin, 1978.

Hunt-Perry, Patricia, and Lyn Fine. "All Buddhism Is Engaged: Thich Nhat Hanh and the Order of Interbeing." In *Engaged Buddhism in the West,* edited by Christopher S. Queen, pp. 59, 61. Somerville, Mass.: Wisdom Publications, 2000.

Hutton, Will. *The State We're In.* London: Jonathan Cape, 1995.

Huxley, Aldous. *Eyeless in Gaza,* chapter 54. London: Chatto & Windus, 1969.

Ikeda, Daisaku. Quoted in *Religion and Society in Modern Japan,* by Edward Norbeck, p. 179. Houston: Tourmaline Press, 1970.

Ives, Christopher A. *Zen Awakening and Society,* pp. 69, 70. Honolulu: University of Hawaii Press, 1982

James, William. *Varieties of Religious Experience,* pp. 416–17. London & New York: Longmans, Green, n.d.

Jayatilleke, K. N. "The Conditioned Genesis of the Individual." *Buddhist Quarterly,* 11 (2–3), 1978–79, pp. 59, 60.

Jenkins, Stephen. "Do Bodhisattvas Relieve Poverty? The Distinction between Economic and Spiritual Development and Their Interrelation in Indian Buddhist Texts." *Journal of Buddhist Ethics* 7 (2000).

Johnston, William, *The Mirror Mind,* p. 99. New York: Fordham University Press, 1981.

———. *The Still Point: Reflections on Zen and Christian Mysticism,* p. xiii. New York: Harper & Row, 1970.

Jones, Ken. "Dumbing Down the Dharma?" *New Ch'an Forum* no. 25 (Winter 2001): 38–42.

Jung, C. G. "Psychology and Religion, West and East." In *Collected Works.* Vol. 11. London: Routledge & Kegan Paul, 1958.

Kabat-Zinn, Jon. "Catalyzing Movement Towards a More Contemplative / Sacred-Appreciating / Non-Dualistic Society." Paper presented at The Contemplative Mind in Society Working Group, 29 September and 2 October 1994, Pocantico, N.Y.

———. "Indra's Net at Work." In *The Psychology of Awakening,* edited by Gay Watson et al., pp. 225–49. London: Rider, 1999.

Kantowsky, Detlef. *Sarvodaya: The Other Development,* p. 67. New Delhi: Vikas, 1980.

Kapleau, Philip. *Zen Dawn in the West,* pp.232, 250. London: Rider, 1980.

Kelsay, John. "The Just-War Tradition and the Ethics of Nuclear Deterrence." *International Journal on the Unity of the Sciences* 2, no. 2 (Summer 1989): 229–52.

King, Sallie B. Conclusion. *Engaged Buddhism: Buddhist Liberation Movements in Asia,* edited by Christopher S. Queen and Sallie B. King, pp. 401–36. Albany: State University of New York Press, 1996.

King, Winston L. *In the Hope of Nirvana: An Essay on Theravada Buddhist Ethics,* p. 43. La Salle, Ill.: Open Court, 1964.

Kornfield, Jack. In *Ken Wilber in Dialogue,* edited by Donald Rothberg and Sean Kelly, p. 162. Wheaton, Ill.: Quest Books, 1998.

————. "Meditation: Aspects of Theory and Practice." In *Beyond Ego: Transpersonal Dimensions in Psychology,* edited by Roger Walsh and Frances Vaughan, pp. 150–53. Los Angeles: J. P. Tarcher, 1980.

————. *A Path with Heart: A Guide through the Perils and Promises of the Spiritual Life.* New York: Bantam, 1993.

————. "Psychological Adjustment Is Not Liberation." In *Zero: Contemporary Buddhist Life and Thought,* vol. 2, pp. 74, 76. Los Angeles, Calif.: Zero Press, 1979.

Korten, David. *When Corporations Rule the World,* pp. 214–18, 232–33. West Hartford, Conn.: Kumarin Press, 1995.

Kraft, Kenneth. "New Voices in Engaged Buddhism." In *Engaged Buddhism in the West,* edited by Christopher Queen, pp. 485–506. Somerville, Mass.: Wisdom, 2000.

————. "Practicing Peace: Social Engagement in Western Buddhism." *Journal of Buddhist Ethics* 6 (June 1999).

————. *The Wheel of Engaged Buddhism: A New Map of the Path.* New York: Weatherhill, 1999.

Laing, Ronald. *The Politics of Experience.* London: Penguin, 1967.

Larkin, Philip. *Collected Poems,* ed. Anthony Thwaite, p. 202, Boston: The Marvell Press, 1988.

Lasch, Christopher. *The Culture of Narcissism.* London: Abacus, 1980. also US imprint. New York: Warner Books, 1980.

Lindblom, Charles. *The Policy Making Process.* Eaglewood Cliffs, New Jersey: Prentice-Hall, 1968.

Ling, Trevor. *The Buddha,* pp. 106, 109, 151, 196. London: Temple Smith, 1973.

————. *The Buddha's Philosophy of Man.* London: Dent, 1981.

————. *Buddhism, Imperialism and War,* p. 147. London: Allen & Unwin, 1979.

Loori, John Daido. *Mountain Record of Zen Talks,* pp. 139–40. Boston: Shambhala, 1988.

Loy, David R. *A Buddhist History of the West: Studies in Lack,* p. 198. Albany: State University of New York Press, 2002.

————. *The Great Awakening: A Buddhist Social Theory.* Boston: Wisdom Publications, 2003.

————. "The Deconstruction of Buddhism." In *Derrida and Negative Theology,* edited by Harold Coward, p. 227. Albany: State University of New York Press, 1992.

Lozoff, Bo. *We're All Doing Time*. Durham, N.C.: Prison Ashram Project, 1987.

Macy, Joanna R. *Despair and Personal Power in the Nuclear Age*. Philadelphia: New Society Publishers, 1983.

————. *Dharma and Development: Religion As a Resource in the Sarvodaya Self-Help Movement*, revised edition, pp. 37, 95. West Hartford, Conn.: Kumarian Press, 1985.

Macy, Joanna R., and Molly Young Brown. *Coming Back to Life: Practices to Reconnect Our Lives, Our World*. Stony Creek, Conn.: New Society Publishers, 1998.

Maslow, Abraham. *Towards a Psychology of Being*, 2nd edition, pp. 71–72. Princeton: Van Nostrand, 1968.

Mason, Michael. Quoted in a report by John Vidal. *Guardian* (London) (31 July 1999): 9.

McClellan, John. Letter to the Editor. *Tricycle* 3, no.3 (Spring 1994): 10–13.

McCormack, Cathy. Quoted in *The Myth of the Market* by Jeremy Seabrook, pp. 102–103. Hartland, Devon: Green Books, 1990.

McIntosh, Sandy. "An Insider's View of Nichiren Shoshu." *Tricycle* 2, no. 2 (Winter 1992): 22.

McNulty, Christine. Quoted in *The Living Economy: A New Economics in the Making*, by Paul Ekins, pp. 63–69. London: Routledge & Kegan Paul, 1986.

Merton, Thomas. *On Peace*, pp. 17, 113, 114. Oxford: Mowbrays, 1976.

Metraux, Daniel A. "The Soka Gakkai." In *Engaged Buddhism: Buddhist Liberation Movements in Asia*, edited by Christopher S. Queen and Sallie B. King, pp. 365–400. Albany: State University of New York Press, 1996.

Milarepa. Quoted in *Tibet's Great Yogi Milarepa*, 2nd edition, edited by W. Y. Evans-Wentz, p. 271. London: Oxford University Press, 1951.

Milgram, Stanley. "Some Conditions of Obedience and Disobedience to Authority." *Human Relations* 18: 57–76. 1965.

Montague, Peter. "One Fundamental Problem." *Rachel's Environment & Health Weekly*, no. 582 (22 January 1998).

Murdoch, Iris. *The Sovereignty of the Good*, pp. 54, 59, 67. London: Routledge & Kegan Paul, 1970.

Myers, Norman. "Problems of the Next Century." Paper presented to United Nations Economic and Development U.K. Committee, Green College, Oxford, 24 June 1996.

Naess, Arne, and George Sessions. Quoted in *Simple in Means, Rich in Ends,* by Bill Devall, p. 14. London: Green Print, 1990.

Nakamura, Hajime. *Ways of Thinking of Eastern Peoples,* revised edition, p. 153. London: Kegan Paul International, 1997.

Needleman, Jacob. *The New Religions,* pp. 16–17. London: Allen Lane, 1972.

Nhat Hanh, Thich. "*Ahimsa*: The Path of Harmlessness." In *Buddhist Peacework: Creating Cultures of Peace,* edited by David W. Chappell, pp. 155–64. Somerville, Mass.: Wisdom Publications, 1999.

———. *Love in Action: Writings on Non-Violent Social Change,* p. 82. Berkeley: Parallax Press, 1993.

———. *The Miracle of Mindfulness.* Berkeley: Parallax Press, 1987.

———. "Nonviolence: Practicing Awareness." In *Seeds of Peace* 1, no.1 (April 2528 [i.e., 1985]):.4.

Nietzsche, Friedrich. "On Truth and Lie in the Extra-Moral Sense." In *The Portable Nietzsche,* edited by W. Kaufmann, pp. 46–47. London: Viking Penguin, 1968.

Nyanaponika Mahathera. *The Power of Mindfulness,* p. 16. Kandy: Buddhist Publication Society (Wheel Publication 121/122), 1976.

Ophuls, William. "Political Values for an Age of Scarcity: Buddhist Politics." *American Theosophist* 69, no. 5 (May 1981): pp.140–47.

Ornatowski, Gregory K. "Continuity and Change in the Economic Ethics of Buddhism: Evidence from the History of Buddhism in India, China, and Japan." *Journal of Buddhist Ethics* 3 (1996).

Orwell, George. *The Collected Essays, Journalism and Letters.* Edited by Sonia Orwell and Ian Angus, vol. 3, pp. 293–99. New York: Harcourt Brace Jovanovich, 1968.

Otto, Rudolf. *Mysticism East and West,* p. 14. New York: Macmillan, 1970.

Queen, Christopher S., ed. *Engaged Buddhism in the West,* pp. 1–2, 25. Boston: Wisdom Publications, 2000.

Queen, Christopher S., and Sallie B. King, eds. *Engaged Buddhism: Buddhist Liberation Movements in Asia.* Albany: State University of New York Press, 1996.

Rahula, Walpola. *What the Buddha Taught,* p. 32. London: Gordon Fraser, 1959.

———. *Zen and the Taming of the Bull.* London: Gordon Fraser, 1978.

Rathana, Athuraliya. Quoted in "In Defense of the Dharma: Just-War Ideology in Buddhist Sri Lanka," by Tessa Bartholomeusz. *Journal of Buddhist Ethics* 6 (1999): 3.

Rewata Dhamma. "Towards a Better Society: A Buddhist Perspective." Paper presented at a United Nations University meeting at Thammasat University, Bangkok, 20–22 March 1985.

Rilke, Rainer Maria. "Tenth Duino Elegy." Translated by Ruth Speirs. In *The Rider Book of Mystical Verse,* edited by J. M. Cohen. London: Rider, 1983.

Rothberg, Donald. "The Parking Lot Sutra." *Turning Wheel: The Journal of Socially Engaged Buddhism* (Winter 2001): 34–37.

Rowe, Dorothy. *Living with the Bomb: Can We Live without Enemies?,* p. 112. London: Routledge & Kegan Paul, 1985.

Sangharakshita. *New Currents in Western Buddhism,* p. 64. Glasgow: Windhorse, 1990.

Santikaro Bhikkhu. "The Four Noble Truths of Dhammic Socialism." In *Entering the Realm of Reality: Towards Dhammic Societies,* edited by Jonathan Watts, Alan Senauke, and Santikaro Bhikkhu. Bangkok: International Network of Engaged Buddhists, 1997.

———. Letter to author. 16 February 2002.

———. "Socially Engaged Buddhism and Modernity." *Think Sangha Journal* 2 (Winter 1999): 141–60.

Schor, Juliet. *Overworked Americans.* Cambridge: Harvard University Press, 1993.

Schutz, Alfred. *On Phenomenology and Social Relations: Selected Writing,* edited by Helmut R. Wagner, p. 80. Chicago: University of Chicago Press, 1970.

Seed, John. *Thinking Like a Mountain.* Philadelphia: New Society Publishers, 1988.

Senauke, Alan. Letter to author. 31 January 2002. <au: pls. confirm, was letter?>

Seng-ts'an. *Hsin-hsin-ming [On Trust in the Heart].* Translated (mainly) by Arthur Waley. In *Buddhist Texts throughout the Ages,* edited by Edward Conze et. al., p. 211. Oxford: Cassirer, 1954.

Sennett, Richard. *The Fall of Public Man,* p. 219. Cambridge: Cambridge University Press, 1977.

Shantideva. *Bodhicaryavatara.* In *World of the Buddha,* edited by Lucien Stryk, p. 303. New York: Anchor Doubleday, 1969.

Sharpe, Gene. *Social Power and Political Freedom.* Boston, Porter Sargent, 1980.

[Shin] Buddhist Churches of American Social Issues Committee. "A Shin Buddhist Stance on Abortion." *[American] Buddhist Peace Fellowship Newsletter* 6, no. 3 (July 1984): 6–7.

Sivaraksa, Sulak. "Buddhism and a Culture of Peace." In *Buddhist Peacework: Creating Cultures of Peace,* edited by David W. Chappell, pp. 39–46. Somerville, Mass.: Wisdom Publications, 1999.

———. *Siamese Resurgence,* pp. 37–38, 77-78, 108. Bangkok: Asian Cultural Forum on Development, 1985.

Skinner, Robyn, "Psychotherapy and Spiritual Tradition." In *Awakening the Heart: Eastern and Western Approaches to Psychotherapy and the Healing Relationship,* edited by John Welwood, pp. 18–32. Boston: Shambhala, 1983.

Smart, Ninian. *Beyond Ideology: Religion and the Future of Western Civilization,* pp. 309, 311. London: Collins, 1981.

Smith, Bardwell L. "Sinhalese Buddhism and the Dilemmas of Reinterpretation," in *The Two Wheels of Dhamma: Essays on the Theravada Tradition in India and Ceylon,* p. 106. Chambersberg, Penn.: American Academy of Religion, 1972.

Snyder, Gary. "Buddhism and the Coming Revolution." In *Earth House Hold,* p. 91. New York: New Directions, 1957.

———. *The Practice of the Wild,* p. 68. San Francisco: North Point, 1990.

Spiro, Melford E. *Buddhism and Society.* London: Allen & Unwin, 1970.

Steiner, George. *Grammars of Creation.* London: Faber, 2001.

Suzuki, D. T., trans. *Avatamsaka Sutra,* in *Essays in Zen Buddhism: Third Series,* p. 83. London: Rider, 1970.

———. *The Field of Zen,* p. 58. London: The Buddhist Society, 1970.

———. "Knowledge and Innocence." In *Zen and the Birds of Appetite,* edited by Thomas Merton. New York: New Directions, 1968.

———., trans. *The Lankavatara Sutra.* London: Routledge & Kegan Paul, 1932.

———. "Self the Unattainable." In *The Buddha Eye: An Anthology of the Kyoto School,* edited by Frederick Franck, p. 16. New York: Crossroad, 1982.

Thomas, Kate. *The Destiny Challenge.* Forres, Scotland: New Frequency Press, 1992.

Thurman, Robert A. F. "Guidelines for Buddhist Social Activism Based on Nagarjuna's *Jewel Garland of Royal Counsels.*" *Eastern Buddhist* 16, no. 1 (Spring 1983), 19–51. Reprinted in *The Path of Compassion: Writings on Socially Engaged Buddhism,* edited by Fred Eppsteiner and Dennis Maloney, pp. 120–44. Berkeley: Parallax Press, 1985.

———., trans. *The Holy Teachings of Vimalakirti: A Mahayana Scripture,* pp. 50–51. Pittsburgh: Pennsylvania State University Press, 1976.

————. "The Politics of Enlightenment." *Lindisfarne Newsletter* 8. 1979.

Tillich, Paul. *The Courage to Be,* p. 190. New Haven, Conn.: Yale University Press, 1959.

Titmuss, Christopher. "A Passion for the Dharma." *Turning Wheel* (Fall, 1991): 19.

Trainer, F. E. *Abandon Affluence!,* pp. 194–96. London: Zed Books, 1985.

Trungpa, Chögyam. Quoted in *Buddhism in America* by Emma McCloy Layman, p. 102. Chicago: Nelson Hall, 1976.

————. *The Myth of Freedom,* p. 70. Boston: Shambhala, 1976.

Tworkov, Helen. Editorial. *Tricycle* 8, no. 4 (Summer 1999).

————. *Zen in America,* p. 258. New York: Kodansha, 1994.

United Nations Development Program. *Human Development Reports.* New York: United Nations Organization. 2001

United States Code. United States Code Congressional & Administrative News, 98th Congress, Second Session, 19 October1984, v. 2, para. 3077, 98 STAT. 2707. St. Paul, Minn.: West Publishing Co., 1984.

Varela, Francisco. From an interview in *Inquiring Mind* 16, no. 1 (Fall 1999): 7.

Victoria, Brian. *Zen at War.* New York: Weatherhill, 1997.

Visvapani. "Buddhism and the New Age." *Western Buddhist Review* 1 (December 1994):11.

Wallace, B. Alan. "Tibetan Buddhism in the West: Is It Working?" *Tricycle* 40 (Summer 2001): 54–63.

Walsh, Roger, and Frances Vaughan. *Paths beyond Ego,* p. 267. Los Angeles: Tarcher/Putnam, 1993.

Walshe, Maurice, trans. *Samyutta Nikaya: An Anthology,* Pt. 3, 12, 15. Kandy: Buddhist Publication Society, 1985 (Wheel Publications).

Warraq, Ibn. *Why I Am Not a Muslim.* Amherst, N.Y.: Prometheus, 1995.

Welwood, John. "Befriending Emotion." In *Awakening the Heart: Eastern and Western Approaches to Psychotherapy and the Healing Relationship,* pp. 84–90. Boston: Shambhala, 1983.

————. "Psychology and Meditation." In *Awakening the Heart: Eastern and Western Approaches to Psychotherapy and the Healing Relationship.* Boston: Shambhala, 1983.

Whitmyer, Claude. *Mindfulness and Meaningful Work: Explorations in Right Livelihood,* pp. 262–63. Berkeley: Parallax, 1994.

Wilber, Ken. *No Boundary: Eastern and Western Approaches to Personal Growth*, pp. 107, 124. Boston: Shambhala, 1981.

————. *Up from Eden: A Transpersonal View of Human Evolution*. London: Routledge & Kegan Paul, 1983.

Wilkinson, Helen, and Melanie Howard. *Tomorrow's Women*. London: Demos, 1997.

Winston, Diana. "Justify Your Love: Finding Authority for Socially Engaged Buddhism." ThinkSangha web publication. <http://www.bpf.org/sebmeth.html> [September 2001].

Woolger, Roger J. *Other Lives, Other Selves: A Jungian Psychotherapist Discovers Past Lives*, pp. 334–35. New York: Dolphin/Doubleday, 1987.

Yarnall, Thomas Freeman. "Engaged Buddhism: New and Improved!? Made in the U.S.A. Out of Asian Materials." *Journal of Buddhist Ethics* 7 (2000): 2.

Zimbardo, Philip G., et al. "Reflections on the Stanford Prison Experiment." In *Obedience to Authority*, edited by T. Blass, pp. 193–237. Mahwah, New Jersey: Eribaum, 2000. (For an internet slideshow of the experiment go to <www. prisonexp.org>.)

FOR FURTHER INQUIRY:

For a further discussion of new Buddhist movements in the United Kingdom, see Ken Jones, "Movements in British Buddhism." *New Ch'an Forum,* no. 13 (Spring 1996). See also issue no. 14 (Spring 1997). The New Kadampa and the Friends of the Western Buddhist Order were the subject of articles by Madelaine Bunting in the London *Guardian* on 6 July and 27 October 1997, respectively. This was the beginning of a long-running controversy around the FWBO and its leader, Sangharkshita. Henry Shukman attempted a balanced assessment in *Tricycle* 8, vol. 4 (Summer 1999), pp. 66–67, 111–18.

There has been some valuable scholarly inquiry into the exotic, devotional, and shamanic attractions of Tibetan Buddhism for the Western psyche, with its empowerments, potent teachings by celebrated gurus, and fascination with Tantrayana. See Peter Bishop, *Dreams of Power: Tibetan Buddhism and the Western Imagination* (London: Athlone, 1993). See also Donald S. Lopez, *Prisoners of Shangri-La: Tibetan Buddhism and the West* (Chicago: University of Chicago Press, 1998).

A broad "antiglobalization" coalition has already proposed policies for moving in that direction. See the companion volumes by Harry Shutt: *The Trouble with Capitalism: An Inquiry into the Causes of Global Economic Failure,* and *A New Democracy: Alternatives to a Bankrupt World Order,* published in 1999 and 2001 respectively by Zed Books, London.

For more information about Aung San Suu Kyi, see Aung San Suu Kyi with Alan Clements, *The Voice of Hope* (New York: Seven Stories Press, 1997).

For further discussion of Buddhist feminism, see the Spring 1999 issue of *Turning Wheel,* which was devoted to the subject. Their reading list includes: Rita Gross, *Buddhism after Patriarchy* (Albany: State University of New York Press, 1992); Marianne Dresser, ed., *Buddhist Women on the Edge* (Berkeley: North Atlantic Books, 1996); and two books by Sandy Boucher: *Opening the Lotus: What Women Want to Know about Buddhism* (Boston: Beacon, 1997), and *Turning the Wheel: American Women Creating the New Buddhism* (Boston: Beacon, 1994).

ThinkSangha is a socially engaged international think tank, which uses the Buddhist *sangha* model to explore pressing issues and concerns. The group's methodology is based on friendship and Buddhist practice as much as theory and thought. Its core activities are networking with other scholar-activists, producing Buddhist critiques and models on social issues, and providing materials and resource persons for conferences and workshops. Web site: <http://www.bpf.org/think.html>.

For a presentation of a Buddhist social theory, see David Loy's *The Great Awakening* (Wisdom Publications, Boston).

INDEX

identity, 72;
practice, 102–3. *See also* mindfulness

B
Ball, John, 58
Banerjee, N. V., 46, 216
bare awareness, 102–3.
  See also awareness; mindfulness
Basham, A. L., 46–47
Batchelor, Stephen, 106–7, 120, 125–26, 238
Bauman, Zygmunt, 165
Beck, Charlotte Joko, 124
Becker, Ernest, 55
behavioral roles, 38–39
Belgrade, 56. *See also* Yugoslav crisis
belief, 93–94. *See also* faith
Bellah, Robert, 75, 93, 115
belongingness, 6–7, 15, 199;
  and antithetical bonding, 54–55;
  and the disembedded self, 76;
  and fundamentalism, 95;
  and history, 52;
  and the Janus syndrome, 64–66;
  and nondualistic spirituality, 93
Berger, Brigitte, 80–81
Berger, Peter, 76, 80–81
Berman, Morris, 97
Berry, Wendell, 232
Beyond Belief: Essays on Religion in a Post-Traditional World (Bellah), 75, 93
Beyond Ideology (Ninian), 92
Bhikkhu, Santikaro, 74–75, 110, 179–81, 183, 220, 230
Big Mind, concept of, 7, 32–35
biocentric egalitarianism, 97–98. *See also* egalitarianism
biography, 114
Blake, William, 212
Blum, William, 145–46, 160
Blythe, R. H., 9
bodhisattvas, 18–20, 47, 178, 212, 222, 236, 241
bonding, antithetical, 54–55, 236
Bondurant, Joan, 149, 150
Bonhoeffer, Dietrich, 95, 138, 148
Bookchin, Murray, 232
brahman, 89
Brahma-vihara meditation, 105
Brandon, David, 69–70, 128, 177

Brazier, Caroline, 206
Brazier, David, 193, 206, 229–30
Britain, 120, 124, 130, 175, 206–8;
  economic conditions in, 167;
  and the United States, war between, 160
Brown, Helen Gurley, 7
Buber, Martin, 91
Buddha (Siddhartha Gautama):
  family background of, 44;
  Fire Sermon, 38, 159;
  on hatred, 38, 146;
  and ideology, 59, 61, 62;
  and Indian Buddhism, 44;
  on liberation, 69;
  noble truths proclaimed by, 3–4, 7–9;
  path of, 121;
  on salvation, 93;
  on suffering, 3, 33;
  and the wheel of the Dharma, 67, 68.
  See also Buddha nature
Buddhadharma, 148–49, 241
Buddhadhasa, Ajahn, 48–49, 190–91, 214
Buddha nature, 7, 14;
  and morality, 128;
  and passion, 35.
  See also Buddha
Buddhism. *See specific forms*
Buddhism and Marxism: A Study in Humanism (Banerjee), 46
Buddhism and the Coming Revolution" (Snyder), 70
"Buddhism and the New Age" (Visvapani), 99
Buddhism without Beliefs (Batchelor), 125
Buddhist Churches of America, 136
Buddhist History of the West: Studies in Lack (Loy), 164
Buddhist Peace Fellowship, 146, 174, 179, 206, 240;
  described, 201–2;
  historical validation sought by, 222–23;
  Senauke on, 182–83
Bultman, Rudolf, 95
Burke, Edmund, 26
Burma, 24, 45, 114, 153, 191–92

E
Easter Island, 27, 168
Eckhart, Meister, 89, 91
ecocentrism, 98
ecology, xvi, 120, 161, 163, 167–80,
175;
deep, 97–98;
and Dharma Gaia, 170–72;
and ecospirituality, 96–99;
and emancipatory movements, 71;
and karma, 27;
and morality, 131;
and nondualistic spirituality, 88
economics, 190, 209, 218, 227, 234–35;
and emancipation, 70–71;
and ideology, 61;
and institutionalized delusion, 54,
58, 61;
Marxian, 58.
See also Capitalism; Socialism
education, 45, 46, 47, 76, 150. *See also*
teachers
egalitarianism, 58, 97–98, 120, 123, 171
ego and the collective unconscious,
34;
and compassion, 177;
and emptiness, 13;
and faith, 94;
and the id, 7;
and ideologies, 60, 61;
and the Janus syndrome, 66;
and Mahayana Buddhism, 12, 13,
15;
and morality, 129;
and the need for inner work, 72;
and the New Age movement,
99–100;
and nondualistic spirituality, 88,
90;
and postmodernism, 79, 80;
and the skandha model, 31, 32;
spiritualized, 96;
and transpersonal psychology,
110–12, 121–22.
See also egoic era; individualism;
self
egoic era, 57, 90. *See also* ego
Ehi-passika, 62
Einstein, Albert, xvi, 120–21
electric shocks, administration of, 57
Eliot, T. S., 91

elitism, 79
Ellul, Jacques, 148, 155
Emancipation, 70–71
emotion: befriending, 102–3;
and mindfulness, 103;
and social action, 105;
and transpersonal psychology, 108,
110
emotional intelligence, 237
empathy, 155, 177–78
empowerment, 54, 124–25
emptiness, 11–18, 20–21, 228–30
energy: attentive, 32, 33;
commitment of, through social
action, 104;
and meaning making, 36;
and mindfulness, 102, 103;
and rebirth, 27
Engaged Buddhism: anatomy of,
173–76;
in Asia, 185–99;
avoiding ideological traps in,
63–64;
and compassion, 176–78;
distinguishing characteristics of,
181–82;
and emptiness, 228–30;
and the fragmentation of organizations, 182–84;
grounding of, 211–20;
and identity politics, 203–4;
overview of, 173–84;
root problems faced by, 221–30;
in the West, 201–9
enlightenment, 213, 216;
and collective awakening, x;
and Indian Buddhism, 45, 47, 49;
and institutionalized delusion, 63;
Kraft on, x;
and Mahayana Buddhism, 14, 18;
and the New Age movement, 100;
and meditation, 102;
quest for, 122–23;
and religious belief, 94;
and transpersonal consciousness,
121–22;
and the yanas, 114
*Entry into the Inconceivable: An Intro-
duction to Hua-yen Buddhism*
(Cleary), 17
environmentalism, 97–98

epistemology, 214
ethics, 15, 181;
and Buddhist precepts, 130–34;
and corporate policies, 162;
environmental, 98;
and Indian Buddhism, 47;
and karma, 23–24, 34–35;
and institutionalized delusion, 52,
63;
and mindfulness, 103;
and nondualistic spirituality, 93;
and peacework, 154–55;
and postmodernism, 80;
and social awareness, 113, 115, 117.
See also morality
ethnicity, 55–56, 70–71, 143, 159, 175
ethnocentrism, 94
evangelical fundamentalism, 95. *See
also* fundamentalism
Evans-Wentz, W. Y., 223–24
evil, 7, 62;
avoidance of, 127, 128;
and Indian Buddhism, 44, 49;
and morality, 127, 128, 129, 135;
ordinary citizens as perpetrators of,
56–57;
and social action, 105;
"war against," 159, 160, 161
existential hunger, 57–58
existentialism, 79, 95
experience, as one of the four states of
spiritual unfolding, 93–94
expressive behavior, 65–66. *See also*
emotion
Eyeless in Gaza (Huxley), 128

F
faith: and contemporary spirituality,
93–94;
and exoteric religion, 95;
and monasticism, 107;
as one of the four states of spiritual
unfolding, 93–94;
and transpersonal consciousness,
121
Fall of Public Man, The (Sennett), 81
false consciousness, 38. *See also* consciousness
family: and Congregational Buddhism, 123;
extended, 82;
loyalty, in Japan, 115;

and morality, 132;
and spiritual community, 107–8.
See also relationships
fascism, 62, 143
fasting, 104
fatalism, 23, 24, 40
Fayan, 8
fear, xvi, 7;
and emptiness, 4, 13;
liberation from, 9;
and morality, 137;
and postmodernism, 80;
repressed, projection of, 38;
and the self, 34;
and the skandha model, 32;
and warfare, 56
feminism, 100, 108, 128, 204
Field of Zen (Suzuki), 33
Fine, Lyn, 194
Fire Sermon (Buddha), 38, 159
Fitzgerald, F. Scott, 54
Flight of the Garuda, The (Dowman),
35
For the Common Good (Cobb and
Daly), 167
form: and emptiness, 13, 15–16;
and phenomenology, 37;
and the yanas, 114
Foster, Nelson, 223
fourth eye, opening of, x, 113–26, 106,
240
Fox, Matthew, 96
fragmentation, 78, 182–84
freedom: and capitalism, 69, 70;
and the disembedded self, 76;
and emancipatory movements,
70–71;
and modernity, 68;
and postmodernism, 80;
and radicalism, 54.
See also liberation
Freud, Sigmund: repetitive compulsions in, 25;
transference in, 55
Friends of the Western Buddhist
Order
(FWBO), 93, 124, 206–8, 229
Froissart, Jean, 58
Fromm, Eric, 16, 37–38, 55
fundamentalism, 62, 94–96, 181

G

scientific socialism, 59. *See also* socialism
scientism, 61
Scott, Michael, 137, 138, 148
"Sea of Faith" (Cupitt), 95
secularization, 91, 126, 127
Seed, John, 98
self: and Buddist social psychology,
31–41;
disembedded, 75–76, 82;
and existential paradoxes, 4–7;
explorers, 237;
and Indra's net, 16–18;
and institutionalized delusion,
53–54, 57–58, 64–66;
and the Janus syndrome, 64–66;
and karma, 25;
and Mahayana Buddhism, 12, 14,
16–18;
and meditation, 32;
and the New Age movement,
99–100;
and physical survival, 57–58;
and postmodernism, 79, 80–81;
question of, 3;
and the remedying of suffering,
7–9;
restoration of, 9;
and the skandha model, 32;
and social awareness, 117–18,
121–22;
social construction of, 35–39;
transcendence, 82;
and transpersonal consciousnesss,
121–22.
See also Ego; Individualism
"Self the Unattainable" (Suzuki),
33–34
Senauke, Alan, 182–83
Sengcan, 13, 14, 62
Sennett, Richard, 81
separation, 14, 128;
and nondualistic spirituality, 89;
and the self, 33
September 11th 2001 terrorist attack,
145, 159–61, 225. *See also* terrorism
Serbs, 56. *See also* Yugoslav crisis
Sessions, George, 98
sexism, 145
sexual: ethics, 131;
harassment, 145
sexuality, 134

shadow, subconscious, 7, 88
Shakespeare, William, 5, 136
Shamatha, 101
Shambhala Training project, 124
Shankara, 89
Shantideva, 18
Sharp, Gene, 146, 150
sheaves, notion of two, 28
Sherif, M., 55
Shin'ichi, Hisamatsu, 54, 117, 226
Shintoism, 119
Shobogenzo, (Dogen) 181, 222
Shotoka (prince), 48
Shramadana, 186
Shunyata, 13. *See also* Emptiness
Siamese Convergnence, 132
Siamese Resurgence (Sivaraksa), 72, 107
Siddhartha Gautama (Buddha): fam-
ily background of, 44;
Fire Sermon, 38, 159;
on hatred, 38, 146;
and ideology, 59, 61, 62;
and Indian Buddhism, 44;
on liberation, 69;
noble truths proclaimed by, 3–4,
7–9;
path of, 121;
on salvation, 93;
on suffering, 3, 33;
and the wheel of the Dharma, 67,
68.
See also Buddha nature
Sigalovada Sutta, 44
Simple in Means, Rich in Ends
(Devall), 98
Sinhala heritage, 181
Sivaraksa, Sulak, 72, 107, 132, 153–54,
189–90
Skandhas, 31, 32–37
"skillful means," concept of, 94, 119,
126
Skinner, Robyn, 111
"small is beautiful," notion of, 17, 209
small mind, concept of, 7, 32–35
Smart, Ninian, 92
Smith, Bardwell, 213
Snyder, Gary, 70, 98–99
*Social Dimensions of Early Buddhism,
The* (Chakravarti), 48
social fallacy, 39–41
socialism, 191, 196, 208, 216, 233
socialization, 65

194–96, 204, 223–24;
and the Dharma of modernity,
120;
and disillusionment, 122;
dzogchen meditation tradition, 35;
and gurus, 106;
and inner Buddhism, 173;
and peacework, 156;
and social awareness, 115–16, 120.
See also Dalai Lama
Tiep Hien Order, 132
Tillich, Paul, 91, 95, 178
time: commitment of, through social
action, 104;
and the disembedded self, 75
Titmuss, Christopher, 130, 131,
225–26
TNCs (transnational corporations),
162, 163
*Tokugawa Religion: The Cultural
Roots of Modern Japan* (Bellah), 115
Tomorrow's Women (Howard and
Wilkinson), 76
"Towards a Better Society: A
Buddhist Perspective" (Dhamma),
87
Towards a Psychology of Being
(Maslow), 112
trace states, 95
Trainer, F. E., 166
tranquility, 101
transcendence, 96
transcendentalism, 45–47, 119
transference, 55
transience, 52, 120
transmutation, 102
transpersonal psychology, 88, 108–12
trauma, 108, 110
Tricyle (journal), 122–23
Trungpa, Chögyam, 88, 103, 124
truth(s), 183–84, 195–96, 211, 230;
and core Dharma, 118;
and creative nonviolence, 150;
and the Dharma of modernity, 119;
and ecospirituality, 98;
and fundamentalism, 94;
and ideology, 62;
and Indian Buddhism, 46, 47;
and institutionalized delusion, 53,
62;
and morality, 133;

noble, declared by the Buddha,
3–4, 7–9;
Russian words for, 183–84;
and social action, 105;
and variable Dharma, 119
Tucker, Mary E., 171
Tworkov, Helen, 122–23, 156–57
typification, concept of, 36

U
Udayi (king), 47
Ulysses (Joyce), 67
uncertainty, 134–38
unemployment. *See* Work
United Nations, 165, 198;
Environment Program, 168;
World Food Program, 169
Unity consciousness, 14, 33–34
*Universal Responsibility and the Good
Heart* (Dalai Lama), 73
universalism, 123
Upaya, 94, 119
Upekkha, 105
Up from Eden (Wilber), 89
utilitarianism, 71, 115
utopianism, 232

V
Vajrayana Buddhism, 102, 180
Varela, Francisco, 79
Varieties of Religious Experience
(James), 89
Vaughan, Frances, 112
Vedana, 31
victimhood, 25
Victoria, Brian, 116
Vietnam, 53, 70, 132, 147, 192–94
Vietnam War, 132
Vijnanavada, 12
Vimalakirti Sutra, xvi, 62
Vimalakirtinirdesha Sutra, 222
violence: avoidance of, 130;
covert, 144;
cultural, 143–46;
direct, 144;
efficacy of, as a means of social
change, 141–42;
Ellul on, 141–42, 155;
establishing peaceful stabilization
instead of, 152–53;
and Indian Buddhism, 44, 46–47;

and phenomenology, 37;
structural, 143–46. *See also*
nonviolence; Warfare
*Violence: Reflections from a Christian
Perspective* (Ellul), 141–42, 155
Vipassana, 101, 109, 204
Virya, 229
void. *See* emptiness

W
Wallace, B. Alan, 122
Walsh, Roger, 112
war: crimes, 59, 148;
and Imperial Way Buddhism,
115–18, 181, 239;
and institutionalized delusion,
54–56;
and the Janus syndrome, 65;
just, notion of, 142–43;
low intensity, 160;
and morality, 134, 138;
preventing, 153–54;
and the social fallacy, 41.
See also terrorism; violence
War Responsibility of Buddhists, The
(Hakugen), 117
Warraq, Ibn, 79
Watts, Alan, 120
wealth, 52, 54;
creation, incentives to, 70;
and creative nonviolence, 149;
and karma, 26;
and morality, 131, 133.
See also economics
Weber, Max, 213
Weil, Simon, 91
welfare states, 38, 48, 45–46, 48
Welwood, John, 102, 110
Western Buddhist Order, 124
What the Buddha Taught (Rahula),
142
Wheel of Engaged Buddhism (Kraft),
101
When Corporations Rule the World
(Korten), 163
White Lotus Society, 142
Whitmyer, Claude, 207
Wilber, Ken, 57, 88, 89, 93
Wilde, Oscar, 60
Wilkinson, Helen, 76
Williams, Duncan R., 171
Winston, Diana, 215, 219–20, 225

wisdom, 155, 177, 212;
compassion as the daily face of,
177;
dawning of, 9;
and faith, 94;
and the higher third, 15;
and Indian Buddhism, 47;
and Mahayana Buddhism, 15,
17–18;
and morality, 127, 129;
and nondualistic spirituality, 89
women's rights, 143
work, 6, 8;
and cultural violence, 145;
and the disembedded self, 76;
ethos of, 107–8;
and the Janus syndrome, 65;
and nondualistic spirituality, 92;
and the social fallacy, 40
World As Lover, World As Self (Macy),
x
World War I, 120
World War II, 67, 117, 120, 137–38,
148
Worldwide Fund for Nature, 169
WTO (World Trade Organization),
163

Y
Yale University, 56
Yanas, 113, 114–16, 180, 230
Yarnall, Thomas, 218–19
Yasutani, Hakuun, 113, 116
Yogachara school, 12–14, 32–35, 114
Yugoslav crisis, 56, 152, 156, 157

Z
Zazen, 137. *See also* Meditation
Zen Buddhism, 181, 202–4, 222, 226;
and the American Dharma Revolution, 122–23;
Big Mind in, concept of, 7, 32–35;
and the Dharma of modernity,
120;
dialogue of, with Christianity, 92;
and ecology, 97, 170;
and the Huayen school, 16;
and ideology, 62;
and the injunction to "kill the
Buddha," 95;
Imperial Way, 115–18, 181, 239;
and inner Buddhism, 173;

ABOUT WISDOM

WISDOM PUBLICATIONS, a not-for-profit publisher, is dedicated to making available authentic Buddhist works for the benefit of all. We publish translations of the sutras and tantras, commentaries and teachings of past and contemporary Buddhist masters, and original works by the world's leading Buddhist scholars. We publish our titles with the appreciation of Buddhism as a living philosophy and with the special commitment to preserve and transmit important works from all the major Buddhist traditions.

To learn more about Wisdom, or to browse books online, visit our website at wisdompubs.org.

You may request a copy of our mail-order catalog online or by writing to:

WISDOM PUBLICATIONS
199 Elm Street
Somerville, Massachusetts 02144 USA
Telephone:(617) 776-7416
Fax: (617) 776-7841
Email: info@wisdompubs.org
www.wisdompubs.org

The Wisdom Trust

As a not-for-profit publisher, Wisdom is dedicated to the publication of fine Dharma books for the benefit of all sentient beings and dependent upon the kindness and generosity of sponsors in order to do so. If you would like to make a donation to Wisdom, please do so through our Somerville office. If you would like to sponsor the publication of a book, please write or email us at the address above.

Thank you.

Wisdom is a nonprofit, charitable 501(c)(3) organization affiliated with the Foundation for the Preservation of the Mahayana Tradition (FPMT).

Mindfulness in Plain English:
Revised and Expanded Edition
Bhante Henepola Gunaratana
224 pages, ISBN 0-86171-321-4, $14.95

"*Mindfulness in Plain English* is a wonderfully clear and straightforward explanation of mindfulness meditation. Venerable Gunaratana has done a valuable service in writing this book. It will be a great help to all who read it."
—Joseph Goldstein, author of *One Dharma*

"Extremely up-to-date, and approachable, this book also serves as a very thorough FAQ for new (and not-so-new) meditators.… . Bhante has an engaging delivery and a straightforward voice that's hard not to like."—*Shambhala Sun*

Zen Meditation in Plain English
John Daishin Buksbazen
Foreword by Peter Matthiessen
128 pages, ISBN 0-86171-316-8, $12.95

"Buksbazen, a psychotherapist and Zen priest, offers practical and down-to-earth advice about the specifics of Zen meditation. The bulk of this primer is concerned with introducing the basics of zazen, or seated meditation: how to position the body; how and when to breathe; what to think about. Helpful diagrams illustrate the positions, and Buksbazen even provides a checklist to help beginners remember all of the steps. He builds a strong case for the powerful effect of being involved with a community of other practitioners and follows this with concrete information about group practice, including meditation retreats and other intensive training periods. This is a fine introduction to Zen meditation practice, grounded in tradition yet adapted to contemporary life."
— *Publishers Weekly*

Beside Still Waters:

Jews, Christians, and the Way of the Buddha
Edited by Harold Kasimow, John P. Keenan, and
Linda Klepinger Keenan
Foreword by Jack Miles, Pulitzer Prize–winning
author of *God: A Biography*
288 pages, ISBN 0-86171-336-2, $14.95

This unprecedented volume goes beyond inter-religious dialogue to offer the personal experiences of fourteen Jews and Christians who may practice and even teach Buddhism. Authors such as Sylvia Boorstein, Norman Fischer, Ruben Habito, and Sister Elaine McInnes relate the impact that Buddhism has had upon their sense of religious identity.

"This book heralds an important new age in interreligious relations, and more than ever it is needed and welcome." —Brother Wayne Teasdale, author of *The Mystic Heart*

Buddhist Peacework:

Creating Cultures of Peace
Edited by David. W. Chappell
256 pages, ISBN 0-86171-167-X, $14.95

Buddhism is known for bringing inner peace, but what about social harmony, human rights, and environmental balance? We have a responsibility today to work directly with our own suffering and the suffering in our communities, the world, and the environment.

Buddhist Peacework collects—for the first time in one place—first-person descriptions of the ideas and work of eminent Buddhist leaders such as the Dalai Lama, Thich Nhat Hanh, Daisaku Ikeda, Robert Aitken, and others. These 18 essays are divided into three sections that explore the newest Buddhist social developments, the principles that guide Buddhist peacework, and the importance of ongoing inner peacework in developing a sense of kinship with all people.

The voices and experiences collected here provide information for Buddhists and non-Buddhists alike, and reveal new models for Buddhist practice in an unstable modern world.

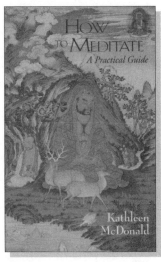

How to Meditate:
A Practical Guide
Kathleen McDonald
224 pages, ISBN 0-86171-009-6, $14.95

What is meditation? Why practice it? How do I do it? The answers to these often-asked questions are contained in this down-to-earth book written by a Western nun in the Tibetan Buddhist tradition with solid experience in both the practice and teaching of meditation.

"An excellent introduction—refreshingly readable, displaying clarity without oversimplification."
—Buddhist Studies Review

"As beautifully simple and direct as its title."—*Yoga Today*

Engaged Buddhism in the West
Edited by Christopher S. Queen
560 pages, ISBN 0-86171-159-9, $24.95

"Chris Queen has done a great service in bringing together a book that is sure to close the gaps that presently exist among the very diverse and widespread groups of Buddhists actively engaged in social action. This well-researched collection of essays makes it clear that a powerful movement is underway." —John Daido Loori, abbot, of Zen Mountain Monastery and editor of *The Art of Just Sitting.*

"This is a deep and rich offering, an important look at the work of engaged Buddhists who have acted from their practice. The chapters in this volume show how engaged Buddhists are offering the fruits of their practice in very concrete ways in the West. These writers help us understand and gain inspiration from engaged Buddhism as it is practiced in daily life and in society today."
— Thich Nhat Hanh

The Great Awakening:
A Buddhist Social Theory
David R. Loy
Foreword by Kenneth Kraft
320 pages, 0-86171-366-4, $16.95

The essential insight that Buddhism offers is that all our individual suffering arises from three and only three sources, known in Buddhism as the three poisons: greed, ill-will, and delusion. In *The Great Awakening,* scholar and Zen teacher David R. Loy examines how these three poisons, embodied in society's institutions, lie at the root of all social maladies as well. The teachings of Buddhism present a way that the individual can counteract these to alleviate personal suffering, and in the *The Great Awakening* Loy boldly examines how these teachings can be applied to institutions and even whole cultures for the alleviation of suffering on a collective level.

This book will help readers to realize the social importance of Buddhist teachings, while providing a theoretical framework for socially engaged members of society to apply their spiritual principles to collective social issues. *The Great Awakening* shows how Buddhism can help our postmodern world develop liberative possibilities otherwise obscured by the anti-religious bias of so much contemporary social theory.

"Loy extends our understanding of Buddha's Four Noble Truths by showing how the three poisons of greed, ill-will and delusion become socially embedded and supercharged. He then enlarges this understanding in examinations of social issues ranging from the 'War against Evil' to the reformation of dangerous criminals. Sophisticated theories like the ones Loy presents here are an urgent requirement if socially engaged Buddhism is to reach its full potential."
—Ken Jones, author of *The New Social Face of Buddhism*